Solutions

Advanced **Student's Book**

2nd edition

Tim Falla, Paul A Davies

OXFORD
UNIVERSITY PRESS

Check your progress

Think about your progress as you work through *Solutions 2nd edition Advanced*. After completing Skills Round-up 1–4 read each statement and write the number of ticks (✓) that apply to you. Do the same again after Skills Round-up 1–10.

✓ = I need more practice.   ✓✓ = I sometimes find this difficult.   ✓✓✓ = No problem!

In English I can …		Skills Round-up 1–4	Skills Round-up 1–10
Listening			
B2	… understand extended discussions on familiar topics and identify speaker viewpoints. **1A, 1B, 1F, 2A, 2F, 3A, 8A**		
B2	… understand and react to current affairs radio programmes. **1C**		
B2	… follow complex lines of argument on familiar topics. **3F**		
B2	… understand detailed and linguistically complex descriptive and narrative passages. **2C, 5A, 8F**		
C1	… follow extended speech even when it is not clearly structured. **2C, 4A, 5F, 7F, 9F**		
C1	… understand a wide range of broadcast material and identify finer points of detail. **3C, 4C, 6C, 7C, 9C, 10C**		
Reading			
B2	… scan quickly through long and complex texts, locating relevant detail. **1D, 2D**		
B2	… read reviews dealing with the content and criticism of cultural topics and summarise the main views. **2G**		
B2	… understand magazine articles about current issues in which writers adopt particular viewpoints. **3D**		
B2	… understand factual articles and reports. **1D, 4E, 6E**		
C1	… understand long and complex factual and literary texts. **2D, 4D, 6D, 7D, 9D, 10D**		
C1	… read reports, analyses and commentaries where opinions and viewpoints are discussed. **5D, 8D, 9G, 10D**		
C1	… recognise the social, political or historical background of a literary work. **4C, 9C**		
Speaking			
B2	… present detailed descriptions on a variety of familiar topics. **1B, 2A, 2G, 3B**		
B2	… take an active part in a discussion on familiar topics. **1A, 1C, 2D**		
B2	… develop a clear argument, supporting my views at some length with relevant examples. **1F, 2B, 2F, 3A**		
C1	… engage in conversation on most general topics. **3D, 4C, 6A, 7C, 9A, 9B**		
C1	… formulate ideas and opinions and present them skilfully and coherently to others. **3C, 4A, 4B, 4F, 5A, 5C, 6C, 6F, 7B, 8B, 9D, 10B, 10C**		
C1	… give a clearly developed presentation, highlighting significant points and relevant supporting detail. **3F, 5F, 7F, 8F, 9F, 10F**		
Writing			
B2	… write a review of a film, book or play. **2G**		
B2	… write detailed descriptions of real or imaginary events in a clear connected text. **1G, 6G**		
C1	… write clear, well-structured texts which expand and support views with subsidiary points, reasons and examples. **4G, 9G, 10G**		
C1	… select a style appropriate to the reader in mind. **5G**		
C1	… put together information from different sources and relate it in a coherent summary. **3G, 8G**		
C1	… write formally correct letters. **7G**		

THIS UNIT INCLUDES

Vocabulary ▪ prefixes ▪ time expressions ▪ adverb collocations ▪ adjectives describing emotional states ▪ similes
Grammar ▪ phrasal verbs ▪ talking about habitual actions
Speaking ▪ talking about childhood memories ▪ talking about inherited characteristics ▪ talking about the origins of languages ▪ discussion: genetic engineering ▪ reacting to opposing views
Writing ▪ a description of an event

Beginnings 1

1A VOCABULARY AND LISTENING Memories

I can talk about childhood memories.

1 SPEAKING Look at the photo of a child's first day at school. Answer the questions.

1 How do you imagine the child is feeling? Use the words below to describe his emotions.

> bewildered   circumspect
> disorientated   distraught
> overawed   overwhelmed
> preoccupied   uneasy
> unnerved   withdrawn

2 What other situations might cause similar emotions?

3 What are your own memories of your first day at school?

▶▶▶ **VOCABULARY BUILDER 1.1: PREFIXES: WORKBOOK PAGE 102** ◀◀◀

2 🎧 1.01 Listen to four speakers talking about aspects of their childhood. Choose the topic which best matches each speaker.

a primary school (classmates, teachers, subjects, etc.)
b best friends
c family relationships
d favourites (games, food, clothes, films, TV shows, books, etc.)
e fears and anxieties
f special occasions (birthdays, festivals, etc.)

Speaker 1 ☐   Speaker 2 ☐   Speaker 3 ☐   Speaker 4 ☐

3 🎧 1.01 Complete the phrases the speakers use with the words below. Listen again and check.

> call   evocative   hindsight   ingrained   picture
> recall   recollection   reminisce   traumatic

1 As I _____ , the trouble started when…
2 With _____ , I suppose it was…
3 I found the whole thing quite _____ .
4 I can still _____ it clearly.
5 … until it became completely _____ in my memory.
6 Christmas is a very _____ time for me.
7 I can't _____ to mind many disappointments.
8 I still have a clear _____ of that smile.
9 It would be fun to _____ about the good old days.

4 Match the expressions (1–10) with the synonymous words and expressions below.

> all the time   finally   for now   immediately   occasionally
> never   never-ending   repeatedly   then   very soon

1 time after time
2 at the time
3 for the time being
4 any moment now
5 the whole time

6 endless
7 once in a while
8 not for a moment
9 at once
10 in the end

5 Complete the text with words and expressions from exercise 4.

A childhood memory

I grew up in central London, where it took two hours to escape from the city by car or bus. ¹_____ , dad used to take us for a drive in the countryside but most of the time, we stayed close to home. So the first time I visited my grandparents' house on the coast, I fell in love with the seaside ²_____ . ³_____ , my grandparents were in their sixties and quite fit and healthy, so they would come with us to the beach every day. I have such vivid memories of those ⁴_____ afternoons that my sisters and I spent playing in the sea. The water was freezing, but ⁵_____ did that put us off! Neither did the large and powerful waves, which used to knock me off my feet ⁶_____ . I would laugh, jump up and rush back into the waves ⁷_____ . We wouldn't want to leave the beach, but ⁸_____ , sunset would force us to return to my grandparents' house for the night.

6 Choose one topic from exercise 2 to talk about. Think of three memories to include.

7 SPEAKING Work in pairs. Take turns to be A and B.

Student A: Tell your partner about your memories. Include as many words and expressions from exercises 1, 3 and 4 as possible. Then try to answer B's questions.
Student B: Listen carefully. Then ask your partner three questions about his or her memories.

1 SPEAKING **Work in pairs. Discuss these questions.**

Twins Ryan and Leo were born in Germany in 2008.

1 What physical and mental traits can be inherited?
2 What physical and mental traits can only be aquired?

2 🎧 1.02 **In pairs, complete the quiz questions using the words below, then choose the correct answers. Listen and check.**

bases   chromosomes   code   genome   helix   trait

1 DNA is often described as the 'double _____' because:
   a every cell contains two genes.
   b its structure is arranged in pairs.
   c there are two different kinds of DNA.
2 How many pairs of _____ are found in most human cells?
   a 23   b 46   c more than a million
3 How many different chemical _____ , the fundamental building blocks of DNA, are there?
   a 4   b 40   c 4,000
4 How many genes, approximately, are described in the human _____ , a complete map of human DNA?
   a 250   b 25,000   c 25 million
5 Humans share about 50 per cent of their genetic _____ with:
   a chimpanzees.   b dolphins.   c bananas.
6 A recessive gene shared by both parents causes offspring to have a personality or physical _____ which:
   a none of their ancestors had.
   b only their grandparents had.
   c certain ancestors had, but not their parents.

3 🎧 1.03 **Listen to a dialogue between three people talking about family similarities. Which of these things do they mention?**

a strong physical resemblance
b similar personality traits
c similar tastes and hobbies
d a shared childhood habit
e similar political views
f a shared talent

4 🎧 1.03 **Listen again. What exact words do the speakers use to express these ideas?**

1 I've got the same kind of nose as my dad.
2 I've inherited my mum's personality.
3 We deal with stressful problems in a very similar way.
4 I look extremely similar to my granddad.
5 Other people can see that my sister and I are from the same family.
6 My brother does not look similar to any other family member.
7 I can see clear similarities between me and my dad.
8 The habit must have been inherited.

5 **Write five sentences comparing yourself to family members. Use expressions from your answers to exercise 4.**

6 **Study these sentences. Underline the verb forms for talking about habitual behaviour. Complete the chart (1–8) with the sentences (a–h) below.**

a My grandmother used to suck the third finger on her left hand.
b I'll often call my mum to talk about my problems.
c People were always mistaking us for twins.
d I'd deliberately wear very different clothes from my brother.
e My sister will phone me late at night for a chat.
f My brother is forever borrowing my clothes.
g My grandfather would insist on driving without a seatbelt.
h I usually like the same music as my dad.

	past		present	
neutral	1_____	2_____	3_____	4_____
expressing disapproval	5_____	6_____	7_____	8_____

>>> GRAMMAR BUILDER 1.1: TALKING ABOUT HABITUAL ACTIONS: PAGE 115 <<<

7 SPEAKING **Work in pairs. Think of five examples of things which a family member often does or often used to do. Then tell your partner, using as many different verb forms as possible from exercise 6.**

8 **Prepare an interview for your partner about mental or physical traits inherited from parents or grandparents. Use the list from exercise 3 to write six questions and try to include expressions from your answers to exercise 4.**

1 Which of your parents or grandparents do you bear the strongest physical resemblance to?

9 SPEAKING **Work in pairs. Take turns to be A and B.**

Student A: Interview B using your questions from exercise 8.
Student B: Answer A's questions. Use expressions and verb forms from exercises 4 and 6 where appropriate.

The origins of English

I can understand and react to an article about the origins of English.

1 Work in pairs. Look at excerpts 1–5 and match them with the works of English literature (a–e) from which they are taken. Which words gave you the clues?

1 'I never had one hour's happiness in her society, and yet my mind all round the four-and-twenty hours was harping on the happiness of having her with me unto death.'
2 'O! she doth teach the torches to burn bright.'
3 'Hwæt! We Gardena   in geardagum,
þeodcyninga,   þrym gefrunon,
hu ða æþelingas   ellen fremedon.'
4 'It was the day my grandmother exploded.'
5 'With us ther was a Doctour of Phisik,
In al this world ne was ther noon hym lik,
To speke of phisik and of surgerye,
For he was grounded in astronomye.'

a *Beowulf*, an epic poem composed by an unknown author some time between 800 and 1200.
b *The Canterbury Tales*, a collection of stories written in the fourteenth century by the poet Geoffrey Chaucer.
c *Romeo and Juliet*, a play by William Shakespeare, written around 1594.
d *Great Expectations*, a novel by Charles Dickens, written in 1860.
e *The Crow Road*, a novel by Iain Banks, written in 1992.

2 🎧 1.04 Listen to a radio programme about the origins of the English language. What are the three main phases in its history? Complete the terms.

1 O_____ English (also known as Anglo-Saxon)
2 M_____ English
3 M_____ English

3 🎧 1.04 Listen again. Complete each sentence with up to three words.

1 Before the fifth century, the inhabitants of Britain spoke various *Celtic languages*.
2 When Britain was invaded by Germanic tribes during the fifth century, the native population went to live in Wales, Cornwall _____ .
3 Many English words derived from Anglo-Saxon are a reflection of their _____ .
4 Along with the word for *school*, one thing which the Anglo-Saxons borrowed from the Romans was _____ .
5 The Viking raiders who came to Britain around 900 mostly settled in the _____ parts of the country.
6 From the eleventh century onwards, English word order became _____ .
7 The words *beef* and *mutton* reflect the fact that, in the Middle Ages, the wealthiest people in Britain were _____ .
8 The era of Modern English is generally accepted to coincide approximately with the invention of _____ .
9 Today, the English language is being shaped not only by people who speak it as a mother tongue, but increasingly by the vast number of _____ .

4 Match the words (1–8), which have all entered the English language recently, with their definitions (a–h). Can you work out how the words were formed?

1 neet   5 newpeat
2 shedquarters   6 slurb
3 peerents   7 glocalisation
4 moregeoisie   8 locavores

a parents who try to be like their children's friends
b a suburban area with very poor housing
c a TV episode which is shown again with extra material not previously included
d young people who are not in employment, education or training
e when multinational companies try to respect local customs and sensitivities
f consumers who strive to acquire more than others
g people who only eat food which is produced near to their home
h a home office in the garden

5 SPEAKING How much do you know about the origins of your own language? Discuss the questions with the class.

1 How much has your language changed over the past 1,000 years? Would you be able to understand a text written 1,000 years ago?
2 Which other languages are most closely related to your own language? Why?
3 Does your language contain words derived from Latin or Greek? Give examples.
4 Does your language contain many words derived from English? Are they old or recent acquisitions?
5 Can you think of any words which have been added to your language in the past 5–10 years?

I can understand an article about the origins of different sports.

1 SPEAKING Read the quotation from British actor, Robert Morley. What do you think it means? Do you agree with it? Give reasons.

> *The ball is man's most disastrous invention.*

2 Work in pairs. How many of the different sports in the photos can you name? Can you think of any other ball sports?

3 Read the texts quickly. What are the three sports, and in what chronological order were they invented?

READING TIP!

When doing a multiple matching task, read through the questions before you read the text carefully. This way, you will know what information you are looking for.

---

4 Read the *Reading tip!*. Then read the texts carefully again. Answer the questions A, B or C.

Which sport:

1 was invented to keep young people entertained? ☐
2 might have been based on an English game? ☐
3 had a special group of experts set up to uncover its origins? ☐
4 is supposed to have resulted from one player breaking the rules? ☐
5 was later prohibited by the organisation where it was invented? ☐
6 was not intended to be played outside? ☐
7 was officially declared to have been invented by a member of the armed forces? ☐
8 was named after the place where it was reputedly first played? ☐
9 was far more successful than its inventor expected? ☐
10 was almost certainly first played in England? ☐

A   A public school product

A new form of football originated in England during the 19th century, taking its name from the place where it was supposedly invented: Rugby School. In the early 1800s, football was played throughout England (and in many other countries too) but there were no standard rules, and in most versions of the game, the ball could be caught as well as kicked. However, running with the ball was largely outlawed. Legend has it that in 1823, a student at Rugby School called William Webb Ellis picked up the ball during a football match and ran with it towards the opposing goal line. This illegal action caused a permanent change in the rules of the game, or so the story goes, and from that day onwards, Rugby School played its own version of football which became known as Rugby Football. (The more familiar kind of football is officially known as Association Football to distinguish it from Rugby Football.) To this day, there is an inscription at Rugby School celebrating William Webb Ellis and his actions, and although the historical truth of the events is highly questionable, the story endures. The plaque reads: 'This stone commemorates the exploit of William Webb Ellis who with a fine disregard for the rules of football as played in his time first took the ball in his arms and ran with it thus originating the distinctive feature of the Rugby game.'

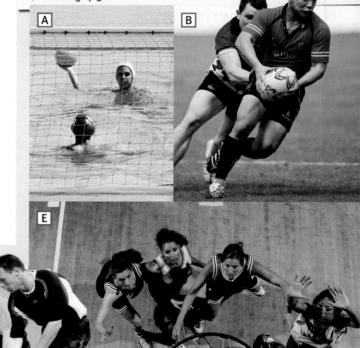

B   A Canadian invention

James Naismith was a Canadian physical education instructor who worked at the YMCA (Young Men's Christian Association) training school in Springfield, Massachusetts, in the USA. In 1891, he was asked to devise a new sport which the students could play indoors during the winter to stave off boredom. Naismith came up with a game which involved two teams of nine players trying to throw a ball into peach baskets which were fixed to the wall at either end of the gym. It was loosely based on a game from his own childhood called 'Duck on a rock'. On 15 January 1892, he published the rules of his new game, which he called basketball. Naismith's handwritten diaries, which were discovered by his granddaughter in 2006, reveal that he was anxious about the new game and thought it would prove a failure, like many other attempts at inventing new indoor sports. On the contrary, the game was a huge success and rapidly became very popular throughout the USA, spreading across the country through the network of YMCA gyms and beyond. (Ironically, the YMCA banned the game from its gyms a few years later because it was too rough.) In 1893, iron hoops with nets were introduced to replace the original baskets. However, it was another ten years before open-ended nets were developed; prior to that, players had to climb up and retrieve the ball from the net whenever a basket was scored.

C   An all-American sport

In 1905, a famous sportswriter named Henry Chadwick wrote an article suggesting that baseball evolved from the old English game of rounders. This upset Albert Spalding, one of the game's earliest players and a manufacturer of sports equipment. He resolutely refused to accept that the great American game did not originate in America. So Spalding organised a commission of seven prominent and patriotic men to determine the 'true origin' of baseball. The project was widely reported in the newspapers. In charge of the commission was Colonel Mills of New York. He had played baseball before and during the Civil War and was the fourth president of the National League in 1884. The commission's investigations were essentially at a dead end until Abner Graves, a mining engineer from Denver who was travelling through Ohio at the time, happened to see a newspaper article about it. He sat down in his hotel room and wrote a long letter to the Mills Commission. In the letter, Graves stated categorically that at Cooperstown in 1839 he had watched a US army officer called Abner Doubleday scratching out a baseball pitch on the ground and instructing other young men how to play baseball with teams of eleven players and four bases. Graves described how the ball that they used was made of roughly-stitched horse-hide and stuffed with rags. The Mills commissioners and Spalding were elated. They promptly proclaimed baseball was invented by an American army officer, Abner Doubleday, in Cooperstown in 1839. The only evidence for this was the testimony of Graves, who was perhaps not the most reliable of witnesses. A year later, he murdered his wife and was committed to an asylum for the criminally insane.

---

5 Match the highlighted adverbs in the text with their equivalents.

1	by and large	7	untidily
2	staunchly	8	paradoxically
3	swiftly	9	extensively
4	purportedly	10	unambiguously
5	effectively	11	forwards
6	thereby	12	vaguely

LOOK OUT!

Words with the same meaning do not always collocate in the same way. For example, we can say *This is your big chance!* but not *This is your large chance!*, even though *big* and *large* are synonyms. A good dictionary will include information about collocations.

---

6 Read the *Look out!* box. Then complete the sentences with the adverb (a–c) that collocates best.

1 The practice of taking drugs to enhance athletic performance is _____ agreed to have begun in ancient Greece.
   a largely   b generally   c chiefly

2 In the 1930s, the first amphetamines were produced, but were not _____ available for a few decades.
   a widely   b broadly   c extensively

3 At the 1952 Olympics, speed skaters who had taken amphetamines became _____ ill.
   a grimly   b gravely   c solemnly

4 In 1968, the International Olympic Committee issued its first list of substances that athletes were _____ prohibited from taking.
   a firmly   b rigorously   c strictly

5 In 1991, twenty ex-East German swimming coaches _____ admitted giving anabolic steroids to their former charges during the 1970s.
   a openly   b overtly   c plainly

6 In 1994, _____ renowned footballer Diego Maradona was banned from the World Cup for taking drugs.
   a globally   b universally   c internationally

7 In 2003, a British sprinter called Dwain Chambers tested positive for THG, a _____ invented steroid.
   a freshly   b lately   c newly

8 Today, while the vast majority of people are _____ opposed to the use of drugs in sport, detection remains a real problem for the governing bodies.
   a staunchly   b securely   c steadily

7 **SPEAKING** Discuss the question in groups. Then compare your ideas with the class.

If you could 'un-invent' one sport so that it no longer existed, which would you choose, and why?

Phrasal verbs

I can use phrasal verbs correctly.

1 Read the text and explain the question in the title. Then sum up the answer the text gives.

What makes you you?

Why do some people **back down** when faced with a threat, while others **stand up to** it? When given a difficult task, why do some people **see** it **through**, while others **give up**? It all comes down to personality. But where does that come from? Some scientists believe that most traits are inherited. Others take the opposite view: personality, they say, is formed by our environment and parents do not **pass** it **on** to their children.

The truth is probably somewhere in between. Some traits are clearly determined by your environment: whatever your genetic background, if you **grow up** in Sweden, you'll probably speak Swedish. On the other hand, when it comes to traits like the colour of your eyes or your blood type, it is clear that genetics alone **accounts for** them. There are also traits which are partly inherited but partly shaped by environment: your weight, and even your height and skin colour, are examples.

Of course, genetics and the environment together are not the full picture. Your free will – your ability to take decisions – is also a factor in shaping your identity, but how big a factor? You'll have to **make** your own mind **up** about that!

2 Read the *Learn this!* box below and match one, two or three examples (a–h) with each type of phrasal verb.

a How well do you **get on with** your siblings?
b **Put** your jacket **on**, we're going outside.
c Who is going to **look after** me when I'm old?
d It's nine o'clock – time **to get up**!
e I don't think many guests are going **to turn up**.
f Don't forget **to take off** your shoes.
g How can you **put up with** that noise?
h I'd like **to think** it **over** for a while.

LEARN THIS!

Phrasal verbs
A phrasal verb is when a verb combines with an adverb or preposition (or sometimes both) to create a new meaning. Phrasal verbs can be divided into four main types:
1 Two-part verbs with no object. **Example(s):** _____
2 Two-part verbs whose object can come between OR after the two parts. (However, when the object is a pronoun, it must come between the two parts.) **Example(s):** _____
3 Two-part verbs whose object cannot come between the parts. **Example(s):** _____
4 Three-part verbs whose object cannot come between the parts. **Example(s):** _____

▶▶▶ **GRAMMAR BUILDER 1.2: PHRASAL VERBS: PAGE 115** ◀◀◀

LOOK OUT!
When phrasal verbs are used in passive structures, the two or three parts stay together.
All the lights had been switched off.
The same is true for infinitive structures unless the phrasal verb belongs to type 2.
Jane is not easy to get on with.   I need to look it up in a dictionary.

3 Read the *Look out!* box. Then find phrasal verbs 1–8 in the text in exercise 1 and decide:

a what each phrasal verb means.
b whether they are type 1, 2, 3 or 4.
c whether they are active, passive or infinitive structures.

1 back down   3 see through   5 pass on   7 account for
2 stand up to 4 give up   6 grow up   8 make up

4 Read the text in exercise 5, ignoring the mistakes. What can identical twins tell us about the effects of genetics and environment?

▶▶▶ **GRAMMAR BUILDER 1.3: PHRASAL VERBS: PASSIVE AND INFINITIVE FORMS: PAGE 116** ◀◀◀

5 Find and correct eight more mistakes with the word order of phrasal verbs.

Most people would agree that human behaviour is made ~~of up~~ up of a mixture of genetics and environment. The question is: can we break down it into its constituent parts and decide which influence is stronger in certain situations? It's an intriguing question, and one which will certainly have important consequences for our society if the scientists who have been looking it into for many years suddenly come with up a definitive answer.

For example, if drug addiction turns out to be largely genetic, can we blame a heroin addict for not being able to give up it? If a man is destined to be a criminal because of his DNA, is it morally right to punish him for his crimes, or should society allow him to get them away with? Calculating the relative importance of genetics and environment is difficult, but in some situations, it is possible to work out it. Of particular interest to researchers are identical twins who have been brought in different families up. It's the differences between these twins which provide the key: only their environments can account them for because identical twins share exactly the same DNA.

6 SPEAKING Work in pairs. Discuss these questions.

1 What kind of people do you get on with best?
2 Which famous people do you look up to, and why?
3 Which of your personality traits were passed on by your parents and which can be accounted for by your experiences?

1 Read the first paragraph of the text. What is unusual about Andi, the monkey in the photograph?

  a Before birth, he was genetically identical to a human embryo.

  b His DNA was genetically engineered to make him immune to certain diseases.

  c His DNA includes a gene from another creature.

2 Read the rest of the text. Which view is closer to your own opinion?

Meet Andi

Although it is illegal in most countries for scientists to alter the DNA of human eggs or embryos, experiments on animals are allowed. In April 2001 the first genetically-modified monkey was born – he was called Andi (representing 'Inserted DNA' backwards). Andi developed from an egg into which scientists had inserted a jellyfish gene; as a result of which Andi glowed green in ultraviolet light.

Dave King, a campaigner against human genetic engineering, said yesterday: 'It is science out of control and at its most irresponsible. People should wake up to the fact that genetic engineering of people could be just around the corner.'

Simon Fishel from the Park Hospital, Nottingham, responded: 'We've been striving for hundreds of thousands of years to eliminate human diseases. If we get to the stage in human development where the only way to do that is to attack the errors in our DNA, then we have to try to attack those errors. I see this as positive research.'

3 🎧 1.05 Listen to a man and a woman discussing the topic of genetic experiments. Answer the questions.

  a Who is in favour and who is against?

  b At what point does the woman think the man is not being serious?

4 Who makes points 1–8, the man or the woman? Complete the points with the adverbs below.

> entirely eventually freely genetically morally
> realistically virtually widely

  1 It's _____ indefensible to use animals in experiments.

  2 If scientists are allowed to create designer babies, then one day, people who haven't been _____ modified will be seen as inferior.

  3 By altering our DNA, scientists will _____ be able to eliminate the most serious diseases.

  4 There's no reason why parents shouldn't be able to choose _____ whether they have a baby girl or boy.

  5 Artificial alterations to our genes may have _____ unforeseen side effects.

  6 _____ , scientists will never find a cure for cancer unless experiments on animals are permitted.

  7 If this kind of experiment is _____ permitted, scientists will go on to create monsters by mixing human and animal DNA.

  8 We have to embrace scientific progress, since it's _____ impossible to hold it back.

5 🎧 1.06 Complete the useful expressions for reacting to an opposing view. Then listen again and check.

  1 I don't really _____ with that.

  2 That's just an opinion – there's no evidence to _____ it.

  3 But where will it _____ ?

  4 That's a fair point, I _____ . But in my view …

  5 That argument doesn't _____ sense.

  6 You don't _____ to _____ things to such an extreme.

  7 I _____ what you mean. But …

  8 You can't _____ serious.

6 Student As work in pairs and Student Bs work in pairs.
Student As: You agree with the statement below.
Student Bs: You disagree with the statement below.
Each write a list of points to support your own position. Use the points from exercise 4 and your own ideas. Compare your list with your partner.

Designer babies will lead to a healthier and happier population.

7 SPEAKING Work in new pairs of one Student A and one Student B. Discuss the statement in exercise 6. Use expressions from exercise 5 to react to opposing points.

I can write an effective description of an event.

1 Read the model. Have you ever experienced a live music gig? If so, were your feelings similar?

My first gig

I first went to hear a live rock concert when I was eight years old. My brother and his friends were all fans of a heavy metal group called Black Wednesday. When they discovered that Black Wednesday were going to perform at our local theatre, they all bought tickets for the gig. However, at the last minute, one of the friends couldn't go, so my brother offered me the ticket. I was thrilled!

I remember the buzz of excitement inside the theatre as we all found our seats. After a few minutes, the lights went down and everybody became quiet. I could barely make out the stage in the darkness. We waited. Then there was a roar from the crowd, like an explosion, as the first members of the band stepped onto the stage. My brother leaned over and shouted something in my ear, but I couldn't hear what he was saying. The first song was already starting and the music was as loud as a jet engine. I could feel the bass notes and the drum beats in my stomach.

I can't recall any of the songs that the band played. I just remember that I didn't want it to finish. But in the end, after three encores, the show finished. We left the theatre and stumbled out onto the pavement. I felt bewildered, as if I had just woken from a long sleep. My ears were still ringing with the beat of the last song.

After the gig, I became a Black Wednesday fan too for a few years before getting into other kinds of music. Once in a while, though, I listen to one of their songs and imagine I'm back at that first gig.

WRITING TIP

You can improve the style of your writing by using sentences of different lengths. Very short sentences can be effective if used occasionally to create emphasis or build suspense or tension.

2 Read the *Writing tip*. Then underline two very short sentences in the model. Which is used for emphasis and which is used to build suspense?

3 Rewrite the sentences to include at least one short sentence. Say whether the effect is building tension or suspense or adding emphasis.

1 When we arrived at the hotel, I went straight to our room. I looked out of the window and there was the sea!

2 As Ben approached the door, he could hear footsteps inside the room. He turned the handle, the door swung open and he finally came face to face with the man who had been following him.

3 The playground was huge and I had never seen so many other children in one place. They were running to and fro, shouting and bumping into each other and it was terrifying.

4 Complete these sentences from the model.

1 Then there was a roar from the crowd, _____ an explosion, as the first members of the band stepped onto the stage.

2 The first song was already starting and the music was _____ loud _____ a jet engine.

3 I felt bewildered, _____ I had just woken from a long sleep.

5 Use your answers to exercise 4 to complete the information about similes.

Similes

Writers often use similes to make their writing more descriptive. A simile makes a comparison using *like* or *as*.

1 *We use* _____ + *noun to express a general similarity between two things.*
   The hospital was _____ **a maze.**

2 *We use* _____ + *adjective/adverb* + _____ + *noun/-ing form to compare a specific aspect.*
   Her face was _____ **white** _____ **snow.**

3 *We use* _____ _____ *to introduce a comparison with a complete clause.*
   The runner fell to the ground _____ _____ **he'd been shot.**

6   **SPEAKING** Work in pairs. Invent similes to complete these sentences.

1 My sister covered her mouth with her hand, as if …

2 The water in the lake where we used to go swimming was like …

3 When I lost my teddy bear, I cried and cried as if …

4 I crept downstairs as quietly as …

5 My mother suddenly began sniffing the air like …

6 The two men stared at each other as if …

1 Look at the adjectives for describing emotional states below and find pairs with similar meanings. Then say when you might experience these states.

~~annoyed~~ apprehensive baffled disenchanted disillusioned eager elated enthusiastic ~~irritated~~ nervous perplexed petrified reluctant remorseful repentant tense terrified thrilled unwilling uptight

annoyed – irritated
You might feel annoyed or irritated if your brother played loud music while you were trying to revise.

> **WRITING TIP**
>
> Use synonyms (words with the same meaning) to avoid repetition. A good dictionary may provide information about synonyms.

2 Read the *Writing tip*. Then look at the extract from the *Oxford Advanced Learner's Dictionary* and answer the questions below.

SYNONYMS

angry

mad · indignant · cross · irate

All these words describe people feeling and/or showing anger.

angry feeling or showing anger: *Please don't be angry with me.* ◇ *Thousands of angry demonstrators filled the square.*

mad [not before noun] (*informal, especially NAmE*) angry: *He got mad and walked out.* ◇ *She's mad at me for being late.* NOTE **Mad** is the usual word for 'angry' in informal American English. When used in British English, especially in the phrase go mad, it can mean 'very angry': *Dad'll go mad when he sees what you've done.* 'Go mad' can also mean 'go crazy' or 'get very excited'.

indignant feeling or showing anger and surprise because you think that you or sb else has been treated unfairly: *She was very indignant at the way she had been treated.*

cross (*rather informal, especially BrE*) rather angry or annoyed: *I was quite cross with him for being late.* NOTE This word is often used by or to children.

irate very angry: *irate customers* ◇ *an irate letter* NOTE **Irate** is not usually followed by a preposition: ~~She was irate with me/about it.~~

Which of the four synonyms of *angry* are you most likely to use:
1 if you're six years old?
2 if you're from New York?
3 if you're describing unfair treatment?
4 if you're describing an extreme feeling?

3 Rewrite the sentences using synonyms to avoid repetition. Use a dictionary to help you, if necessary.
1 The room was very large with very large windows.
2 She was a thin woman with a thin face.
3 My clothes were wet and my hair was wet.
4 I could see the beautiful mountains and beautiful lakes.

5 When the phone rang, I answered it immediately and knew immediately that something was wrong.
6 I found my father's diary and found an old postcard inside it.

4 **SPEAKING** Work in pairs. Choose two 'firsts' from the list below and discuss your personal memories. Use adjectives from exercises 1–3 where appropriate.
1 your first day at a new school
2 your first trip abroad
3 the first time you met a close friend
4 the first CD or DVD you ever bought
5 your first romantic date
6 your first day at work
7 your first visit to a large city
8 the day you got your first pet

5 You have been asked to write an article for your school magazine. Follow the plan below to describe one of the events that you chose in exercise 4.

> 1 When and where did it happen? How old were you? Who else was there?
>
> 2 What are your strongest memories? What happened? How did you feel?
>
> 3 What other memories do you have of the occasion? How did it end?
>
> 4 What happened afterwards? How do you feel about it now, looking back?

6 Work in pairs.
1 Look at your partner's notes from exercise 5 and write down three questions to ask.
2 Ask and answer the questions you wrote down.
3 Use your answers to your partner's questions to add more details to your plan.

7 Write an article of 200–250 words following your plan. Remember to use synonyms to avoid too much repetition and to include at least one simile.

8 Check your work using the list below.

> **CHECK YOUR WORK**
>
> **Have you:**
> ☐ followed the plan correctly?
> ☐ written the correct number of words?
> ☐ used synonyms?
> ☐ included at least one simile?
> ☐ used at least one short sentence to add emphasis or build suspense?
> ☐ checked the spelling and grammar?

1 Get ready to READ Read the definition and think of arguments for and against cloning.

> **clone** /kləʊn; NAmE kloʊn/ noun, verb
> ■ noun **1** (biology) a plant or an animal that is produced naturally or artificially from the cells of another plant or animal and is therefore exactly the same as it
> ■ verb [VN] **1** to produce an exact copy of an animal or a plant from its cells: *A team from the UK were the first to successfully clone an animal.* ◇ *Dolly, the cloned sheep*

2 Look quickly through the text in the Reading exam task, ignoring the gaps. What two arguments in favour of cloning are implied by the text? Do you agree with them?

3 Do the Reading exam task.

READING exam task

Read the text carefully and decide which sentence (A–F) best fits each gap (1–5). There is one sentence that you do not need.

$150,000 for a pet dog, just like your last one

Snuppy: the first cloned dog in the world

A Californian dog-lover has agreed to pay $150,000 to have her dead pit bull recreated in the world's first commercial pet cloning project. ¹☐ South Korean scientists will now use the tissue to attempt to create an exact replica of the pet.

RNL Bio, based in Seoul, said it is already working on the order. The work will be carried out by a team of Seoul National University (SNU) scientists under the direction of professor Lee Byeong-chun, a key member of the research team headed by disgraced stem cell scientist Hwang Woo-suk. ²☐ But the SNU team was successful in creating the world's first dog clone, an Afghan hound named 'Snuppy'.

Bernann McKunney is the American woman who really misses her dead dog. ³☐ Specific breeds of pit bull are banned or restricted in several countries including the UK, New Zealand and Canada, but not in the USA.

Cho Seong-ryul, RNL's marketing director, said the company's success rate for producing dogs by cloning was high with around one out of every four surrogate mother dogs producing cloned puppies. ⁴☐ The scientists and Mrs McKunney are hoping that at least one of these will develop into a healthy puppy.

'If successful, this will mark the first time that a dog has been cloned in a commercial contract,' Cho said. 'But it won't be the last. Cloning is fast becoming an industry. ⁵☐' RNL Bio plans eventually to focus on cloning not only pets, but also special dogs like those trained to sniff out bombs.

A She is thought to have become especially attached to it after the pit bull saved her life when another dog attacked her.

B The latter achieved notoriety when his well-publicised breakthroughs in cloning human stem cells were discovered to be fake.

C Increasing demand means the cost for cloning a dog may come down to less than $50,000.

D The dog, named Booger, died a year and a half ago but his owner kept part of the dog's ear in cold storage.

E Nevertheless, some people are worried that human cloning is an inevitable development.

F In this case, cells have been extracted from Booger's ear tissue and inserted into the eggs of living dogs.

4 Look at the photo of Frankenstein below. Discuss the questions.

1 What do you know about the story?
2 How does it portray science and scientists?

5 Do the Use of English exam task.

USE OF ENGLISH exam task

Complete the text. Write one word only in each gap.

Many people regard the possibility of human clones ¹＿＿＿ horror and see it as a sign that scientific progress is spiralling ²＿＿＿ of control. Although this initial revulsion is understandable, it is perhaps taking things ³＿＿＿ an extreme. After all, human clones already exist in nature: they're called identical twins, and ⁴＿＿＿ though some people find identical twins unnerving, few are actually disgusted by the very idea of them.

It's all ⁵＿＿＿ easy to dismiss cloning ⁶＿＿＿ the work of mad scientists trying to create Frankenstein-like monsters. This image has very little to ⁷＿＿＿ with the truth. ⁸＿＿＿ reality, the aim of scientists is to find new ways to combat disease and repair the human body. Some scientists have suggested that by cloning our own cells, we could halt or maybe ⁹＿＿＿ reverse the ageing process. The ultimate prize would be a kind of immortality. ¹⁰＿＿＿ that would be a good thing in practice is another question.

6 Do the Speaking exam task.

SPEAKING exam task

Read the following statement. Do you agree or disagree with it? Discuss the issue with your partner, responding to any counter-arguments they have.

The cloning of humans should never be allowed.

THIS UNIT INCLUDES
Vocabulary ▪ compound adjectives ▪ compound nouns ▪ verb-noun/adjective-noun collocations ▪ phrasal verbs ▪ aspects of films ▪ adjectives describing films ▪ modifying adverbs
Grammar ▪ *like, unlike* and *as* ▪ narrative tenses ▪ simple and continuous forms ▪ speculating
Speaking ▪ talking about characters in films and books ▪ talking about TV viewing habits ▪ reacting to literary texts
Writing ▪ a film review

Stories 2

2A VOCABULARY AND LISTENING Compound adjectives
I can talk about various aspects of stories.

1 🎧 1.07 Listen to three people describing the kind of films they like. What aspects of the films do they particularly like?

2 🎧 1.07 Complete the compound adjectives that the speakers use with the words below. Then listen again and check.

action cool engineered heart man moving narrow raising run self time witted

1 genetically-_____ 7 _____-headed
2 _____-packed 8 all-_____
3 _____-warming 9 _____-down
4 slow-_____ 10 hair-_____
5 _____-made 11 _____-minded
6 quick-_____ 12 _____-assured

3 Which adjectives in exercise 2 can be used to describe:
a character? b aspects of films?

LEARN THIS! Compound adjectives
1 Many compound adjectives consist of
a a noun, adjective or adverb plus present participle.
thirst-quenching easy-going never-ending
b a noun, adjective or adverb plus past participle.
tongue-tied left-handed well-paid
2 When the first element of the compound is an adjective, the past participle can be formed from a noun rather than a verb.
thick-skinned tight-fisted thin-lipped flat-footed
3 Another common pattern is adjective/number + noun. The noun is always singular.
deep-sea last-minute ten-storey

▶▶▶ **VOCABULARY BUILDER 2.1: COMPOUND ADJECTIVES: WORKBOOK PAGE 102** ◀◀◀

4 How many compound adjectives can you make using the adjectives and nouns below? How many more can you add using different adjectives and nouns?

big broad cold empty fair kind long narrow single thin wide

blood eyed hair hand head heart leg mind shoulder skin

5 Rewrite the text by replacing the underlined words with compound adjectives. You may need to make other changes.

Of Mice and Men is a novel by the Nobel Prize-winning author John Steinbeck.

Of Mice and Men is a novel by the author John Steinbeck, <u>who won the Nobel Prize.</u> It is set in 1930s California and is the story of two migrant farm workers, George Milton and Lennie Small. George <u>thinks quickly, and has a kind heart,</u> and looks after his friend Lennie Small, who is <u>like a child</u> and has a simple mind. Physically they are different too; George is small, <u>with a slim build,</u> while Lennie is tall and <u>his shoulders are broad.</u> They share a dream that one day they will own their own ranch. But it all goes wrong when Lennie accidentally kills someone. The ending <u>breaks your heart</u>, as George kills Lennie in order to save him from a lynch mob. <u>The novel only has 100 pages</u>, but it is a fantastic read.

6 SPEAKING Work in pairs. Think of someone or something that can be described using the compound adjectives below. Explain why they can be described like this.
1 cold-blooded 5 time-consuming
2 absent-minded 6 cut-price
3 light-hearted 7 remote-controlled
4 long-lasting

7 Make notes under the headings below about a character from a story, film or TV programme that you know. Use some of the compound adjectives on this page.
1 Character: positive aspects
2 Character: negative aspects
3 Appearance

8 SPEAKING Work in pairs. Describe the character to your partner. Can your partner guess who it is?

▶▶▶ **VOCABULARY BUILDER 2.2: COMPOUND NOUNS: WORKBOOK PAGE 102** ◀◀◀

1 Complete the text with appropriate words. Write one word only in each gap.

Too much TV may result ¹_____ academic failure

Teenagers who watch several hours ²_____ television a day do worse at school and are less likely to graduate ³_____ their peers, a new study suggests. The 20-year study involving nearly 700 families in the USA found that those watching more than three hours of TV a day were half as likely ⁴_____ continue their education past high school.

In the mid-1980s scientists began interviewing 14-year-olds from 678 families about their television viewing habits. They also asked the teens' parents as ⁵_____ whether the youngsters had any behavioural or academic difficulties. The researchers continued collecting information from the parents and interviewed the teens again at age 16, and again at ages 22 and 33.

At age 14, most of the children watched ⁶_____ one and three hours of television each day, while thirteen per cent watched more than four hours, and ten per cent watched less than one hour. The scientists found that 30 per cent of students who watched more than three hours of television at age 14 had attention problems ⁷_____ subsequent years, and fell behind or failed to graduate by age 22. ⁸_____ comparison, only fifteen per cent of those who watched less than one hour of TV at age 14 showed the same attention deficits later ⁹_____.

Other experts, however, say the link is unclear and maintain that the study does not provide strong evidence ¹⁰_____ a causal relationship between television viewing and subsequent attention difficulties. Teens ¹¹_____ learning disorders might simply be more likely to watch a lot of TV because they find activities ¹²_____ as reading textbooks too challenging.

2 SPEAKING Discuss this question: Should parents restrict the amount of TV their children watch? Justify your opinions.

3 🎧 1.08 Listen to three people discussing television. What reasons for watching TV do they mention? Choose from:

boredom   cultural and aesthetic enjoyment   escapism   family activity   filling time   getting news   relaxation   satisfying curiosity and general interest   seeking advice   self-education   social activity

4 Complete the questions with the words below. Use the correct form of the verbs.

portray   rubbish   set   slushy   unwind   well-drawn

1 Do you watch TV _____ ?
2 Do you agree there's a lot of _____ on TV?
3 Do you like _____ romantic comedies?
4 Are you critical of the way women _____ on TV?
5 Can you think of a really _____ character in a TV series?
6 Do you prefer fantasy series to TV dramas _____ in the real world?

5 SPEAKING Ask and answer the questions in exercise 4. Give reasons and examples.

6 🎧 1.08 Complete these sentences from the listening with *like*, *unlike* or *as*. Then listen again and check.

a And she's _____ , 'Why are you watching that rubbish?'
b My parents are a bit _____ that too.
c I don't have a TV in my bedroom, _____ Chris does.
d We watch dramas and films mainly, and series, _____ *Heroes*.
e The stories are fascinating, _____ are the characters.
f _____ *Heroes*, *Lost* is set in the real world.

7 Read the *Learn this!* box. Match the sentences (a–f) from exercise 6 with uses 1–6.

> **LEARN THIS!**
>
> **like, unlike and as**
> We can use *like* or *as* to describe similarities.
> 1 *like* is a preposition and comes before a noun or pronoun.
>   *You're **like** a child!*   1 _____
> 2 *as* is a conjunction and comes before a clause (subject and verb / auxiliary).
>   *She's scared, **as** we all are.*
> 3 We often use *like* as a conjunction instead of *as*. It's less formal.
>   *He fooled me, **like** he fooled everybody.*   2 _____
> 4 We sometimes invert the subject and verb after *as* (but never after *like*).
>   *He's tall, **as** is his father.*   3 _____
> 5 We use the preposition *unlike* to describe differences.
>   ***Unlike** you, I love American comedies.*   4 _____
> 6 We use *like* to give examples.   5 _____
> 7 In very informal speech, we can use *be + like* to introduce somebody's words.
>   *He was **like**, 'I'm so happy!'*   6 _____

⟫ GRAMMAR BUILDER 2.1: *AS* AND *LIKE*: PAGE 116 ⟪

8 SPEAKING Discuss with a partner. Do you think men and women have different tastes in films and TV programmes? Give reasons and examples.

1 Read the definition of the 'Great American Dream'. To what extent do you believe that the dream is (a) admirable and (b) achievable?

The Great American Dream is the belief that every citizen can achieve prosperity and happiness through their own efforts and abilities, irrespective of class or race.

2 Complete the text with the correct form of the words in brackets.

Arthur Miller and *Death of a Salesman*

Arthur Miller (1915–2005) is universally recognised as one of the greatest ¹_____ (drama) of the twentieth century. Miller's father had emigrated to the USA from Austria-Hungary, drawn like so many others by the 'Great American Dream'. However, he experienced severe ²_____ (finance) hardship when his family business was ruined in the Great Depression of the early 1930s.

Miller's most famous play, *Death of a Salesman*, is a powerful attack on the American system, with its aggressive business tactics and its ³_____ (insist) on money and social status as ⁴_____ (indicate) of worth. In Willy Loman, the hero of the play, we see a man who has fallen foul of this system. Willy is 'burnt out' and in the ruthless world of business there is no room for sentiment: if he can't do the work, then he is no good to his ⁵_____ (employ), the Wagner Company, and he must go. Willy is ⁶_____ (pain) aware of this and bewildered at his lack of success. He hides behind a smokescreen of lies and ⁷_____ (pretend) to disguise the fact to himself and others that he has failed.

When it was first staged in 1949, the play was greeted with ⁸_____ (enthuse) reviews, and it won numerous ⁹_____ (prestige) literary awards. However, Miller's views attracted the attention of the Un-American Activities Committee, which had been set up to investigate American artists suspected of having communist sympathies. Miller was found ¹⁰_____ (guilt) by the UAAC of undermining the American way of life. The verdict was, however, later overturned and Miller went on to write over fifty plays.

3 Make collocations with the words below. Use verbs for 1–4 and adjectives for 5–8. Find them in the text.

1	_____ hardship	5	_____ hardship
2	_____ attention	6	_____ status
3	_____ a committee	7	_____ award
4	_____ a verdict	8	_____ sympathies

4 Make new collocations. Match 1–8 in exercise 3 with the verbs and adjectives below. Choose three and write sentences.

a	reach	**c**	cause	**e**	marital	**g**	coveted
b	serve on	**d**	draw	**f**	right-wing	**h**	considerable

5 🎧 1.09 Read the glossary, then listen to the opening of *Death of a Salesman*. Why does Willy arrive home late? Choose the correct answer.

> **Glossary**
> shoulder = side of the road
> Studebaker = a make of car
> arch supports = things you put in shoes to give support and comfort
> windshield = car window

1 He couldn't concentrate while he was driving.
2 He fell asleep while he was driving.
3 He was involved in a car accident.

6 🎧 1.09 Listen again. Answer the questions, giving reasons for your answers when appropriate.

1 How would you describe Willy's physical and mental state?
2 How would you describe Linda's attitude to Willy?
3 What reasons does Linda suggest for what happened to Willy in the car?
4 What remedies does Linda suggest?

7 🎧 1.10 Read the glossary, then listen to the second extract. What two topics do Linda and Willy discuss at length?

> **Glossary**
> to send a wire = send a telegram
> to show the line = show new products
> accommodating = willing to adjust to the needs of other people
> crestfallen = sad and disappointed after an unexpected failure
> to tramp around = travel around; move about

8 🎧 1.10 Listen again and answer the questions.

1 What does Linda suggest that Willy should do in order to improve his working life?
2 How does Willy react on the three occasions that Linda makes this suggestion?
3 What did Willy and his son Biff argue about earlier?
4 Can you identify three occasions when Willy is indecisive and quickly changes his mind?

9 SPEAKING Work in pairs. Discuss the questions.

1 Do you feel sympathy for Willy and Linda? Why?/Why not?
2 Is there similar pressure on business people to succeed in your country?
3 To what extent do you believe that your future prosperity and happiness depend on your own efforts?
4 Do you agree with Willy that it's good for young people to move around and try out lots of different jobs?

1 SPEAKING Work in pairs. Imagine you and a group of friends were marooned on a small island in the middle of the ocean. Discuss the questions.

1 What would you do in order to: (a) survive? (b) get rescued?
2 What rules, if any, would you establish? How would you agree on them?

2 Read the extract from *Lord of the Flies* by William Golding, ignoring the gaps. Answer the questions.

1 Where are the boys and how did they get there?
2 Why is Ralph angry at the start of the extract?
3 What was the purpose of the fire?
4 Whose responsibility was it to keep the fire going?
5 What was Jack doing instead of looking after the fire?
6 How does he justify his behaviour?
7 Who had the boys chosen as their leader?
8 What possession of Piggy's did Jack break?
9 Who helps Piggy to find his glasses?
10 What does Jack apologise for?

3 Match the sentences (a–h) with the gaps (1–7) in the extract. There is one sentence that you do not need.

a Piggy grabbed and put on the glasses.
b He took a step, and able at last to hit someone, stuck his fist into Piggy's stomach.
c Jack turned to Piggy and apologised for his cruel behaviour.
d They might have seen us.
e They waited for an appropriately decent answer.
f He went on scrambling and the laughter rose to a gale of hysteria[10].
g Jack was loud and active.
h Then his voice came again on a peak of feeling.

4 Explain in your own words these sentences from the text.

1 The dismal truth was filtering through to everybody. (line 23)
2 There was the brilliant world of hunting, tactics, fierce exhilaration, skill; and there was the world of longing and baffled common-sense. (line 32)
3 He resented, as an addition to Jack's misbehaviour, this verbal trick. (line 84)
4 By the time the pile was built, they were on different sides of a high barrier. (line 105)

5 Find examples of the following behaviour in the text:

1 Jack's violence and aggressiveness.
2 Jack's cruelty.
3 Ralph's indecision.
4 Piggy's defiance.
5 Ralph's inflexibility.
6 Simon's concern for others.
7 the hunters' quickly changing moods.

6 SPEAKING Discuss the questions. Justify your opinions.

1 Do you think that a group of twelve-year-old boys is likely to behave in the way described in the extract?
2 If left to their own devices, do you think a group of twelve-year-old boys is capable of living peacefully with one another?

A group of boys have been marooned on a desert island, following a plane crash, and are waiting to be rescued. In this extract Jack and Ralph, strong characters who both want to be leader of the group, come into conflict.

1 Ralph flung back his hair. One arm pointed at the empty horizon. His voice was loud and savage, and struck them into silence.
'There was a ship.'
5 Jack, faced at once with too many awful implications, ducked away from them. He laid a hand on the pig and drew his knife. Ralph brought down his arm, fist clenched, and his voice shook.
'There was a ship. Out there! You said you'd keep the
10 fire going and you let it out!' He took a step towards Jack, who turned and faced him.
'1 ☐ We might have gone home – '
This was too bitter for Piggy, who forgot his timidity in the agony of his loss. He began to cry out, shrilly:
15 'You and your blood, Jack Merridew! You and your hunting! We might have gone home –'
Ralph pushed Piggy on one side.
'I was chief; and you were going to do what I said. You talk. But you can't even build huts – then you go off
20 hunting and let out the fire –'
He turned away, silent for a moment. 2 ☐
'There was a ship – '
One of the smaller hunters began to wail.[1] The dismal[2] truth was filtering through to everybody. Jack went

²⁵ very red as he hacked³ and pulled at the pig.
'The job was too much. We needed everyone.'
Ralph turned.
'You could have had everyone when the shelters were finished. But you had to hunt – '
³⁰ 'We needed meat.'
Jack stood as he said this, the bloodied knife in his hand. The two boys faced each other. There was the brilliant world of hunting, tactics, fierce exhilaration, skill; and there was the world of longing and baffled⁴
³⁵ common-sense. Jack transferred the knife to his left hand and smudged⁵ blood over his forehead as he pushed down the plastered hair.
Piggy began again.
'You didn't ought to have let that fire out. You said
⁴⁰ you'd keep the smoke going – '
This from Piggy, and the wails of agreement from some of the hunters drove Jack to violence. The bolting look came into his blue eyes. ³☐ Piggy sat down with a grunt. Jack stood over him. His voice was
⁴⁵ vicious⁶ with humiliation.
'You would, would you? Fatty!'
Ralph made a step forward and Jack smacked Piggy's head. Piggy's glasses flew off and tinkled⁷ on the rocks. Piggy cried out in terror:
⁵⁰ 'My specs!'
He went crouching and feeling over the rocks but Simon, who got there first, found them for him. Passions beat about Simon on the mountain-top with awful wings.
⁵⁵ 'One side's broken.'
⁴☐ He looked malevolently at Jack.
'I got to have them specs. Now I only got one eye. Jus' you wait – '
Jack made a move towards Piggy who scrambled⁸
⁶⁰ away till a great rock lay between them. He thrust his head over the top and glared at Jack through his one flashing glass.
'Now I only got one eye. Just you wait – '
Jack mimicked⁹ the whine and scramble.
⁶⁵ 'Jus' you wait – yah!'
Piggy and the parody were so funny that the hunters began to laugh. Jack felt encouraged. ⁵☐ Unwillingly Ralph felt his lips twitch;¹¹ he was angry with himself for giving way.
⁷⁰ He muttered.
'That was a dirty trick.'
Jack broke out of his gyration and stood facing Ralph. His words came in a shout.

'All right! All right!'
⁷⁵ He looked at Piggy, at the hunters, at Ralph.
'I'm sorry. About the fire, I mean. There. I – '
He drew himself up.¹²
' – I apologise.'
The buzz from the hunters was one of admiration
⁸⁰ for this handsome behaviour. Clearly they were of the opinion that Jack had done the decent thing, had put himself in the right by his generous apology and Ralph, obscurely,¹³ in the wrong. ⁶☐
Yet Ralph's throat refused to pass one. He resented, as
⁸⁵ an addition to Jack's misbehaviour, this verbal trick. The fire was dead. The ship was gone. Could they not see? Anger instead of decency passed his throat.
'That was a dirty trick.'
They were silent on the mountain top while the
⁹⁰ opaque look appeared in Jack's eyes and passed away. Ralph's final word was an ungracious¹⁴ mutter.
'All right. Light the fire.'
With some positive action before them, a little of the tension died. Ralph said no more, did nothing,
⁹⁵ stood looking down at the ashes around his feet. ⁷☐
He gave orders, sang, whistled, threw remarks at the silent Ralph – remarks that did not need an answer, and therefore could not invite a snub;¹⁵ and still Ralph was silent. No one, not even Jack, would ask him to
¹⁰⁰ move and in the end they had to build the fire three yards away and in a place not really as convenient. Ralph asserted his chieftainship and could not have chosen a better way if he had thought for days. Against this weapon, so indefinable and so effective, Jack was
¹⁰⁵ powerless and raged without knowing why. By the time the pile was built, they were on different sides of a high barrier.

Glossary
1 (to) wail = (make) a long, high cry of pain or sadness
2 dismal = miserable
3 to hack = cut with rough, heavy blows
4 baffled = confused
5 to smudge = make a dirty mark
6 vicious = cruel and aggressive
7 (to) tinkle = (make) a light, high ringing sound
8 to scramble = move quickly and with difficulty, using your hands to help
9 mimic = copy in a funny way the way sb speaks and acts
10 a gale of hysteria = the sound of people laughing uncontrollably
11 (to) twitch = (make) a sudden, small movement without meaning to
12 to draw oneself up = stand up to one's full height
13 obscurely = for a reason that was difficult to identify
14 ungracious = ill-mannered and unfriendly
15 a snub = an insult

1 Read the Aesop's fable and choose the moral (a–c) which you think best fits the story.

a Don't try to achieve the impossible.

b It is easy to despise what you cannot have.

c Don't underestimate the difficulty of a task.

The Fox and the Grapes

There was once a fox that used to wander far and wide to find food. He would sometimes walk for days in order find a nice meal. One day, he came across a vine branch from which were hanging bunches of ripe, black grapes which no one had yet picked. The fox had been searching for food for many days and was almost dying of hunger. He stood on tip-toe and stretched as high as he could, but he couldn't reach the grapes. He tried jumping but still without success. The fox had thought that it would be easy to reach the grapes, and to hide his disappointment he said to himself, 'What a fool I am! The grapes are sour. I was going to eat them, but I've changed my mind.' And with that, he walked off.

2 Find examples of verb forms 1–7 in the fable in exercise 1. When do we use them?

1 past simple	5 *would*
2 past continuous	6 *used to*
3 past perfect	7 future in the past
4 past perfect continuous	

3 Explain the difference in meaning in these sentences.

1 a When Joe arrived, I'd made some coffee.
   b When Joe arrived, I made some coffee.
   c When Joe arrived, I was making some coffee.
   d When Joe arrived, I'd been making some coffee.

2 a He spoke Japanese because he'd lived in Japan for two years.
   b He spoke Japanese because he'd been living in Japan for two years.

3 a What was that book you read on holiday?
   b What was that book you were reading on holiday?

4 a George used to smoke in the office.
   b George *would* smoke in the office.

5 a Kim and Ben met in 2010 and were to get married in 2012.
   b Kim and Ben met in 2010 and were to have got married in 2012.

>>> GRAMMAR BUILDER 2.2: NARRATIVE TENSES: PAGE 117 <<<

4 Complete the fable with the correct form of the verbs in brackets. Sometimes two answers are possible. Justify your choices. Then in pairs, write a moral for the fable.

The Hare and the Tortoise

One day a hare ¹_____ (run) along a path when he ²_____ (come) across a tortoise. The hare ³_____ (follow) the same route every day and ⁴_____ (never come) across a tortoise before. The tortoise ⁵_____ (walk) slowly and the hare ⁶_____ (begin) to laugh at her. Irritated by the hare, the tortoise ⁷_____ (challenge) him to a race. The hare ⁸_____ (never have) any doubt that he was the fastest animal around, so he ⁹_____ (accept) the challenge. After the hare ¹⁰_____ (run) for a while, he realised that he ¹¹_____ (leave) the tortoise far behind, and ¹²_____ (sit) down under a tree to relax for a while. It wasn't long before he ¹³_____ (fall) asleep. Although the tortoise ¹⁴_____ (not hurry), she overtook the hare. When the hare ¹⁵_____ (wake up), he ¹⁶_____ (realise) that the tortoise ¹⁷_____ (beat) him to the finishing line. The hare ¹⁸_____ (remember) this experience for the rest of his life.

5 Use the notes below to write the fable *The boy who cried wolf*. Use a variety of narrative tenses and make any necessary changes to the text. Begin *There was once … .*

The Boy Who Cried Wolf

A shepherd boy lived in a village. His family lived there for many years. He looked after a flock of sheep. Every day he went to the hillside above the village. He was bored. He left his sheep. He ran to the village. He shouted, 'Wolf! Wolf!' The villagers heard his cries. They ran to help him. They wasted their time. He laughed at them. He did this two or three times. A wolf really did come. He shouted 'Wolf! Wolf!' The villagers ignored him. The wolf killed the whole flock of sheep. The boy didn't cry wolf again.

6 Complete these sentences in your own words. Use as many verb forms as you can from exercise 2.

1 … because it had been raining.
2 I'd had a terrible day at school …
3 When I last spoke to you …
4 I hadn't been feeling well …
5 I'd never thought …
6 As I was walking through the park, …
7 I was to have …

7 **SPEAKING** Work in pairs or small groups. Invent a fable to illustrate one of these sayings. Tell it to the class.

Make hay while the sun shines.   Look before you leap.
Don't judge a book by its cover.   A stitch in time saves nine.

>>> GRAMMAR BUILDER 2.3: SIMPLE AND CONTINUOUS FORMS: PAGE 118 <<<

1   **SPEAKING** Work in pairs. Discuss the questions.

  1 What problems do homeless people face?

  2 Why do people become homeless?

2   Work in pairs. If you had to interview a homeless person, what questions would you ask? Note them down.

3   🎧 1.11 Listen to the interview. Were any of your questions asked? How did the girl answer them?

4   🎧 1.11 Complete the phrasal verbs (1–6) with the correct prepositions, and match them with the definitions (a–f). Then listen again and check.

1 get sb _____	**a** start taking (e.g. drugs)
2 hang _____	**b** stay in a place
3 get _____ sth	**c** leave suddenly
4 walk _____	**d** spend time with (people)
5 kick sb _____	**e** make sb leave
6 hang out _____	**f** depress sb

5   Match 1–5 with a–e to make collocations from the listening.

1 skip	**a** one's drug habit
2 loose	**b** rough
3 feed	**c** change
4 kick	**d** one's drug habit
5 sleep	**e** school

> **SPEAKING TIP!**
>
> When comparing photos, start by saying what is similar and different about what you can see before you start to offer opinions or speculate about other aspects of the photos.

6   **SPEAKING** Work in pairs. Read the *Speaking tip!* and the task in the box below. Talk about the main similarities and differences between the photos. Use the phrases below to help you.

> The photos show homeless people. Compare and contrast the photos, and say what you think life is like for these people and why they might be homeless.

Describing similarities and differences
The most obvious similarity between the photos is (that)...
The photos are similar in that...
The most obvious difference between the photos is (that)...
In the first picture, ...while/whereas in the other,...
Photo 1 shows... Photo 2, on the other hand, shows...

> **SPEAKING TIP!**
>
> We often use the present perfect simple and continuous when speculating about photos.

7   🎧 1.12 Listen to someone saying what she thinks life is like for the person in the first picture and why he might be homeless. Do you agree with her opinions?

8   🎧 1.12 Complete the speculative sentences. You can use more than one word in a gap. Then listen again and check.

  1 This man _____ quite young.

  2 It _____ he's had a particularly hard life.

  3 It _____ he has enough layers to keep warm.

  4 He's sitting on a bunk bed in what's _____ a night shelter of some kind.

  5 I _____ he hasn't been sitting there for long, and he _____ doesn't spend his days there.

  6 He _____ to have any possessions with him.

  7 I _____ life is pretty tough for him.

  8 I _____ if he's run away from home for some reason.

⟫⟫ **GRAMMAR BUILDER 2.4: SPECULATING: PAGE 118** ⟪⟪

9   **SPEAKING** Work in pairs. Say what you think life is like for the person in the second picture and why he might be homeless.

10   **SPEAKING** In your pairs, turn to page 151 and do the picture comparison task.

1 Work in pairs. Discuss the questions.

1 Have you seen any films recently, in the cinema or on the TV? Did you enjoy them? Why?/ Why not? Use the ideas below to help you.

acting   locations   soundtrack   special effects
storyline   screenplay

2 Who are your favourite film stars? What do you like about them?

2 Read the film review. How would you describe it? Find evidence in the text for your opinion.

1 very positive
2 fairly positive
3 lukewarm
4 negative

FILM
Review

A I am a big fan of the James Bond movies, so I was first in the queue at the box office when *Skyfall* was screened at our local cinema. It is directed by Sam Mendes and, like its two immediate predecessors, *Casino Royale* and *Quantum of Solace*, it stars Daniel Craig in the title role as the British secret agent and Judi Dench as the enigmatic spy-chief, M.

B Set in the present day, the action takes place in locations as far apart as Istanbul, Shanghai and the Scottish Highlands. The plot revolves around the race to prevent the chilling arch villain Silva (Javier Bardem) from revealing the identities of undercover NATO agents. Needless to say, at the end of the film Bond triumphs and Silva gets his come-uppance.

C Under the extremely stylish direction of Sam Mendes, Craig, Dench and Bardem give superb performances. As you'd expect, the film is thrilling, fast-moving and visually spectacular, with state-of-the-art special effects, hair-raising chases and jaw-dropping stunt scenes. A bonus is the superb new Bond theme song from Adele. However, like all Bond films it has one weakness: the rather convoluted and far-fetched plot, which begins to unravel in the final quarter of the film.

D That said, this is the best Bond movie for many years, and far more entertaining than its pretty powerful immediate predecessor, *Quantum of Solace*. If it is pure escapism you're after and you love action spectaculars, this film is definitely for you.

3 In which paragraph (A–D) does the writer:

1 talk about the film's strengths?
2 give a brief summary of the plot?
3 give background detail about the film, such as the title and director?
4 give his/her overall verdict on the film?
5 talk about the film's weaknesses?

4 Complete the sentences with the words below.

adaptation   box-office   delivered   enhanced   gross
location   miscast   sequel   sequence   setting
supporting   twists   unfolds

1 As the story _____ , the pace of the action quickens.
2 The film is an _____ of Ian Fleming's best-selling novel.
3 There is a car chase in the opening _____ of the film.
4 The film was shot on _____ in the mountains of Scotland.
5 Keira Knightley was badly _____ in the role of the villain.
6 An instant _____ hit when it was released, the film went on to _____ over $200 million.
7 The film was let down by below-average performances by the _____ cast.
8 After numerous _____ and turns, there's a nail-biting finale.
9 The back streets of New York provide the perfect _____ for this *film noir*.
10 Brad Pitt _____ a fine performance in the leading role.
11 The movie is beautifully filmed and _____ by digital technology.
12 *The Two Towers* is the _____ to the highly-acclaimed *Fellowship of the Ring*.

5 What is the function of the sentences in exercise 4? Put them under the correct heading.

1	describing the plot
2	describing the acting
3	describing the filming and how the film looks
4	giving general and background information about the film

WRITING TIP

In a review, we use the present simple tense to describe the plot of a film, book or play.

6 SPEAKING Work in pairs. Read the *Writing tip*, then describe the plot of a film to your partner, without using the names of any of the characters or actors. Can your partner guess the film?

I can write a film review.

1 In pairs, look at the adjectives for describing films. Which aspects of films (1–5) can they be used to describe? (Some adjectives can describe more than one aspect.)

Adjectives describing films

big-budget disappointing edgy epic far-fetched fast-moving flawed frightening gripping light-hearted low-budget moving powerful predictable serious third-rate thought-provoking violent wacky X-rated

1 the performance of the actors
2 the story
3 the film in general
4 the screenplay
5 special effects

WRITING TIP

You can describe aspects of a film more accurately and subtly by combining adjectives with modifying adverbs such as:
a (little) bit not particularly not very quite fairly pretty rather very extremely
Remember that the adverb *quite* comes <u>before</u> the indefinite article:
It's **quite a** slow-moving film.

2 Read the *Writing tip* and rank the modifying adverbs in order, from the strongest to the weakest. Then find examples of some of them in the text on page 22.

>>> VOCABULARY BUILDER 2.3: MODIFYING ADVERBS: WORKBOOK PAGE 103 <<<

3 SPEAKING Work in pairs. Think of a film that you have both seen. Talk about the film using adjectives from exercise 1 and modifying adverbs.

I thought the acting in 'Twilight' was pretty third-rate.

WRITING TIP

We can use participle clauses to improve our writing style.
This film was released in 2002 and was an instant success.
→ *Released in 2002, this film was an instant success.*
'Hancock' stars Will Smith and is a superhero adventure that left me cold.
→ *Starring Will Smith, 'Hancock' is a superhero adventure that left me cold.*

4 Use participle clauses to rewrite these sentences that introduce films.
1 *Saving Private Ryan* was directed by three-time Academy Award winner Steven Spielberg and is one of the most gripping war films ever made.

2 *The Incredible Hulk* was panned by the critics when it was first released, but it was a box office hit.
3 *Titanic* is one of the most successful films of all time, and won eleven Oscars.
4 *Forrest Gump* features Tom Hanks in the title role and is my favourite movie of all time.
5 *The Mist* was adapted from the Stephen King novel and is a terrifying horror film.

5 Match 1–8 with a–h to make sentences that give overall opinions of films. Which ones are (a) positive? (b) negative? (c) lukewarm?

1 If you have an aversion to pointless special effects,
2 Not the greatest film ever made,
3 For hardcore fantasy fans,
4 This movie is, quite simply, fantastic and
5 There are some nice moments,
6 If, like me, you are a lover of feel-good movies,
7 The film is well worth seeing,
8 Despite being a low-budget art-house film,

a this is one of the most impressive movies you'll see.
b this film is not for you.
c but it's marred by poor a performance from the lead.
d this film won't live up to all the hype surrounding its release.
e if only for the dazzling special effects.
f then you won't regret going to see this film.
g but worth the price of admission.
h I thoroughly recommend it.

6 Make notes about a film that you have seen. Follow the plan below.

1 Background information about the film (title, genre, director, based on a book? date? other interesting facts?).
2 A brief summary of the plot.
3 The film's strengths and weaknesses.
4 Your overall verdict on the film and a recommendation (positive or negative).

7 Write your review (200–250 words). Use the notes you made in exercise 6.

8 Check your work using the list below.

CHECK YOUR WORK

Have you:
☐ followed the plan correctly?
☐ written the correct number of words?
☐ included at least one modifying adverb?
☐ checked the spelling and grammar?

Vocabulary

1 Add a prefix to the words below and use them to complete the sentences.

awed ~~easy~~ occupied orientated nerved

Harry knew he'd made a mistake, so he felt very uneasy when his boss called him into his office.

1 Jack soon became _____ in the narrow streets of the city. He realised he was completely lost.
2 Olivia was too _____ with her new boyfriend to notice that her mother was ill.
3 It was the first time she'd sung in public, so she was completely _____ when she walked out on stage.
4 The doctor's failure to meet her eyes during the appointment _____ Grace considerably.

Mark: ___ /4

2 Use the words in brackets to form compound adjectives which are synonyms of the first word.

artificial (make)   man-made

1 intolerant (mind)   _____
2 pleasing (warm)   _____
3 sensible (head)   _____
4 mean (fist)   _____
5 intelligent (wit)   _____
6 scary (raise)   _____

Mark: ___ /6

3 Match the adjectives (1–5) with their opposites (a–e).

1 serious   a gripping
2 believable   b flawed
3 dull   c third-rate
4 perfect   d far-fetched
5 high-quality   e light-hearted

Mark: ___ /5

4 Complete the sentences with the adverbs below.

categorically ironically loosely promptly widely

1 The film *A Beautiful Mind* is _____ based on the life of John Forbes Nash.
2 The athlete finished the race and _____ collapsed onto the track.
3 The idea that human actions are responsible for climate change is now _____ accepted.
4 William's boss _____ refused to give him a pay rise. He said it was impossible.
5 Van Gogh is one of the world's most famous painters, yet _____ he only sold one picture when he was alive.

Mark: ___ /5

Grammar

5 Complete the sentences. Use a past or present form for describing habitual actions in the first gap and *like* or *as* in the second gap.

1 When my grandfather was younger, he _____ work _____ a tennis coach every summer.
2 My sister _____ losing her temper these days, just _____ our mum!
3 Tom's a good tennis player, but he _____ behave _____ a child whenever he loses a game.
4 Don't worry. I _____ making mistakes _____ that when I was your age.

Mark: ___ /8

6 Complete the sentences with the correct form of the phrasal verbs below. Where possible use an object pronoun.

look after   look into   make up   put on   stand up to   think over

1 My sister's got two children, so when she goes out I always _____ .
2 I was going to carry my jacket, but when I saw it was raining I decided _____ .
3 Police have not yet found the person responsible for the burglary but the case _____ .
4 Her father is very domineering, but she's started _____ and tell him what she thinks.
5 The court proved that she had lied. The story of her husband's disappearance _____ to obtain his life insurance money.
6 When Mike asked Holly to move in with him she said she _____ .

Mark: ___ /6

7 Complete the text with the correct past tense form of the verbs in brackets.

Gary was fed up. He [1]_____ (wait) for his girlfriend for over an hour and she still [2]_____ (not turn up). Just as he [3]_____ (contemplate) going home, she walked round the corner looking pleased with herself. Her smile [4]_____ (vanish), however, when she saw the expression on Gary's face.

'What's wrong?' she asked.

'You're late again,' he said.

'No, I'm not,' she replied, 'The clocks [5]_____ (go back) last night. You [6]_____ (be) early!'

Mark: ___ /6

Total: ___ /40

Speaking

1 Work in pairs. Decide what the three most important personality traits are for working in a large, office-based company.

2 Compare your ideas with another pair. Can you agree on a joint 'top three'?

Reading

3 Look quickly at the four extracts written by four different people and decide:

a what type of text they are all from.

b what the topic of each paragraph is.

A I consider myself to be a self-starter who can show initiative when appropriate. I am also a team player with excellent communication skills and a sense of humour. As my references will indicate, I am well-organised in my approach to work and have the ability to manage large and complex projects with the minimum of fuss. I have a pragmatic approach to problem-solving and believe that almost nothing is impossible, given the right attitude and abilities.

B Having worked at a comparably-sized logistics company in Riga for more than three years, I firmly believe that I have the necessary programming skills for this position at InterPost. I am familiar with all of the programming languages most widely-used in this field, including XHTML, CSS2/3 and JavaScript. I have also acquired a good understanding of how the logistics and distribution industry functions. As well as being a fluent English-speaker, I am also fluent in Latvian (my mother tongue) and Russian, and I have a sound knowledge of French.

C Although my current job offered a degree of challenge at the start, I have now reached a stage where I need to broaden my professional horizons in order to develop my skills further. That is why I am keen to move to a larger company. In addition, I am aware that a high level of fluency in English is a great asset professionally, which is why I intend to spend a minimum of two years in an English-speaking country to perfect my language skills.

D After graduating with a degree in Computer Science from Vilnius University in my home country of Lithuania, I completed a post-graduate diploma in web design at the University of Manchester. This led to a teaching post at the same institution. After four years in academia, I decided on a change of direction and applied for various jobs in the commercial sector. I relocated to Madrid to work for a large advertising agency as their head of web development, a position I found both challenging and enjoyable.

4 For questions 1–8, choose the correct extract (A–D).

Which writer says that he or she:

1 responds well in difficult situations?

2 does not find his/her current job demanding enough?

3 has lived in several different countries?

4 has the technical skills necessary?

5 co-operates well with other workers?

6 initially worked in education?

7 is keen to raise his/her level of English?

8 has a good knowledge of the business as a whole?

Listening

5 🎧 1.13 Listen to a job interview. Which of the extracts in exercise 3 did Edgars write?

6 🎧 1.13 Listen again. Answer the questions.

1 What is the main purpose of Edgars's visit to the UK?

2 What joke does the interviewer make when they're talking about visits to Edgars's homeland?

3 Why does the interviewer continue the interview when the fire alarm first sounds?

4 Why does the interviewer offer Edgars the job and press him for a response, rather than waiting for a letter to be sent?

5 What assistance does the interviewer offer Edgars in relation to accommodation?

Writing

7 Imagine you are Edgars. Write an account of your job interview as part of an email to a friend. Write about:

• your feelings before the interview.

• what happened during the interview.

• what happened at the end of the interview.

• how you feel about it now, looking back.

1 Can you give any examples of: (a) 'urban myths' (strange well-known stories that many people believe but are unlikely to be true) and (b) 'Internet myths' (stories spread via the Internet which turn out not to be true)?

2 Do the Use of English exam task.

USE OF ENGLISH exam task

Complete the text with the correct form of the words in brackets.

In 2007 a rumour spread by chatrooms and text message hit the price of bananas from China's Hainan island. The messages claimed the fruit contained viruses that bore a strong ¹_____ (similar) to SARS, the severe respiratory ²_____ (ill) which has killed hundreds of people worldwide. ³_____ (produce) of the bananas in Hainan say the ⁴_____ (result) price slump cost them up to 20 million yuan (US$2.6m) a day. China's Agriculture Ministry dismissed the SARS claim as completely ⁵_____ (true). Officials claimed that there was no ⁶_____ (science) evidence to support the rumour and that it was ⁷_____ (total) without foundation. They added that it was ⁸_____ (possible) for humans to contract a plant virus. The banana fears come amid international concerns over tainted Chinese exports, including ⁹_____ (allege) of poisons in pet food and toothpaste. The state-owned China Daily newspaper ¹⁰_____ (recent) criticised China's food safety regulators and called on the government to do more to protect Chinese consumers.

3 🎧 1.14 Do the Listening exam task.

LISTENING exam task

Listen to a radio programme about an urban myth. Choose the correct answer (A–D).

1 The New York Times report about alligators stated that
  A the first alligator sighting took place in sewage.
  B one of those who first saw an alligator was killed.
  C one was first seen during a period of cold weather.
  D local authorities refused to investigate the matter.

2 Some of the people at Brooklyn Museum station
  A said the animal they'd seen was extremely big.
  B witnessed an alligator transported on a train.
  C tried to trap the animal in a rubbish bin.
  D provided an explanation for the animal's presence.

3 According to a popular myth, alligators in the sewer
  A reproduced and lived in large groups.
  B had been introduced to fight rats.
  C were of a type specific to New York.
  D climbed up into people's toilets.

4 Scientists think
  A alligators grow too big to fit into sewers.
  B there's no food for alligators in sewers.
  C sewers are too cold for alligators to breed.
  D they need to do more research into the myth.

4 Do the Reading exam task.

READING exam task

Read the text. Decide which sentence part (A–J) best fits each gap (1–8). There are two options that you do not need.

An article in the Japanese *Mainichi Daily News* (which claims merely to ¹_____ that appeared in a magazine called *Fushigi Knuckles*) tells the story of the attempt to introduce Worm Burgers in Japan. A food company, so the story goes, tried to market worms as food for human consumption because of their high nutritional value. Worm Burgers contained ground worms (instead of beef), chopped onions, wheat, flour and egg – with a little milk to make it go down more easily. The magazine notes that ²_____ the Worm Burger ended up as a major flop. The company had been targeting women and young people, but appear to have struggled to overcome the image of worms ³_____.

It's possible that the story is true, but it is more likely a recycling of the old Worm Burger urban myth ⁴_____. This urban myth started when papers reported that food scientists were experimenting with earthworms as a source of protein. Take, for instance, this article that appeared in a number of American newspapers in mid-December, 1975.

'The lowly earthworm, ⁵_____ the fisherman, is burrowing its way into the world of big business, and may be put to work soon to help man grow crops, dispose of garbage and even satisfy his dietary need for protein. If produced in sufficient quantity at a cost competitive with other protein materials, worms could be used as feed for pets, poultry, fish and other animals, ⁶_____. Seventy-two per cent of a worm's dry weight is protein.'

After a few articles like this had appeared, it was simply a matter of time before tales began to spread of McDonalds and other fast-food chains ⁷_____. However, worms are a much more expensive source of protein than beef, so there's little reason to fear that fast-food chains will start padding their burgers with worms ⁸_____.

A in the near future
B secretly using worms in their burgers
C instead of protein
D from the late 1970s
E ignored by almost everybody but
F replacing the beef with worms
G despite the best intentions
H be repeating a report
I as a bizarre food
J as well as food for people

THIS UNIT INCLUDES

Vocabulary ■ verb (+ adjective) + noun collocations ■ set phrases ■ phrases related to friendship ■ literal and figurative language ■ comparative phrases ■ phrases for negotiating ■ adjectives for describing places ■ dependent prepositions (1)
Grammar ■ contrast: present perfect simple and continuous ■ verb patterns
Speaking ■ talking about relationships ■ negotiation
Writing ■ an article about a place

Partners 3

3A VOCABULARY AND LISTENING Relationships

I can talk about different kinds of relationship.

1 **SPEAKING** Work in groups. Look at the photos and answer the questions.

1 What kind of partnership does each photo show?
2 What qualities are needed to make each partnership successful?
3 What other kinds of partnership can you think of? What qualities do they require to be successful?

2 🎧 1.15 Listen to five people talking about their partners. Match the speakers (1–5) with the kinds of partnership (a–e) they are describing. Which words gave you a clue?

a co-presenters of a news programme ☐
b joint owners of a clothes shop ☐
c a composer and lyricist ☐
d co-stars of a stage play ☐
e a rally driver and a navigator ☐

3 🎧 1.15 Listen again. Say which speaker (1–5) mentions these things. Then answer the questions.

a getting depressed ☐ (About what?)
b being like a married couple ☐ (In what way?)
c their different backgrounds ☐ (What are they?)
d a partner's irritating habit ☐ (What is it?)
e having to be careful about what she says ☐ (Why?)

4 Match the verbs (1–9) with the nouns (a–i) to form common expressions.

Collocation: verb + noun

1	voice	a	a friendship
2	form	b	your mind
3	offer	c	a dispute
4	pay	d	the favour
5	take	e	a setback
6	resolve	f	attention
7	return	g	advice
8	speak	h	control
9	suffer	i	an opinion

LEARN THIS!

Some verb + adjective + noun collocations are also common. Look for these in your dictionary and in texts you read.
Over the years, they suffered some major setbacks.
Pay close attention to what I'm about to tell you.

5 Read the *Learn this!* box. Then complete the sentences with expressions from exercise 4.

1 It's impossible to _____ a close _____ with somebody unless you have a lot in common.
2 In any friendship, one partner is always stronger and tends to _____ _____ of the relationship.
3 If you're with a friend, it's always OK to _____ an honest _____ .
4 A friendship that has _____ a major _____ is stronger than one which has not.
5 A friend will never get annoyed or upset with you for _____ constructive _____ .
6 The easiest way to _____ a _____ is to ignore it and pretend that nothing is wrong.

6 **SPEAKING** Work in pairs. Do you agree or disagree with the statements in exercise 5? Give reasons and examples.

> I disagree with number one. I think it's perfectly possible to form a close friendship with somebody who is very different from you. In fact, some people say that 'opposites attract'!

>>> VOCABULARY BUILDER 3.1: SET PHRASES: WORKBOOK PAGE 103 <<<

I can discuss the meaning and importance of friendship.

1 SPEAKING In pairs, discuss this quotation by C.S.Lewis, author of The *Chronicles of Narnia*. Do you agree with it? Can you give any examples of how friendships in your own life began?

> *Friendship is born at that moment*
> *when one person says to another: 'What!*
> *You, too? I thought I was the only one.'*

2 Read the song. How would sum up the meaning of the lyrics?

I turn to you

When I'm lost in the rain,
In your eyes I know I'll find the light to light my way.
When I'm scared, [1]losing ground,
When my world is going crazy, you can [2]turn it all around.
And when I'm down you're there; pushing me to the top.
You're always there; giving me all you got.
For [3]a shield from the storm,
For a friend; for a love
To keep me safe and warm,
I turn to you.
For the strength to be strong;
For [4]the will to carry on,
For everything you do,
For everything that's true,
I turn to you.
When I lose the will to win,
I just reach for you and [5]I can reach the sky again.
I can do anything,
'Cause your love is so amazing; 'cause your love inspires me.
And when I need a friend, you're always on my side,
Giving me faith to get me through the night.
For the arms to be my shelter through all the rain,
For truth that will never change,
For [6]someone to lean on,
For a heart I can rely on through anything,
For [7]the one who I can run to ...
I turn to you.

3 Explain the underlined phrases in your own words.

4 SPEAKING Work in pairs. How many other songs can you think of about friendship? Compare your ideas with the class.

5 🎧 1.16 Listen to a woman describing a friend. Which of these words and phrases best describe that friend, and why?

an acquaintance   an associate   a childhood friend
a classmate   a crony   a fair-weather friend
a family friend   a friend of a friend   a soulmate
a workmate   one of a close-knit circle (of friends)

6 🎧 1.16 Complete these excerpts from the description using the words below. (You need to use some words more than once.) Then listen again and check.

back   down   inside   out   through   to   up

1 As friends, we go _____ more than ten years and we've known each other even longer than that.
2 We haven't fallen _____ at all in recent years, but in the past, we've had our _____s and _____s.
3 We've even had the odd set-_____ over the years.
4 We've been _____ so much together.
5 Recently, problems at work have been getting me _____ .
6 She's always been somebody I can really open _____ _____ .
7 It's easy to talk to close friends because they know you _____ _____ .
8 She's very dependable, and honest _____ and _____ .

7 Look at the examples of the present perfect in exercise 6. Try to explain the choice of the simple or the continuous form. Use Grammar Reference 3.1 on page 119 to help you.

>>> GRAMMAR BUILDER 3.1: PRESENT PERFECT SIMPLE AND CONTINUOUS: PAGE 119 <<<

8 Explain the difference in meaning between sentences a and b in each pair, if there is any.

1 a I've spent a lot of time with my best friend.
  b I've been spending a lot of time with my best friend.
2 a We've drifted apart since leaving school.
  b We've been drifting apart since leaving school.
3 a How long have you been working in IT?
  b How long have you worked in IT?
4 a Have you seen the girl in the flat below us?
  b Have you been seeing the girl in the flat below us?
5 a Have you been wearing the coat I bought you?
  b Have you worn the coat I bought you?

9 Look at the words and phrases in exercise 5 and choose one type of friend from your own life. Write down five key points about your relationship with that person. Try to include appropriate phrases from the song and from exercise 6.

10 SPEAKING Work in pairs. Take turns to be A and B.

Student A: Using your notes from exercise 9 to tell your partner about your friend. Then answer B's questions.

Student B: Listen carefully to your partner's description. Then ask three questions about the friend using the present perfect simple or continuous. For example:

> What have you been doing together recently?
> What's the biggest argument you've ever had?

3C CULTURE Marriage in the UK

I can express my opinions on marriage.

1 SPEAKING Explain this slightly altered quotation from the Irish writer Oscar Wilde in your own words. What does it tell you about his attitude to marriage?

> *Bigamy is having one husband or wife too many. So is monogamy.*

2 SPEAKING Work in pairs. Look at the chart about weddings in Britain. Present the information it contains to another pair.

WEDDING VENUES

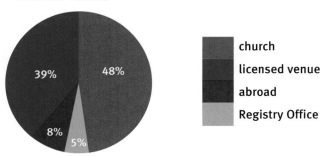

- church
- licensed venue
- abroad
- Registry Office

licensed venue = a non-religious venue (e.g. hotel or restaurant) which has been granted a licence to perform wedding ceremonies
Registry Office (or Register Office) = a municipal office which performs non-religious wedding ceremonies and also officially records births, deaths and marriages

3 SPEAKING Work in pairs. Compare the information in exercise 2 with your own country. Answer the questions.

1 Are the basic choices of venue the same? Explain any differences.
2 Do you think church weddings are more or less popular in your country? Why?

4 🎧 1.17 Listen to a news report. What is it chiefly about?

a the rising cost of weddings in Britain
b British habits and attitudes concerning weddings
c the declining popularity of weddings in Britain

5 🎧 1.17 Listen again. Are the sentences true or false according to the report? Correct the false ones.

1 42 per cent of men and women would like to lose weight before their wedding.
2 Couples getting married intend the wedding to cost, on average, £10,600.
3 The survey only included men and women between the ages of 20 and 34.
4 Nearly a quarter of brides pay more towards the wedding than the groom does.
5 Younger couples tend to have shorter engagements than older couples.
6 A lot of men said they would most like their bride to look like Kate Winslet on their wedding day.

6 SPEAKING Work in pairs. Answer the questions and justify your answers.

1 Would you pay for any beauty treatments before your wedding day? Would you want or expect your fiancé(e) to?
2 If you get married, which celebrity would you most like to resemble on your wedding day? Which celebrity would you most like your fiancé(e) to resemble?

7 🎧 1.18 Listen to six people talking about different aspects of weddings and marriage. Choose the correct answers.

1 A man is talking about weddings. What often spoils them, in his opinion?
a the music during the evening
b the standard of food at the reception
c a family argument
2 A woman is talking about the age you can legally marry in the UK. What is her opinion of the law?
a She thinks the age should be raised.
b She doesn't think parental consent should be needed.
c She believes the existing law should remain.
3 A man is complaining about couples who choose to marry in a church. Why is he critical?
a He thinks everyone should have a civil ceremony.
b He thinks they choose it for the wrong reasons.
c He doesn't believe in making religious vows.
4 A woman is discussing superstitions surrounding marriage. What is her attitude to them?
a She is determined to follow them as much as possible.
b She doesn't believe in them but thinks they're worth following as part of tradition.
c She thinks they're ridiculous and refuses to follow them.
5 A man is explaining the traditional order of speeches at a British wedding reception. Which three people give speeches?
a the best man, the bride and the groom
b the bride's father, the groom and the best man
c the bride, the bride's father and the best man
6 A woman is talking about unusual wedding venues. What is her attitude to them?
a She thinks that the more unusual the venue is, the better.
b She thinks it's very romantic.
c She thinks people just do it for publicity.

8 SPEAKING Work in pairs. Answer the questions.

1 What is the ideal age to get married, in your opinion?
2 Do you know any superstitions connected to weddings in your country?
3 What happens at a typical wedding in your country? (Think about the ceremony, the reception, the guests, gifts, etc.)

1 SPEAKING Work in pairs. Discuss what problems might be experienced by two people wanting to be a couple if:

a they're from different continents.
b they follow different religions.
c one is from a rich family and the other from an ordinary working-class family.

2 SPEAKING Share your ideas from exercise 1 with the class. Decide whether a, b or c would create the most problems. Would you personally be willing to face these problems for the right person?

3 Read the text quickly. Which of the problems from exercise 1 did Ehdaa and Sean face?

4 Read the text again. Are the sentences true or false? In which paragraph A–K can you find evidence to support your answers?

1 At their first meeting the attraction between Sean and Ehdaa was physical.
2 The writer finds it surprising that the army was not more supportive of the relationship between Sean and Ehdaa.
3 Sean's commanding officer made it impossible for Sean and Ehdaa to see each other after the wedding.
4 As Ehdaa set off to be reunited with Sean, she was preoccupied with the risks of the journey.
5 Members of Sean's patrol knew that the secret wedding was going to take place.
6 Sean took time off from his army duties in Iraq in order to be with Ehdaa.
7 The fact that there has been media interest in Ehdaa's story makes it easier for her to enter Jordan.
8 Sean and Ehdaa found it difficult to communicate with each other when they were face to face.
9 The army overestimated the strength of feeling between Sean and Ehdaa.
10 The rules of the military forbid soldiers from marrying local civilians while on active service.
11 Sean feels slightly awkward when he is reunited with Ehdaa in Jordan.
12 Sean changed his religious beliefs before marrying Ehdaa.

READING TIP

Many military words and phrases can be used in a **literal** sense to describe military events, or in a **figurative** sense to describe other kinds of events.
Literal: *Caesar's armies outflanked their enemy and attacked them from behind.*
Figurative: *The Prime Minister's announcement has outflanked his opponents, who were planning to raise this very issue themselves.*

Love and War

A They say all's fair in love and war; unless, perhaps, it involves the US Army. A year ago, when an American soldier fell in love in Baghdad, his commander ordered him not to marry. What was a heartsick soldier to do? Well, Sgt Sean Blackwell launched a secret mission to marry the Iraqi woman he loved. That's when the Army came down with both boots and ordered Blackwell home, 11,000 kilometres from his bride, Ehdaa, apparently never to see her again.

B But there was one thing the Army didn't count on. It's something else they say about romance – that love, of course, conquers all. It's 6 a.m. in Baghdad and Ehdaa Blackwell is donning a bullet-proof vest. She's filled with hope for a new future, even as she waves goodbye to everything she has ever known. Ehdaa is making a run of 500 kilometres through the dangers of the Sunni Triangle, trying to reach her new American husband, the one that the Army ordered out of her life. 'Sometimes, you just fall in love and you don't know why. I think it's our fate,' says Ehdaa. 'I think we're meant to be together. I just can't wait to see him.'

C The dream is to bring together two lives that couldn't be more different. Ehdaa grew up wealthy in a country at war. Sean grew up peacefully, in a working-class area in Florida. He listened to country music; she listened to Saddam. She went to medical school; he held to a family tradition, following his father and six uncles into the military.

D After the fall of Baghdad, Blackwell landed in one of those places where the tension was greatest, Baghdad's biggest hospital. One day, amid the chaos, in walked Ehdaa, a young Iraqi doctor. 'To be honest, when I first met her, I was like, you know, she's very, very attractive, but you know, what's the point of trying to start a relationship over here?' recalls Blackwell. 'And the more we talked, the more we started to learn about each other, and it didn't take long for, you know, emotional attachment to grow there.'

E 'I saw a tall, shy, handsome soldier. He had the most beautiful eyes I had ever seen,' says Ehdaa. Ehdaa had never met an American before in her life. But soon, she was seeing this American every few days. Blackwell had been in Iraq only a few weeks, but between patrols and weapons raids, she'd bring him home-cooked meals and hours of conversation. 'I started thinking, what we are doing is impossible. I'm Muslim and he's a Christian. I'm Iraqi and he's American. It just can't happen,' says Ehdaa. 'It did. Love can produce miracles. I do believe this now.'

F After three months of war-zone dating, Blackwell took the plunge – keeping, of course, with local tradition, where a marriage proposal is a question asked man-to-man. Blackwell asked Ehdaa's brother, who told him, 'I'd be honoured for you to marry my sister.' But under local law, a Muslim woman can marry only a Muslim man. So Blackwell stood before an Iraqi judge and said in Arabic: 'There's only one God and that's God and Mohamed is the messenger of God.' Through those words, Blackwell became a Muslim. It was a conversion of convenience, not conviction.

G The couple was ready to say 'I do' when Blackwell's commanding officer stepped in. There was no regulation against a marriage, but the battalion commander was worried that, in a war zone, it would be a dangerous distraction. So he ordered Blackwell not to get married. 'We were brought together by some, some higher force than ourselves, and it was meant to be,' says Blackwell. 'And I wasn't going to let anybody stop that.' For the first time in his career, Sgt Blackwell set out to disobey an order. On a sizzling August morning, he went out on patrol with a small team. The soldiers responded to a rocket attack. But on the way back to base, the patrol made an unauthorised detour to a restaurant.

H Two soldiers with heavy weapons stood guard outside. Blackwell went into the courtyard where Ehdaa was waiting with her family, a judge, and a pair of rings. Friends translated the Arabic vows and recorded on tape one small moment of peace in a larger war. It ended with a kiss on the forehead, and then Blackwell went back on patrol with his team. Once the battalion commander found out about the wedding, Blackwell was exiled to Baghdad Island in the Tigris River. However, no charges were filed against Blackwell, and it may be that the Army just wanted the whole thing to go away. Blackwell got away with no more than a reprimand and left the military with an honourable discharge.

I But six months after his wedding, Blackwell said goodbye to his mother and headed back towards the war zone he had recently left. Ehdaa, escorted by her little brother, sped past the war zones of Fallujah and Ramadi towards the rendezvous on the border between Iraq and Jordan. Soon, the 11,000-kilometre separation is cut down to a stretch of highway, 80 kilometres long.

J At the border, guards search the car three times, and Jordanian intelligence pulls Ehdaa and her brother aside for questioning. There is no guarantee that she will make it out of Iraq – Saddam didn't allow doctors to have passports. She spends three hours going nowhere, when the improbable happens: one of the guards recognises her from an article he read about an Iraqi woman who married an American soldier. And in this dusty little outpost, fame is a passport. Ehdaa continues on her journey and at last, in Jordan, the couple are reunited. 'She looks just as beautiful as the first time I saw her. I feel so comfortable. It's like I haven't been away from her for six months,' says Blackwell.

K In a sense, the Blackwells are exactly what the Pentagon had dreamed of at the start of the war – American soldiers embraced by Iraq. It seems ironic that when the military got what it wanted, at least on a small scale, it manoeuvred to divide, only to be outflanked by a soldier who would not disobey the orders of his heart.

5 Read the *Reading tip* on page 30. Complete these verb-noun collocations from the text.

  a to _____ a (secret) mission
  b to _____ a bullet-proof vest
  c to _____ an order
  d to _____ on patrol
  e to _____ to an attack
  f to _____ a detour
  g to _____ guard
  h to _____ charges

6 Complete the sentences with collocations from exercise 5. Are the phrases used literally or figuratively?

  1 On the way home from school, we _____ into town to buy a new video game.
  2 The chief executive was accused of negligence, but _____ by pointing out that the events in question occurred before his term of employment began.
  3 Three members of the battalion were severely reprimanded for _____ after they gave unauthorised interviews to the press.
  4 Some African governments _____ to eradicate malaria by 2015.
  5 They met on the steps of the Art Institute of Chicago, where two bronze lions _____ outside the entrance.
  6 Some areas of town are considered so lawless that police officers are instructed to _____ before going on foot patrol.

7 SPEAKING Work in pairs. Think about a story you know which involves love triumphing over obstacles. It could be a true story, a book or a film. Answer the questions.

  1 What exactly were the obstacles?
  2 How did the couple manage to overcome them?
  3 What is your opinion of the story?

8 SPEAKING Work in pairs. Present your story to the class.

1 **SPEAKING** When you work closely with someone, what kind of person do you work better with? Give reasons.

a a family member
c an acquaintance
b a close friend
d a stranger

2 Complete the text with the infinitive, base form (infinitive without *to*), past participle or *-ing* form of the verbs in brackets. Then describe the twins' working relationship in your own words.

Like many identical twins, Helen and Morna Mulgray are used to ¹_____ (do) things together. They have always enjoyed ²_____ (watch) the same television programmes and have tended ³_____ (read) the same books too. They even chose ⁴_____ (pursue) the same career as teachers. Now, at the age of 73, being retired has allowed them ⁵_____ (focus) on a mutual hobby: writing.

'We both spent 31 years ⁶_____ (work) as English teachers, so we've always been keen on ⁷_____ (write),' said Morna.

It took the twins five years ⁸_____ (get) their novel, which is entitled *No Suspicious Circumstances*, ⁹_____ (accepted) by a publisher, although they have since had three further novels ¹⁰_____ (publish).

Morna, who is the elder by ten minutes, said: 'We both sit at the laptop, and whoever happens ¹¹_____ (be) closest to the computer or feels like ¹²_____ (type) just starts.' Helen added: 'Occasionally there are small disagreements over the text but ... ' She lets her sister ¹³_____ (finish): 'It rarely happens.'

3 Find one verb in the text for each verb pattern (1–5). Use the verb to make your own example sentence.

1 verb + infinitive
decide: *We decided to get married in June.*
_____ : _____

2 verb + object + infinitive
persuade: *My sister persuaded me to take up aerobics.*
_____ : _____

3 verb + object + base form
make: *My parents made me learn the piano.*
_____ : _____

4 verb (+ object) + *-ing* form
imagine: *I can't imagine (my brother) becoming rich.*
_____ : _____

5 verb + object + past participle
have: *She had her car stolen last weekend.*
_____ : _____

>>> GRAMMAR BUILDER 3.2: VERB PATTERNS (1): PAGE 119 <<<

4 Look at the dictionary entry. Does this verb take an infinitive or *-ing* form? How do you know?

post·pone /pə'spəʊn; NAmE poʊ'spoʊn/ *verb* ~ **sth (to/until sth)** to arrange for an event, etc. to take place at a later time or date **SYN** PUT OFF: [VN] *The game has already been postponed three times.* ◇ *We'll have to postpone the meeting until next week.* ◇ [V -ing] *It was an unpopular decision to postpone building the new hospital.*—compare CANCEL ▶ **post·pone·ment** *noun* [U,C]: *Riots led to the postponement of local elections.*

5 Use a dictionary to find out if the verbs below:

1 take an infinitive.
2 take an *-ing* form.
3 take either, with no difference in meaning.
4 take either, but with a difference in meaning.

claim   demand   fail   guarantee   hate   love   refuse   remember   risk   stop   try

LOOK OUT!

Verb patterns can include passive, perfect and continuous forms of the infinitive or *-ing* form.
She claims to have met Leona Lewis. (perfect infinitive)
The window appears to have been broken deliberately. (passive perfect infinitive)

6 Read the *Look out!* box. Then complete the text with the infinitive or *-ing* form of the verbs in brackets. You may need to use passive and/or perfect forms.

Sam and Dave were one of the most popular singing duos of the 1960s. Their live performances were so good that some other stars of their day refused ¹_____ (book) on the same bill in case they were made ²_____ (look) second-rate. In his autobiography, the boss of Atlantic Records remembers ³_____ (impress) by Sam and Dave's 'harmony and goodwill' on stage. In fact, the two performers were only pretending ⁴_____ (have) a good relationship. Off stage, they were hardly managing ⁵_____ (stay) on speaking terms. When Dave shot and injured his own wife in a domestic dispute, Sam gave up ⁶_____ (try) ⁷_____ (maintain) any kind of relationship with his partner. Although Dave seems ⁸_____ (forgive) by his wife shortly after the shooting, Sam recalls ⁹_____ (disgust) so much by the event that he told Dave: 'I'll sing with you but I'll never speak to you again.' And although they went on ¹⁰_____ (perform) together, he claims ¹¹_____ (not speak) a word to Dave for the next twelve years.

>>> GRAMMAR BUILDER 3.3: VERB PATTERNS (2): PAGE 120 <<<

7 **SPEAKING** Work in pairs. Tell your partner something that you:

1 regret not having done.
2 can imagine having been said about you.
3 were taught to do by a relative.
4 would hate being made to listen to.
5 hope to be doing in five years' time.

I can discuss suggestions and negotiate a course of action.

1 SPEAKING Work in pairs. Look at the photos in exercise 2. Match 1–8 with a–f to make comparative phrases and decide which café each phrase is likely to apply to. You can use words a–f more than once.

1 more attentive
2 livelier
3 more affluent
4 larger
5 more affordable
6 higher standards of
7 more laid-back
8 more up-market

a portions
b hygiene
c staff
d atmosphere
e clientele
f drinks

2 SPEAKING Work in pairs. Compare and contrast the photos. What kind of people would you expect to find at each café? Which café would you prefer to visit, and why?

3 SPEAKING Work in pairs. Imagine you are business partners who plan to buy a café. Which of the factors below do you think is most important? Give reasons.

1 location
2 size
3 internal decoration
4 external appearance
5 name
6 quality of staff

4 🎧 1.19 Listen to two business partners discussing three cafés. Which do they decide to buy? Which two factors from exercise 3 lead to the decision?

a The Soup Bowl   b Mario's   c The Corner Café

5 🎧 1.19 Complete these useful phrases from the dialogue. Then listen again and check.

1 So, let's look at the different _____ .
2 What puts me _____ is …
3 All in _____ , it isn't very appealing.
4 I think we should _____ onto the next option.
5 This one has quite a lot _____ for it, in my opinion.
6 Can you think of any _____ ?
7 I suppose there are _____ around that.
8 I think it's definitely _____ considering.
9 On reflection, maybe we should _____ that option.
10 So, have we _____ a decision?
11 I'll go _____ with that.

6 SPEAKING Work in pairs. Ask and answer the questions.

1 What features would your ideal nightclub have?
2 What do you imagine are the best and worst aspects of working in a nightclub?
3 Do you think owning a nightclub is an easy way to make money? Why?/Why not?

7 SPEAKING Imagine that you and your partner are going to open a new nightclub. Decide on:

1 a name.
2 the type of clientele you wish to attract.
3 the type of music you will play.
4 the image: internal decoration and external appearance.
5 what food and drink you will offer.

8 SPEAKING With your partner, imagine now that you have received the suggestions (1–5) below from a marketing agency for improving the profitability of your new club. Discuss each suggestion and decide which one you are going to choose. Think about questions (a–e) below and include phrases from exercise 5.

a Will it be popular with your clientele?
b Will it be easy/difficult/cheap/expensive to organise?
c Will it be popular/unpopular with local residents?
d Will it be more attractive to people on their own/ in groups?
e Will it be profitable? Why?/Why not?

1 **Fancy dress night!**

Every Thursday
Different theme each week
£5 entry fee
£50 prize for the winning costume

2 **Live music every Saturday night. 10 p.m. – 2 a.m. Local bands. Free entry!**

3 **Happy hour!** Half price drinks from 7 – 8 p.m. every evening.

4 **Free Wi-Fi!** Come in, sit down, log on. Catch up with work or emails.

5 *Singles night*

Half-price entry fee for anyone arriving alone. A great way to make new friends!

1 **SPEAKING** Look at the photos in the article. Which town would you prefer to visit? Give reasons.

2 Read the article. For each town, say which of the topics below are mentioned.

a eating out   e sport
b architecture   f excursions
c nightlife   g culture and arts
d shopping   h surrounding landscape

WRITING TIP

You can liven up a description by going beyond basic vocabulary and using more elaborate words and phrases. This also helps to avoid repetition. Compare:

There are a lot of shops in the town centre.
The town centre boasts an impressive array of shops.

3 Read the *Writing tip*. Then look through the article and find:

1 at least four different ways of saying that there is/are a lot of something.
2 as many different adjectives as possible which have a base meaning of 'attractive'.

4 Work in pairs. Using a dictionary to help you, decide which synonym (a–c) is least likely to be applied to a town or city. What else might it describe?

1 interesting: a captivating   b fascinating   c gripping
2 large: a considerable   b immense   c vast
3 old: a ancient   b antique   c historic
4 modern: a up-to-date   b current   c contemporary

5 Rewrite the sentences, going beyond basic vocabulary. Try not to use the same phrase more than once.

1 There are a lot of old, attractive buildings on the High Street.
2 There are a lot of large, modern buildings in the financial district.
3 The port has a lot of interesting history.
4 There's a lot for young people to do in the town centre.
5 There are a lot of modern Internet cafés near the station.
6 A lot of culture is on offer in the theatre district.

6 **SPEAKING** Work in pairs. Describe some of the attributes of your own town or city, or a place you know well, using these expressions from the article.

1 If _____ is your thing, then …
2 If _____ is/are more your scene, then …
3 For those seeking _____ , …

Come to the Cotswolds!

The Cotswolds region in the centre of England boasts some of the most exquisite scenery in the country, as well as some of the quaintest villages, renowned for their golden Cotswold stone. Alternatively, if shopping and nightlife are more your scene, both are readily available in some of the larger towns. Why not base a visit around two contrasting towns? They make perfect partners for the ideal holiday!

Burford

Rich in history, Burford is situated twenty miles north of Oxford and is reminiscent of a town from a storybook. The High Street, which slopes gently down to the willow-fringed River Windrush, is lined on either side with golden stone houses, some of which date back to the fifteenth century.

Often described as the southern gateway to the Cotswolds, Burford is ideally placed for excursions, whether it be on foot, by car or by bicycle. Explore the picturesque countryside of central England, where idyllic villages tucked away in wooded valleys are waiting to be discovered.

Burford

Cheltenham

If shopping is your thing, then Cheltenham, on the western edge of the Cotswold region, has a great deal to offer, from fashion to furniture and from accessories to antiques. The Beechwood Shopping Centre, a stone's throw from the train station, has a wealth of well-known stores, while for those seeking a more individual purchase, Suffolk Street has a parade of small, independent shops.

By night, the streets of Cheltenham are teeming with life, and thanks to the wide variety of venues offering after-hours entertainment, clubbers are well provided for. The town also caters for couples, and whether you wish to dine at a romantic hide-away or a busy bistro, you'll find yourself spoiled for choice.

Cheltenham

3G WRITING TASK An article

I can write an article about a popular tourist destination.

1 Work in pairs. Look at the adjectives for describing places. Divide them into two groups: positive and negative. Which adjectives could go in either group, depending on your opinion?

Adjectives for describing places

affluent bustling cosmopolitan crowded deprived desolate high-rise hilly historic industrial isolated picturesque remote rundown sprawling thriving touristy vibrant well-connected

2 **SPEAKING** Compare and contrast the two photos using adjectives from exercise 1. Answer questions 1–4 below.

1 Which place would you prefer to visit? Give reasons.
2 Which place would you prefer to live in? Give reasons.
3 What do you imagine would be the advantages and disadvantages of living somewhere isolated?
4 What do you imagine would be the advantages and disadvantages of living somewhere touristy?

STUDY TIP

A dictionary entry will often include information about prepositions that go with that word. Try to learn the word and the preposition together as a phrase. Make a note of them as you come across them. Writing an example sentence can help to fix it in your memory.

3 Read the *Study tip*. Then complete this sentence using information from the dictionary entry below.

Cheltenham benefits _____ excellent transport connections.

bene·fit 0-- /'benɪfɪt/ *noun, verb*

■ *verb* (-t- or -tt-) **1** [VN] to be useful to sb or improve their life in some way: *We should spend the money on something that will benefit everyone.*

2 [V] ~ **(from/by sth)** to be in a better position because of sth: better position because of sth: *Who exactly **stands to benefit** from these changes?*

4 Find expressions 1–12 in the article on page 34 and write the missing preposition.

1 renowned _____
2 rich _____
3 reminiscent _____
4 lined _____
5 to date back _____
6 ideally placed _____
7 a stone's throw _____
8 teeming _____
9 thanks _____
10 well provided _____
11 to cater _____
12 spoilt _____ choice

5 Complete these expressions with a preposition. Use a dictionary.

1 buzzing with
2 to play host _____
3 steeped _____
4 to hark back _____
5 to be home _____
6 blessed _____
7 to date _____
8 to take pride _____

6 Complete the sentences with expressions from exercise 5.

a Cheltenham is [1]_____ to the world-famous Cheltenham racetrack. Every March, the racetrack [2]_____ _____ to the annual Cheltenham Festival, which [3]_____ _____ to 1902.
b The residents of Burford [4]_____ _____ in their town, which is [5]_____ in history. The Bay Tree Hotel, which [6]_____ from the sixteenth century, maintains many original features such as stone floors and open fireplaces.

7 Read the task below. In pairs, choose the two towns you are going to write about and make notes. Use the topics in exercise 2 on page 34 for ideas.

> Write an article for an in-flight magazine extolling the virtues of two contrasting towns in your region.

8 Work in pairs. Write your article (200–250 words).

1 Use your notes to write about one town each. Try to go beyond basic vocabulary.
2 Swap your work and make suggestions for improving your partner's writing.
3 Work together to write the introduction.

9 Check your work using the list below.

CHECK YOUR WORK

Have you:
☐ mentioned a range of attractive features for each town?
☐ written the correct number of words?
☐ gone beyond basic vocabulary?
☐ used the correct prepositions?
☐ checked the spelling and grammar?

1 [Get ready to READ] Look at the photo from a newspaper story. What do you think the story might be? Use the expressions below to help you.

childhood sweethearts romance blossomed drift apart
mutual love to tie the knot

2 Do the Reading exam task.

READING exam task

Read the text. For questions 1–8, choose the correct couple (A–C). The couples may be chosen more than once.

A Beatrice Ballott, 84, first met 87-year-old Ivan Hicks in 1942 when she was a clerk in a bank in Oudtshoorn and he was stationed near the town as part of his training for the RAF. The pair met at a party and their romance soon blossomed, but when Mr Hicks was stationed back in England they drifted apart. Eventually, they both married, although they stayed in touch over the years with letters and cards. However, when Mr Hicks's wife passed away last year he set about going through his diary and it was then that he came across Ms Ballott's telephone number. After his daughter Hazel contacted her for him, the two arranged to see each other. They quickly realised that their mutual love for each other was still present. The pair happily tied the knot on Saturday, 26th September.

B Childhood sweethearts Sue Hammond and Chris Osment have married after being reunited via the Internet 30 years after they first met. Romance first blossomed between the couple when they were 15-year-old pupils at Highfield Comprehensive School in Newcastle, in the north-east of England. But after they left school they didn't set eyes on each other again until last year, when they made contact on the Friends Reunited website. Both Chris and Sue were single following the break-up of their marriages. They chatted to each other every day for two months using webcams before Susan travelled to Chris's new home on the opposite side of the world. She spent two weeks in Sydney before returning to the UK, but then after four painful months apart from Chris, she made the decision to emigrate to Australia for a new life with the man she loved.

C A man has left his wife after meeting a childhood sweetheart he had not seen for nearly half a century. John Pearce walked out on his wife of twenty years to meet up with old friend Jackie Butt and never went back home. They met each other on the Friends Reunited website, the Internet site which puts old school friends back in touch with each other.

Jackie and John met at primary school in Plymouth in 1952 at the age of five and quickly became friends. The two lost touch when Jackie moved on to secondary school. For 26 years Jackie ran a rescue home for rabbits in Hythe, a couple of hundred miles away from John. After being reunited on the Internet, the couple arranged to meet up in Southampton. 'We knew we loved each other before we even met up,' said John. So, taking drastic steps, John resigned from his job and stayed in Southampton. Despite the obstacles they had to overcome, and the people they hurt, Jackie and John both firmly believe it was all worth it.

Which couple:

1 never had a period when they were not in contact? ☐
2 prioritised their own relationship over the feelings of others? ☐
3 first met outside England? ☐
4 were temporarily separated after seeing each other again? ☐
5 both got divorced before getting back in touch? ☐
6 did not re-establish contact online? ☐
7 met at secondary school? ☐
8 lived in the same country while apart? ☐

3 Do the Use of English exam task.

USE OF ENGLISH exam task

Some lines of the text are correct and some contain an extra word which should not be there. Cross out the extra words and tick the lines which are correct.

0	There are many customs and superstitions associated	✓
00	with weddings, most of which had originated centuries	___
1	ago. In the past, a wedding was seen as a time when	___
2	people that were particularly susceptible to bad luck and	___
3	evil spirits. Some traditions, such as the bride is not being	___
4	seen by the groom in her wedding dress before the	___
5	ceremony, are known throughout the UK and many other	___
6	parts of the world too. Others may be regional or can even	___
7	maintained within families from generation to generation.	___
8	Whether they are widespread or specific to a small group,	___
9	they are maintained in the belief that they will bring the	___
10	good luck and happiness to the couple at a time when	___
11	their lives are changing, hopefully for the better. In the	___
12	days gone by, when marriage proposals were more	___
13	formal, the prospective groom sent his friends or his	___
14	members of his family to represent his interests to the	___
15	prospective bride and her family. If they saw a blind man,	___
16	a monk or a pregnant woman during their journey it was	___
17	thought that the marriage would be doomed to failure as if	___
18	they continued their journey, so they had to go home and	___
19	start again! If, however, they saw goats, pigeons or	___
20	wolves, these were good omens which would not bring	___
21	good fortune to the marriage.	___

THIS UNIT INCLUDES

Vocabulary ▪ synonyms of change ▪ nouns formed from verbs ▪ expressions with change ▪ adjective-noun collocations ▪ expressing opinions ▪ linking words ▪ *neither/nor, either/or, not only/but also* ▪ speculating (degrees of probability)
Grammar ▪ comparative and superlative forms ▪ reduced relative clauses ▪ conditionals
Speaking ▪ talking about change ▪ talking about protest and protest songs ▪ discussion: plans for urban development
Writing ▪ a discursive essay

Changes   4

4A   VOCABULARY AND LISTENING   Describing change

I can describe the process of change.

1 **SPEAKING** Read the quotation from George Bernard Shaw and answer the questions.

> *Some people see things as they are and say, 'Why?' I dream of things that never were and say, 'Why not?'*

1 How could you paraphrase the writer's attitude to change? Is he generally in favour of it or against it?
2 What is your own attitude to change? Which parts of your life do you prefer to remain constant?

2 Complete each pair of sentences with one verb below in the correct form. Use a dictionary to help you.

adapt   adjust   alter   convert   evolve   modify
refine   transform

1 a This sofa _____ into a bed.
  b Last year my uncle _____ to Catholicism.
2 a The novel was _____ for the screen.
  b My cousin couldn't _____ to life in France.
3 a Nothing can _____ the fact that the world's population is increasing rapidly.
  b When I met Harry, he had _____ beyond recognition.
4 a Yoga has _____ her life. She's become much calmer and more positive.
  b Scientists can now _____ human cells from one type into another.
5 a Zoologists believe that birds _____ from dinosaurs.
  b American football _____ from rugby and soccer.
6 a Crude oil is _____ to make petrol and diesel.
  b The law needs _____ if it's to be completely effective.
7 a This knob _____ the volume on the TV.
  b It took a moment for my eyes to _____ to the bright light.
8 a In Brazil, many cars have been _____ to run on ethanol.
  b It's possible to genetically _____ crops to make them more resistant to disease.

3 🎧 1.20 Listen to four speakers talking about things and people that have changed in some way. Say if the speakers are:

1 positive about the changes.
2 negative about the changes.
3 neutral.

4 🎧 1.20 Write nouns formed from the verbs in brackets. Then choose which collocation the speakers used. Listen again and check.

1 film/screen _____ (adapt)
2 significant/minor _____ (alter)
3 complete/radical _____ (transform)
4 slight/small _____ (modify)
5 process/period of _____ (adjust)
6 make/require some _____ (refine)
7 undergo/experience a _____ (convert)
8 theory/process of _____ (evolve)

5 **SPEAKING** Work in pairs. Describe the changes that have taken place in the photos. Use verbs and nouns from exercises 2 and 4. Give your personal opinion of the changes.

⫸ **VOCABULARY BUILDER 4.1: EXPRESSIONS WITH** *CHANGE*: **WORKBOOK PAGE 104** ⫷

4B REAL ENGLISH Life changes

I can talk about changes that occur at different stages of life.

1 Compare the two photos and use the words below to say what image they convey of childhood and teenage years. Do you think it is accurate? If not, suggest what other words would give a more accurate portrayal.

carefree   frustrating   idle   idyllic   innocent   joyful   listlessness

2 Read the opinions (a–h) about how people change as they become teenagers. Say whether you agree or disagree with them, and try to think of examples.

a Emotionally, you are probably at your least stable during your teenage years.

b One of the hardest things about being a teenager is leaving behind the security and comfort of childhood.

c During your teenage years, you become more and more aware of the world around you.

d When you're a teenager, the more friends you have the better.

e As a teenager, you aren't quite so willing to involve your parents in your social life.

f You become less and less likely to accept your parents' opinions without questioning them.

g The older you get, the more you start to have your own opinions.

h The worst thing about being a teenager is that you have to work more and adults help you less.

3 Rewrite the sentences using the words in brackets, and the examples in exercise 2 to help. Don't change the meaning! Then say whether you agree or disagree with each one. Give reasons.

1 It becomes steadily more difficult to make new friends during your teenage years. (less and less)

2 As you start to go out more, money becomes more central to your life. (the more)

3 Few things are more important to teenagers than friendship. (one of)

4 Teenagers want to have the most fashionable clothes possible. (the better)

5 As a teenager, you are more sensitive to criticism than at any other time. (at your most)

6 As a teenager, you become a bit more unwilling to follow orders. (not quite so)

>>> GRAMMAR BUILDER 4.1: COMPARATIVE AND SUPERLATIVE FORMS: PAGE 120 <<<

4 🎧 1.21 Listen to three teenagers talking about how their lives have changed since childhood. Match two sentences (a–f) with each speaker (1–3).

a He/She claims to be less childish than most teenagers.

b He/She sees family members far less and friends far more.

c He/She has become slightly more independent by working.

d He/She thinks parents are generally to blame for arguments with their teenage children.

e He/She does not have so many family arguments as before.

f He/She believes that having more money would mean fewer family rows.

5 Look at these phrases the teenagers use for modifying comparative and superlative adjectives. Use them to complete the *Learn this!* box below.

a good deal   a bit   so   a long way   marginally   far and away   only   very

LEARN THIS!

modifying superlatives
¹_____ / easily the best
the ²_____ best
the best by far / by miles / by a mile / by ³_____

modifying comparatives
no better (than…) / ⁴_____ as good (as…)
⁵_____ / very slightly better
a little /⁶_____ / a little bit better
rather better
not quite as / not quite / not ⁷_____ bad (as…)
(quite) a lot better
much / far / a far sight / an awful lot / ⁸_____ better

LOOK OUT!

We can only put *very* before a short superlative form, not a superlative with *most*. We also use it with *first*.
My parents walked in at the very worst moment.
It was the very first time I'd spent a night away from home.

6 SPEAKING Read the *Look out!* box. Then discuss your own ideas about how people change as they become adults rather than teenagers. Use expressions from exercise 5 and discuss the topics below or your own ideas.

family relationships   fashion   freedom   friendship   money   work

1 SPEAKING Work in pairs. Read the lyrics of *Strange Fruit*. Discuss what you think the 'strange fruit' are and what the song is about. Then share your ideas with the class.

Strange Fruit

Southern trees bear strange fruit
Blood on the leaves, and blood at the root
Black bodies swinging in the southern breeze
Strange fruit hanging from the poplar trees
Pastoral scene of the gallant south
The bulging eyes and the twisted mouth
The scent of magnolia sweet and fresh
Then the sudden smell of burning flesh
Here is a fruit for the crows to pluck
For the rain to gather, for the wind to suck
For the sun to rot, for the tree to drop
Here is a strange and bitter crop

2 🎧 **1.22** Listen to part one of a radio programme about *Strange Fruit*. Were your ideas in exercise 1 correct?

LISTENING TIP

Names of people and places can be difficult to understand when you hear them. Before listening, look through the questions and pronounce any names in your head.

3 🎧 **1.22** Read the *Listening tip*. Then listen again and answer the questions using the names below. One of the answers requires two names.

Abel Meeropol   Abram Smith   Laura Duncan
Lewis Allan   Thomas Shipp

1 Under whose name was the song *Strange Fruit* first published? _____
2 What was the real name of the writer? _____
3 On whose murder was the song based? _____
4 Who first sang *Strange Fruit*? _____

4 🎧 **1.23** Read the sentences below. Then listen to part two of the radio programme. Are the sentences true (T), false (F) or is the answer not stated (NS)?

1 Barney Josephson told Billie Holiday about the song.
2 In most nightclubs at that time, black and white customers were segregated.
3 Holiday was too frightened to sing *Strange Fruit* in Josephson's nightclub.
4 The song received a very good reception the first time Holiday performed it.
5 Holiday blamed racial prejudice for the death of her father.
6 Recording *Strange Fruit* led to the termination of Holiday's recording contract with Columbia.
7 *Strange Fruit* was generally regarded as one of Holiday's finest recordings.
8 For Holiday, the emotional effect of performing the song became even stronger as the years passed.

5 Complete the text with the correct form of the words in brackets.

SINGING FOR CHANGE

The story of the American protest song goes back [1]_____ (significance) further than *Strange Fruit*. After the founding of the United States in 1776, songs were written by slaves in protest against their [2]_____ (captive). Songs like *We Shall Be Free* and *Steal Away* had their roots in religious music, but their message was more [3]_____ (politics). One song, called *Follow the Drinking Gourd*, even contained code words that helped slaves escape to [4]_____ (free) in the North by describing landmarks along the route they needed to follow.

During the nineteenth century, protest songs featured a variety of subjects, including the [5]_____ (abolish) of slavery and votes for women. [6]_____ (perform) often took well-known existing songs and wrote their own words, a tradition which continues to this day.

The [7]_____ (economy) hardship of the Great Depression in the 1930s proved fertile ground for the protest song and a new theme emerged: unionism and workers' rights. Later, in the 1960s and 1970s, singers from different musical genres united in their [8]_____ (condemn) of the war in Vietnam and in their support for Martin Luther King Jr and the Civil Rights movement.

Today, American musicians of every genre continue to write protest songs. Some have an [9]_____ (environment) message, others campaign for social justice or against wars. Whether it is possible to change the world with a song is hard to say, but songwriters who are part of this tradition certainly feel that it is their duty to try.

6 SPEAKING Work in pairs. Discuss the questions. Give examples where possible.

1 How many protest songs do you know? What are they protesting about?
2 Are songs an effective method of protest? What advantages might songs have over other forms of protest?
3 What other methods of protest are there and which is the most effective, in your opinion?
4 Are there any singers, past or present, from your own country whose songs often have a serious message?
5 If you were going to write a protest song, what would it be about? Invent a title and think of some possible lines for your song.

I can understand and react to an article about radical life changes.

1 SPEAKING Work in pairs. Read the quotation from Raymond Chandler. Do you agree with it? Give reasons.

Ability is what you're capable of doing. Motivation determines what you do. Attitude determines how well you do it.

2 Look at the photo and the first two lines of the article. Predict what the text is about. Then skim-read it and check your ideas.

3 Read the text and choose the best answers.

1 **As a child, Jaeger played tennis because**
   a she wanted to be the best in the world.
   b her parents put pressure on her to play.
   c she wanted to escape from her overbearing father.
   d she wanted to develop a 'killer instinct'.

2 **Jaeger gave up tennis when she**
   a started a children's charity.
   b got fed up with the competitive atmosphere on the tennis circuit.
   c suffered an injury.
   d realised that she wanted to help people.

3 **When she stopped playing tennis, she was pleased because she**
   a had put her amazing talent to good use.
   b had achieved her ambition of beating Billie-Jean King.
   c no longer enjoyed the applause.
   d could do something different with her life.

4 **What did Andrea Jaeger keep secret for nearly twenty years?**
   a her frequent arguments with her father
   b the fact that she deliberately lost an important match
   c a close friendship with Martina Navratilova
   d her ambition to do something different with her life

5 **When Jaeger looks back at the past, she**
   a believes she could have won a lot of Grand Slams.
   b wonders how successful she might have become.
   c has no regrets.
   d wishes she hadn't been injured.

6 **When Jaeger returned to Wimbledon, she**
   a was surprised that the guards didn't know who she was.
   b was overwhelmed by the fact that the guards treated her like royalty.
   c was bitter about the fact that she had wasted her youth.
   d was delighted at the way that the guards treated the children she was with.

4 Match the adjectives (1–8) with the nouns (a–h) to make collocations from the text.

1 enforced	a teenager
2 uplifting	b environment
3 impressionable	c father
4 stormy	d childhood
5 overbearing	e journey
6 brief	f retirement
7 competitive	g row
8 protracted	h relationship

5 SPEAKING Work in pairs. Retell the story of Jaeger's life so far using the collocations from exercise 4.

6 Look at the example of a reduced relative clause from the text. Expand it into a full relative clause.

Jaeger lacked the killer instinct required of great champions.

7 Find three more examples of reduced relative clauses in the text (lines 15–18, 25–29, 60–65) and expand them into full relative clauses.

>>> GRAMMAR BUILDER 4.2: REDUCED RELATIVE CLAUSES: PAGE 121 <<<

8 SPEAKING Work in pairs. Answer the questions.

1 Do you admire Andrea Jaeger? Why?/Why not?
2 Why don't more famous people devote their lives to good causes?
3 Do you think that you would be willing to give up fame and fortune and devote your life to people less fortunate than yourself? Why?/Why not?
4 'Kids should be driven by their own goals and their own passion, not by someone else's. That's when it becomes dangerous.' To what extent do you agree or disagree with Jaeger's view?

Little stars

1 Andrea Jaeger was a tormented teenager lost in the world of professional tennis. Now she's at peace with herself.

At the age of 47 and more than two decades after her
5 enforced retirement from the game, Jaeger now runs a charity that she set up to help children with cancer. It has been a long, sometimes tortuous, often uplifting journey of sacrifice on the road to a destiny she dimly glimpsed as an impressionable teenager lost in an adult world.

10 Along the way she had to reconcile a stormy relationship with her overbearing father, Roland, and admit to losing matches on purpose, among them the Wimbledon final of 1983. Through a painful and all too brief childhood, Jaeger discovered she had few equals at hitting tennis
15 balls, but lacked the killer instinct required of great champions. In the women's locker-room, inhabited by Chris Evert, Billie-Jean King and Martina Navratilova, the fifteen-year-old found herself out of step with a ruthlessly competitive environment.

20 'I didn't join the circuit to be number one', she says. 'I joined because I was good enough to.' She also played the game to please her parents. 'Kids should be driven by their own goals and their own passion, not by someone else's. That's when it becomes dangerous,' she says.

25 Jaeger took the first opportunity offered to her by a shoulder injury, sustained at the French Open in 1984, to pursue the life that secretly she had always been wanting to lead. She set up the Little Star Foundation – initially with her career earnings of $1.38m – to help children with
30 cancer or at risk in the community.

'When I got injured, to be honest, I was relieved', she explains. 'Everyone was applauding me for playing tennis, but when I was injured I thought, "Finally, I can go and be me." I was given a gift to play tennis, but it wasn't
35 my right to say whether I had it for five years or 50 years. I beat Billie-Jean King on Centre Court at Wimbledon – how many people can even say they played Wimbledon?

'My dad was a brilliant coach and my mum enjoyed how well we were doing. My sister was at Stanford and I was

40 sitting in my hotel room all night, going, "Well, everybody thinks I'm great because I won the match, but what about the person I beat? How's she feeling?"' She minded losing less than her opponents did. Only in 2008, though, did Jaeger admit to deliberately losing the final of the
45 1983 Wimbledon Championships, a tournament she had blasted through without losing a set. On the eve of the final, after a protracted row with her father, she was shut out of the family's rented house in Wimbledon. Jaeger went to knock on the door of the only person she knew
50 in the street, which happened to be Navratilova. The next day the three-time champion finished Jaeger off in 54 minutes.

'I never looked back on my tennis career until this year and I've never wondered how good I could have been,'
55 she says. 'If I'd stayed out there for ten years and not been injured and won all the Grand Slams, I think I would have lost a bit of my soul. Professional tennis was my teenage calling; this is my adult calling. When my teenage years were done, it was time to move on to something else.'

60 Success is now measured in less stark ways than the numbers on a scoreboard. Raising money for her charity requires preparation and discipline, qualities easily transferable from the tennis court, but the sound of laughter coming from the children on holiday at the
65 foundation's ranch near Aspen in Colorado echoes through each day. Many of them have never seen a mountain, let alone experienced rafting down the Roaring Fork River, with Jaeger as guide. Recently she was recognised by a fellow passenger on a plane not for
70 being a former tennis champion, but for running a cancer charity. That pleased her, a sign of progress in her own life too.

A few years ago Jaeger returned to Wimbledon with some of her terminally ill kids and the guards on the gate
75 not only recognised her but gave the children bags of sweets. 'There were these guards all dressed in uniform practically saluting the kids. My kids thought they were the king and queen of England,' Jaeger says. 'If it took all those hours of training and discipline, all the anguish,
80 to get to this, it was worth it. I didn't lose anything by losing a Wimbledon final.'

1 Work in pairs. Try to answer the questions.

1 Were dinosaurs warm-blooded or cold-blooded?
2 When and why did they become extinct?

2 Read the text and find the answers to the questions in exercise 1.

It is a scientific fact that dinosaurs suddenly became extinct about 65 million years ago. Many palaeontologists believe that the extinction was caused by a giant meteor crashing into the Earth. On the face of it, it sounds an unlikely explanation, but dinosaurs were a highly successful species that had ruled the Earth for about 160 million years, and it's difficult to account for their sudden disappearance unless something pretty drastic took place.

But an equally intriguing question is what would have happened if the meteor had missed its target? Suppose dinosaurs were still roaming the Earth today, would the human race have managed to evolve alongside them? It was thought for a long time that dinosaurs were cold-blooded and would never have survived an Ice Age. However, more recent research has revealed that dinosaurs were in fact very adaptable, and some may even have been warm-blooded. Some palaeontologists believe that, had the meteor not hit the Earth, dinosaurs would have continued to thrive, meaning it's unlikely that we'd see many of the mammals that we now rely on for food and company! And if there were no sheep, cows and dogs, we wouldn't have wool, milk or 'man's best friend'. In all likelihood, if the meteor hadn't struck the Earth, we wouldn't be around today to speculate on how things might have turned out.

3 In the text, find examples of structures 1–5. Which refer to (a) the past (b) the present or (c) the past and the present?

1 a second conditional
2 a third conditional
3 two mixed conditionals
4 two conditional clauses introduced by words other than *if*
5 a conditional clause where *if* is omitted and the subject and verb are inverted

>>> **GRAMMAR BUILDER 4.3: CONDITIONALS: PAGE 121** <<<

4 Rewrite the sentences using mixed conditionals.

1 You didn't listen, so you don't know what to do.
If you'd listened, you'd know what to do.
2 Kate failed her driving test last week so she's retaking it in July.
3 He's being prosecuted because he refuses to pay any tax.
4 I don't like him because he was rude to me.
5 His injuries are more serious because he wasn't wearing a seatbelt.
6 I forgot my keys so I can't get back into the house.

5 Rewrite the sentences using an inversion in the conditional clause and omitting *if*.

1 If you should need to make any photocopies, there's a photocopier outside my office.
2 Please contact head office if you should need to make a complaint.
3 If Kurt Cobain were alive today, he'd be over 40.
4 If it weren't for the fact that she's married to the boss, she'd never have got the job.
5 If I'd known it would rain, I'd have taken an umbrella.
6 If it hadn't been for my parents' generosity, I could never have afforded a new car.

6 SPEAKING Complete the sentences in your own words. Compare your answers with your partner.

1 If only I had more time, …
2 If I hadn't studied English, …
3 If teenagers aren't allowed enough freedom, …
4 Unless we act now, …
5 As long as the weather doesn't change, …
6 How I wish …

7 Rewrite the sentences using the words in brackets.

1 I'd never have finished the job without your help. (if)
I'd never have finished the job if you hadn't helped me.
I'd never have finished the job if it hadn't been for your help.
2 If we don't hurry, we won't get to the airport on time. (unless)
3 You can borrow my MP3 player, but you must give it back to me tomorrow. (provided that)
4 Even if there were intelligent life out there, how could we make contact? (supposing)
5 Follow the directions I gave you and you can't go wrong. (as long as)
6 For him to have admitted he was wrong would have been totally out of character. (if/it)

8 SPEAKING Work in pairs and discuss the questions.

How might things be/have been different if
1 we could travel back in time?
2 we stopped eating meat?
3 we could live for ever?
4 computers hadn't been invented?
5 Columbus had not discovered America?
6 dinosaurs were still alive?

I can discuss the merits of proposed changes to a town centre.

1 SPEAKING **Work in pairs. Answer the questions.**

1 How has your town or city changed (a) over the last few years? (b) over the last few decades?

2 Are the changes for the better? Justify your opinion.

3 In general, are you in favour of renovating old, dilapidated buildings or of knocking them down and replacing them? Give reasons for your opinion.

2 Look at the plans for the redevelopment of a town centre. How many of the buildings and facilities below can you find? Which can you find in your town or city?

arts centre   chain store   cycle racks   disabled access
independent shop   landscaped area   open-air market
multi-storey car park   pavement café   pedestrian crossing
pedestrianised street   period buildings   shopping mall
skateboard park   water feature

3 How would you describe the plans? Use the adjectives below to help you.

charming   chic   child-friendly   contemporary   drab
full of character   functional   impersonal   old-fashioned
quaint   soulless   state of the art   trendy

4 🎧 1.24 Listen to two people talking about the changes that are being proposed in picture 2. What benefits and drawbacks for the new buildings do they mention?

5 🎧 1.24 Complete these expressions from the dialogue. Then listen again and check.

1 (that) would seem like the best _____ to me.
2 To my _____ , building a car park…
3 That's not how I _____ it at all.
4 That's a _____ point.
5 I couldn't _____ more.

6 Put the expressions from exercise 5 in the correct group (A–D) in the chart below.

A Giving opinions
one advantage of…is (that)…
one drawback of…is (that)…
Personally, I think that…

B Agreeing/Partially agreeing
That's how I see it too.
I go along with that.

C Disagreeing
I don't accept that.
I disagree with the view that…

D Conceding a point
True.
Yes, I suppose you're right.
Yes, I hadn't thought of that.

7 Work in pairs. Each choose one plan from exercise 2 and think about its merits. Consider the questions below and make notes. Your answers to exercise 4 will help.

1 Which would be better for (a) young people (b) families (c) elderly people?
2 Which is visually more attractive?

8 SPEAKING Discuss the plans with your partner using your notes from exercise 7. Think about the drawbacks of your partner's plan. Give your opinion and react to your partner's points using expressions and phrases from exercises 5 and 6.

1 Work in pairs and discuss the question. Think about the topics below.

How might the world be different a hundred years from now?

clothes communications computers education environment family life food health language leisure money politics religion transport work

2 Read the model essay, ignoring the gaps. Match paragraphs 2–4 with three of the topics from exercise 1.

1 ☐ Science and technology will continue advancing at an ever-increasing pace, and there will doubtless be inventions and discoveries every decade which will affect every aspect of our lives.

2 ☐ A hundred years from now, they will in all probability be far more intelligent than humans. Consequently, our attitude towards them may change: we may regard them either as friends or as potential rivals! We will use them not as only as sources of information, but also as sources of wisdom and advice.

3 ☐ New forms of synthetic material will no doubt have been invented, and these could revolutionise clothing in the same way that the invention of both nylon and Lycra did in the twentieth century. Having said that, designers have a habit of looking to the past for inspiration, so in the twenty-second century, people could be wearing jeans or even nineteenth-century suits and dresses.

4 ☐ Particularly popular will be vehicles which allow commuters to fly to work rather than sitting in a traffic jam. The vehicles will as likely as not be powered by magnetism or some other force which neither requires fuel nor creates pollution.

5 ☐ However, some may make it worse. It is impossible to predict the future with any certainty. There will be many unforeseen developments in the world and some of these will more likely than not be negative.

WRITING TIP

Each paragraph in an essay should contain a 'topic sentence' which expresses the main idea of that paragraph. This usually goes at the beginning. Topic sentences make the essay easier to follow for the reader.

3 Read the *Writing tip*. Match five of sentences a–f with the gaps in the model essay. Which topic from exercise 1 does the other sentence match?

a Assuming that the processing power of computers continues to increase at its current rate, their importance in the world will also grow.

b Within a hundred years, scientists will almost certainly have eradicated most common diseases.

c The increasing congestion on our roads will have led scientists to develop new forms of transport.

d If I am still alive a hundred years from now, I imagine the world will be a very different place from how it is today.

e Broadly speaking, the kinds of changes that I envisage happening will make the world a better place to live.

f I imagine that, a hundred years in the future, fashions will have changed hugely.

4 Work in pairs. Choose three topics from exercise 1 which are not in exercises 2 or 3. Write a topic sentence to begin a paragraph for each one.

WRITING TIP

Make your writing more fluent by using the following linking words to join ideas together:
neither…nor…   *…or even…*
either…or…   *both…and…*
…rather than…   *not only…but also…*

5 Read the *Writing tip*. Then find an example of each expression in the model essay. Which two are similar in meaning? Explain the meaning of the others.

6 Rewrite the two sentences as single sentences using expressions from the *Writing tip*.

1 Computers are becoming more powerful. They're becoming cheaper.

2 Soon computers may be able to hold conversations with humans. Telling jokes may also be possible.

3 We may not have to use a mouse or keyboard. We may be able to control it with our mind.

4 Computers may demand better treatment. They may demand equal rights!

5 Some people maintain that computers will never think like people. They say that computers will never have emotions.

6 Super-powerful computers will be incredibly useful. Or perhaps they'll be incredibly dangerous to mankind.

7 SPEAKING Work in pairs. Discuss the questions, then compare your ideas with the class.

1 If a new kind of material for clothing were to be invented, what do you think it might be like?

2 What new kind of vehicle would be most useful, in your opinion?

3 Do you think it matters if computers become more intelligent that humans? Give reasons.

1 🎧 **1.25** Listen to two teenagers discussing what life might be like a hundred years from now. Number the ideas in the order that your hear them.

a Humans might have cross-bred with aliens and developed green skin, scales and antennae. ☐

b Humans might have become extinct. ☐

c A chip in the brain might allow 24/7 Internet access in your head. ☐

d Humans might have moved to another planet. ☐

e Humans might be bald and very pale as a result of living in space. ☐

f Cars might have been banned completely. ☐

g Children might be able to plug something into their brain instead of going to school. ☐

2 Work in pairs. Decide which ideas in exercise 1 are the most and least likely to happen, in your opinion. Order them from 1 (most likely) to 7 (least likely).

We can use a range of expressions for speculating about events in the future, depending on how likely we believe them to be.
It could/might happen.
It may well happen.
It's bound to happen.
It's very likely to happen.
It will (almost definitely) happen.
It will probably happen.
There's a (faint) chance it might happen.
There's (almost) no chance of it happening.

3 Read the *Learn this!* box. Put the phrases in approximate order of likelihood. (Some expressions are almost synonymous.)

4 Rephrase the ideas from exercise 1 using suitable expressions from the *Learn this!* box, depending on how likely you think each event is.

> There's a faint chance that humans might have cross-bred with aliens.

5 Look back at the model essay on page 44. Complete these words and phrases which all mean *(very) probably*.

1 _____less
2 as _____ as _____
3 more _____ _____ not
4 no _____
5 _____ _____ probability

6 Work in pairs. Plan the following essay:
How might the world be different a hundred years from now?

1 Use your topic sentences from exercise 4 on page 44.
Paragraph 1 Introduction
Paragraph 2 _____
Paragraph 3 _____
Paragraph 4 _____
Paragraph 5 Conclusion

2 Brainstorm ideas for each paragraph and add them to the essay plan. Decide how likely each event is, in your opinion.

7 Working individually, write an essay of 200–250 words following your plan. Remember to use suitable expressions from the *Learn this!* box and exercise 5.

8 Work in pairs. Swap essays and check your partner's work.

CHECK YOUR WORK
Have you:
☐ followed the essay plan correctly?
☐ written the correct number of words?
☐ used expressions from the *Learn this!* box?
☐ used linking words from the writing tip on page 44?
☐ checked the spelling and grammar?

Vocabulary

1 Complete the sentences with a suitable form of the verbs below.

~~offer~~ pay resolve return speak suffer

Dora had had enough of people offering her advice on how to bring up her son.

1 Kieran's relationship _____ a setback recently. His girlfriend has been transferred to Boston.
2 When choosing furniture for a new house it's important to _____ your mind and make a joint decision.
3 Last summer our neighbours watered our garden. We _____ the favour by looking after their dog.
4 The dispute over custody of the children _____ last week in court.
5 Tina gets furious with her boyfriend because he never _____ attention when she tells him what to do.

Mark: ____ /5

2 Match the adjectives (1–6) with their opposites (a–f).

1 well-connected   a old-fashioned
2 affluent   b drab
3 chic   c thriving
4 picturesque   d soulless
5 run down   e remote
6 full of character   f deprived

Mark: ____ /6

3 Complete the sentences with a suitable preposition.

There's a new Asian restaurant a stone's throw [1]_____ my house. Thanks [2]_____ an effective advertising campaign, it was teeming [3]_____ people on the opening night last week. It caters [4]_____ all tastes in Asian food – Chinese, Japanese, Thai and Vietnamese – and the owner takes pride [5]_____ greeting all the guests as they arrive.

Mark: ____ /5

4 Complete the sentences with the noun form of the verbs below.

adapt ~~adjust~~ convert modify transform

Entering the hall, he made a small adjustment to his tie.

1 The town centre had undergone a complete _____ since I was there last.
2 There has been a small _____ to the plans for the new station.
3 It was the author himself who wrote the stage _____ of the novel.
4 I'm looking for a firm to carry out the loft _____ .

Mark: ____ /4

Grammar

5 Complete the sentences with the present perfect simple or continuous form of the verbs below.

clean go know rain retire stay

1 My boyfriend _____ to the gym recently to get fit.
2 We _____ each other since we started school.
3 Sarah _____ out her cupboards so her clothes are all over the floor.
4 My parents _____ to their second home on the coast.
5 It _____ every day this week and the forecast for tomorrow is also pretty bad.
6 I _____ with a cousin while I look for a flat.

Mark: ____ /6

6 Complete the sentences with the correct form of the verbs.

1 He claims _____ (play) basketball with Kobe Bryant.
2 The travelling isn't much fun, but I don't mind _____ (take out) for dinner when I go away on business.
3 The detective's first impression was that the victim appeared _____ . (push)
4 Ignore her. She's only pretending _____ . (cry)
5 I truly admire Ingrid Betancourt. Imagine _____ (keep) hostage in the jungle for six years!

Mark: ____ /5

7 Choose the correct adverb.

1 He finished the race in just under twenty seconds. He was **easily / by a mile** the fastest.
2 Football is **a long way / a good deal** more tiring than cricket.
3 We beat them by 10–1. Our team was the best **far and away / by miles**.
4 A broken rib is only **marginally / quite** more painful than just bruising it.

Mark: ____ /4

8 Complete the sentences with the correct form of the verbs.

If I'd had (have) my car serviced, it wouldn't have broken down (not break down).

1 That accident _____ (not happen) if you _____ (look) at the road!
2 If penicillin _____ (not discover) people _____ (still die) from simple infections.
3 Supposing oil _____ (run out), how will electricity _____ (generate)?
4 People _____ (use) cars less if more _____ (invest) in public transport.
5 Had the area _____ (not evacuate), more people _____ (die).

Mark: ____ /5

Total: ____ /40

Reading

1 Do you think you would be an easy or difficult person to share a flat with? Give reasons.

2 Read the text. In what way is Flat Night Fever similar to a speed-dating event?

Renting: Speed-date your way to a flatmate

Stuart Kelly, 31, earns £28,000 a year, yet he can't find anywhere decent to live in London. 'Back home in Edinburgh I'd be rich, but here my money goes nowhere,' he laments. 'I started out renting a grubby room with no lock in an old mansion in Lewisham, then I moved to Belgravia, where I had problems with the landlady. I am currently paying £800 per month for a rather small single room in Whitechapel. In the process, I have lost about £500 in non-returned deposits and the like. Now my girlfriend wants to come down to London but she won't be earning any money to start with, and I just can't find a double room we can afford. I'm in pretty dire straits, to be honest.' Which is why he is spending the evening at Sound, a West End nightclub in Leicester Square, the venue for a new and unusual type of event called Flat Night Fever.

This is the property world's version of speed-dating. People with rooms to let put on orange-coloured name badges and sit at tables labelled north, south, east or west, according to the part of town where their accommodation is located. Those who are looking for places to live (white name badges) circulate round those tables, in the hope of convincing their orange-badged counterparts that they would make the ideal flatmate.

'It works both ways, of course,' explains the event's organiser, Paul Curry, of accommodation website easyroommate.co.uk. 'The person looking for the room might not hit it off with the person offering the room, either. That is the purpose of this event: to prevent having to do that thing we've all done, which is trek halfway across London to see a flat you hate, lived in by people you wish you'd never met.'

'This isn't an evening we make any money out of,' says EasyRoommate's founder Karim Goudiaby, who usually charges for this introduction service via email, with subscribers getting the contact details of the flat-seeker or flat-owner they want to see. 'This shows we are more than just a property bulletin board: we want to ensure that the people we match up are compatible. Just as you would choose a wife with great care, so you should choose a flatmate with great care, too.'

3 Say whether sentences 1–7 are true (T) or false (F).

1 Stuart could afford better accommodation in Edinburgh.
2 He used to live in a small flat in Lewisham.
3 Initially, Stuart and his girlfriend plan to split the rent.
4 Stuart believes his situation is very problematic.
5 At Flat Night Fever, people with orange badges are looking for somewhere to live.
6 Flat Night Fever is a 'live' version of a process that also happens electronically.
7 Karim Goudiaby argues that choosing a flatmate is just as difficult as finding the right wife or husband.

Listening

4 🎧 1.26 Listen to a dialogue between Edgars and two other people in his new flat. Who are they? Choose from:

a bank employee   a housemate   a neighbour
the landlady   the letting agent   the postman

5 🎧 1.26 Listen again. Are the sentences true (T), false (F) or is the answer not stated (NS)?

1 Most of Edgars's possessions are still in Latvia.
2 Tomas has been living in the house for more than a year.
3 The bank won't let Edgars open an account until he has a formal job offer in writing.
4 Edgars has to pay a larger deposit on the flat because he doesn't have a bank account.
5 Tomas has not had any problems with the neighbours.
6 The landlord sometimes calls by unexpectedly.
7 Edgars's letter is from the person that interviewed him.

Speaking

6 Work in groups of four.

- **Students A and B:** You are flatmates, looking for one more tenant.
- **Students C and D:** You are both prospective tenants, keen to share with students A and B. You can invent new personas.
- **Students A and B:** Interview students C and D one at a time. Ask them questions about their personality, their habits and anything else that occurs to you. Then talk about the two candidates and agree which one to accept.

Writing

7 Read the task below and make notes.

You have been asked to write a short article for a travel magazine about the different areas of your town and where the best places to rent would be.

8 Write your article. Remember to include one or two recommendations and give reasons for them.

⟫⟫⟫ CHECK YOUR PROGRESS: PAGE 4 ⟪⟪⟪

1 Get ready to READ You are going to read a text called *Tropical weather at the Poles*. Do you think it will be mainly about the future or the past? Give reasons for your answer.

2 Read the text in the Reading exam task quickly and check your answer.

EXAM TIP

Always read true/false statements before reading the text closely. That way, you know what information you are looking for. Remember that in order to be 'true' or 'false', the information in the whole sentence has to match exactly what is in the text or be explicitly contradicted by it. If neither is the case, choose 'not stated'. Do not be misled by individual words and phrases.

3 Do the Reading exam task.

READING exam task

Tropical weather at the Poles

WHEN Ernest Shackleton and his men marched towards the South Pole in December 1908, they came across something entirely unexpected. After scaling the vast Beardmore glacier on the edge of the polar plateau, they found seams of coal amid the snow and ice. They also found impressions of leaves in sandstone boulders nearby and even fossilised wood from a coniferous tree.

The conclusion was extraordinary but inescapable: Antarctica was once warm and forested, conditions that could hardly be more different to the far-below-freezing midsummer weather that forced Shackleton's team to turn back before reaching their goal. How was this possible?

Four years later, Alfred Wegener put forward his theory of continental drift which, it was later realised, could explain the balmy climate: Antarctica had been warmer because it was once much closer to the equator. Even today, some schoolchildren are taught that continental drift provides a complete explanation for a warmer Antarctica.

However, the fossil trees Shackleton's team discovered grew around 250 million years ago, when Antarctica was barely closer to the equator than it is today. What's more, the continent reached its current position roughly 100 million years ago, and an ever-growing list of fossil finds date from 100 to 40 million years ago. During this time, when dinosaurs roamed the almost subtropical forests of an ice-free Antarctic, conditions on the other side of the planet were even more remarkable: the Arctic Ocean was a gigantic freshwater lake infested with crocodile-like reptiles.

The most evocative image of a warm Arctic has emerged from the work of John Tarduno of the University of Rochester, New York. For more than a decade, Tarduno has been hunting for fossils on Axel Heiberg Island in the Canadian Arctic, just west of Greenland. The island was already well within the Arctic Circle 90 million years ago. His team has found bones and even partial skeletons of a crocodile-like creature called a champsosaur from this period. The champsosaur was a fish-eating reptile up to 2.4 metres long that probably looked much like the gharials of India. Because these reptiles would have relied on their environment to stay warm, conditions in the far north must have been far hotter than today.

Read the text. Decide whether the information in each sentence (1–8) is true, false or not stated.

	True	False	Not stated
1 Shackleton and his men were surprised to find coal at the Antarctic.	☐	☐	☐
2 The fossils that they found could only have been created in a warmer climate.	☐	☐	☐
3 Shackleton achieved the main objective of his expedition.	☐	☐	☐
4 Most scientists believe that continental drift explains the fossils that were found in Antarctica.	☐	☐	☐
5 The dinosaurs that used to live in Antarctica became extinct when the climate became much colder.	☐	☐	☐
6 The Arctic was once inhabited by freshwater crocodiles.	☐	☐	☐
7 John Tarduno is a Canadian scientist employed by a university in New York.	☐	☐	☐
8 Scientists are not exactly sure what a champsosaur looked like.	☐	☐	☐

EXAM TIP

Do not be thrown by unknown words. You can often use the context to guess their meaning, either precisely or approximately.

4 Read the *Exam tip*. Then find words 1–3 in the text and choose the meaning which makes most sense in the context.

1 scaling: **a** finding   **b** climbing   **c** leaving
2 balmy: **a** warm   **b** cold   **c** freezing
3 a gharial is a type of: **a** lake   **b** bone   **c** reptile

5 Do the Use of English exam task.

USE OF ENGLISH exam task

Complete the second sentence in each pair so that it means the same as the first.

1 We'd have arrived on time if our car hadn't broken down.
   Had _____ arrived on time.
2 As I spend more time online, I'm finding it easier and easier to use search engines.
   The more _____ to use search engines.
3 I'll meet you in town unless it's raining.
   Provided _____ in town.
4 I only recognised George because he was wearing the jacket I'd given him.
   If George _____ recognised him.
5 Skiing is more difficult when the snow is very soft.
   It isn't _____ is very soft.
6 She writes songs and plays several instruments too.
   Not only _____ instruments.

Vocabulary ▪ war and war idioms ▪ verb-noun collocations ▪ sexual discrimination ▪ phrases for structuring a presentation ▪ personal qualities ▪ word formation (1) ▪ linking words: addition
Grammar ▪ *for* + noun/pronoun + infinitive ▪ ellipsis (reduced infinitives, omission of verbs)
Speaking ▪ talking about armed conflict ▪ discussing family tensions ▪ discussing gender equality ▪ a presentation
Writing ▪ a description of a person

Battles | 5

5A   VOCABULARY AND LISTENING   War and peace

I can talk about military conflict.

1 **SPEAKING** Work in pairs. Discuss the meaning of the quotations and sayings. Do you agree with them? Why?/Why not?

1 'One man's terrorist is another man's freedom fighter.'
2 'The pen is mightier than the sword.'
3 'The direct use of force is such a poor solution to any problem that it is generally employed only by small children and large nations.'
4 'We make war so that we can live in peace.'

2 Complete the text with the words below.

allies   coalition   insurgents   mass destruction
security   suicide bombers   troops   violation
weapons inspectors

The Iraq War began in 2003 when a multinational ¹_____ of forces led by the USA invaded Iraq. The reason for the invasion was America and Britain's belief that Saddam Hussein possessed and was developing weapons of ²_____ (nuclear, biological and chemical weapons) in ³_____ of a 1991 agreement. In the event, UN ⁴_____ found no evidence of such weapons. The Iraqi military forces were quickly defeated by America and her ⁵_____ , and thousands of Iraqi ⁶_____ were captured and disarmed. However, the victory was short-lived as ⁷_____ began to attack the occupying forces in an attempt to liberate the country, frequently employing roadside bombs and ⁸_____ . US troops finally withdrew in December 2011, when Iraqi troops took responsibility for ⁹_____ in the fledgling democracy.

3 Find words in the text in exercise 2 that have the opposite meaning to the words below.

advance (v)   arm (v)   civilian (adj)   defeat (n)   defend
enemies   occupy   release (v)

4 🎧 2.01 Listen to an account of the Battle of the Somme in the First World War. Complete the missing information with no more than four words.

Soldiers climbing out of the trenches on the first day of the battle

1 The war had started _____ years before the battle began.
2 The land between the two armies was called _____ .
3 The speaker expresses great surprise that some British and French soldiers were told _____ when they advanced towards the German lines.
4 The bombardment didn't kill many German soldiers because they had hidden _____ .
5 At first, British generals didn't know how many men they had lost because of _____ .
6 German resistance in the weeks after the battle prevented the British and French from making _____ .
7 In the autumn, the weather made it impossible to _____ .
8 _____ could say that they had won the battle.

5 Complete the collocations from the listening exercise with the verbs below.

break   call up   claim   give   grind   inflict   launch
make   put up   suffer

1 _____ a breakthrough   6 _____ casualties
2 _____ an attack   7 _____ losses
3 _____ the stalemate   8 _____ reinforcements
4 _____ orders   9 _____ to a halt
5 _____ resistance   10 _____ victory

6 **SPEAKING** 🎧 2.01 Work in pairs. Retell the story of the Battle of the Somme using the collocations in exercise 5 to help you. Then listen again and check.

7 **SPEAKING** Work in pairs or small groups. Think of:

1 two sets of circumstances in which a country would be justified in going to war as a last resort.
2 two sets of circumstances when a declaration of war would be unjustified.

⯈⯈⯈ VOCABULARY BUILDER 5.1: IDIOMS: WORKBOOK PAGE 104 ⯇⯇⯇

1 SPEAKING Discuss these questions: Do you think it is good to argue? If not, why not? If so, why and in what circumstances?

2 Read the text. How would Tabitha Holmes have answered the questions in exercise 1?

There may be nothing worse than slammed doors, raised voices and tears but, according to new research, it's actually a good idea for parents who want to be close to their teenage children to have a row a day. Instead of causing alienation, conflict can strengthen parent-adolescent relationships, says Tabitha Holmes, a specialist in adolescent development. 'It was a complete surprise to me to discover during my research that teenagers themselves saw heated arguments as something that brought them closer to their parents,' said Holmes. 'Whereas their parents talked about how upsetting and destructive arguing with their child was, the adolescents were able to see how locking horns helped them to understand their parents' points of view more clearly. They were also very aware that a good row forced them to think through, articulate and defend their opinions and desires.' According to Holmes, it is the day-to-day conflicts – the very ones that can be so draining – that are most constructive: the endless rows over homework, clothes, curfews and friends. It's vital for conflicts to be heated: calm discussion or animated debate does not count. 'Adolescents said they only told their mothers what they really felt and thought when they were forced to defend their position. If your teenager is rowing with you, it's actually a mark of respect,' Holmes said. 'It shows they value you enough to tell you their genuine feelings and thoughts.' To be positive, conflicts have to be handled in the right way, Holmes admitted. Parents need to listen genuinely to their teenager's viewpoint; it's necessary for them to be able to modify their own position in the light of what their child tells them; and they need to be respectful, to go into the row acknowledging that their child's point of view is worthwhile.

3 Compare these sentences with the sentences in blue in the text. What structure is used in the text to express the same ideas?

1 Parents who want to be close to their teenage children should actually have a row a day.
2 It's vital that conflicts should be heated.
3 Parents need to be able to modify their own position in the light of what their child tells them.

LEARN THIS!

for + noun/pronoun + infinitive
1 We use this structure when an infinitive needs its own subject.
It's important for Jane not to fail her exams. (*Jane* is the subject of the verb *fail*.)
2 It is frequently used after adjectives and nouns.
I'm unhappy for the children to miss school.
It's time for us to go.
3 It can be the subject of a sentence.
For him to apologise would be unthinkable.
4 It is often used in place of a *that*-clause with *should* or the subjunctive and is less formal.
It's essential that Sue ring her dad.
It's essential for Sue to ring her dad.

>>> GRAMMAR BUILDER 5.1: *FOR* + NOUN/PRONOUN + INFINITIVE: PAGE 122 <<<

4 Read the information in the *Learn this!* box. Then rephrase the sentences using *for* + noun/pronoun + infinitive.

1 It's important that she say sorry.
2 My idea is that we should leave before dawn.
3 I was anxious that he shouldn't feel offended.
4 It would be a disaster if we lost the match.
5 It won't snow – it isn't cold enough.

5 🎧 2.02 Listen to three people talking about family arguments. Write M (Mandy), S (Simon) or T (Tina). Who:

1 feels that experiencing arguments has brought benefits?
2 doesn't think it's surprising that families argue a lot?
3 has a theory about why boys and men are quite likely to argue with one another?
4 feels that being similar to another family member gives rise to arguments?
5 had a competitive relationship with a sibling?
6 used to try to stop family members arguing?

6 🎧 2.02 Complete these discourse markers, which indicate the speaker's attitude. Then listen again and check.

doubtless	fortunately	1_____ enough	2_____	frankly
3_____ honestly	4_____ to my annoyance			
no 5_____ surprisingly 6_____	thank 7_____			
to be 8_____ honest	to my 9_____ astonishment			

7 Which discourse markers indicate that the speaker:

1 believes they are being sincere?
2 is surprised?
3 thinks something is probable but not certain?
4 approves of something?
5 disapproves of something?

8 SPEAKING Recount an argument that you once had, or witnessed. Try to use discourse markers to show the attitude of the people who were arguing, or your attitude as the witness.

I can understand and react to an article about civil rights campaigners.

1 What does the graph below show? How does your country compare with others? What is your reaction to the statistics?

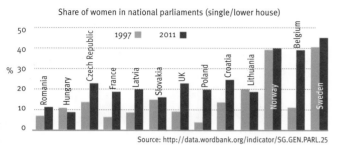

Share of women in national parliaments (single/lower house)

Source: http://data.wordbank.org/indicator/SG.GEN.PARL.25

2 Complete the text with appropriate words. Use one word only in each gap.

The SUFFRAGETTES

From the middle of the nineteenth century many women campaigned peacefully to obtain ¹_____ right to vote in British elections. They organised themselves into groups, held meetings, sent petitions to Parliament and tried to persuade MPs to change the law to enable ²_____ to vote. However, the government ignored their plea.

In 1903, the campaign ³_____ the right of women to vote took an important new turn. ⁴_____ year Emmeline Pankhurst (1858–1928) and her daughters, Christabel and Sylvia, started the Women's Social and Political Union in Manchester ⁵_____ the motto: 'Deeds not words'. They were referred ⁶_____ as the 'Suffragettes'. The Pankhursts and their supporters declared that the situation was ⁷_____ serious that they would have to pursue extreme measures of civil disobedience. They campaigned tirelessly and sometimes violently ⁸_____ achieve their aim: chaining themselves to the railings outside Parliament, disrupting political meetings and even committing acts of arson. Many women ⁹_____ imprisoned and, when they went on hunger strike, were force-fed. In 1913 Emily Davison died for the cause, ¹⁰_____, at a horse race, she rushed out on to the course and stepped in front of the King's horse.

In 1914 the First World War broke ¹¹_____. In the interests of national unity the Suffragettes suspended their campaign of direct civil action. Instead, they urged women to take over men's jobs, so ¹²_____ the men could go and fight in the war. Women were able to prove how indispensable they were in the fields and armaments factories. In March 1918 the government gave in ¹³_____ the pressure, and passed a law giving women over 30 the right to vote. Later that year, it allowed women over 21 to become Members of Parliament, but they still couldn't vote in elections if they were ¹⁴_____ 30! It ¹⁵_____ take a further ten years to amend the age qualification and put men and women on an equal footing.

3 Read the text and answer the questions.

1 What was the result of the nineteenth-century campaign to gain the vote for women?
2 How did the Suffragettes' campaign differ from the methods used before?

3 Can you explain the motto: 'Deeds not words'?
4 Why did the Suffragettes put their campaign on hold in 1914?
5 What was strange about the position of women MPs between 1918 and 1928?

4 🎧 2.03 Read and listen to the song. Do you think the song is anti-men? Why?/Why not? Sum up the message of the song in a few words.

Sisters are doing it for themselves (The Eurythmics)

Now, there was a time when they used to say
That behind every great man
There had to be a great woman.
But in these times of change,
You know that it's no longer true.
So we're comin' out of the kitchen
'Cause there's somethin' we forgot to say to you.

We say, sisters are doin' it for themselves.
Standin' on their own two feet.
And ringin' on their own bells.
Sisters are doin' it for themselves.

Now, this is a song to celebrate
The conscious liberation of the female state.
Mothers, daughters and their daughters too.
Woman to woman, we're singin' with you.
The inferior sex has got a new exterior
We've got doctors, lawyers, politicians too.
Everybody, take a look around.
Can you see, can you see, can you see
There's a woman right next to you?

Chorus
Now we ain't makin' stories
And we ain't layin' plans
Don't you know that a man still loves a woman
And a woman still loves a man
Just the same.

5 SPEAKING Work in pairs. Discuss the questions. Justify your opinions.

1 Should husbands and wives share the housework?
2 Do you think school classes should be single-sex or mixed?
3 Would you prefer a male or a female boss?
4 Would you employ a man to look after your child?
5 In what other ways are there inequalities between men and women in your country? Why do such inequalities exist? Use the ideas below to help you.

discriminate against sb   equal pay and conditions
glass ceiling   maternity leave   opportunities for promotion
positive action   role models   sex discrimination
sexist stereotyping

1 SPEAKING Work in pairs. Describe what is happening in the photo. Why is the man acting in this way, do you think? What do you think of his behaviour?

2 SPEAKING Work in pairs. Answer the questions.

1 Do you enjoy watching wildlife programmes on TV? What do/don't you like about them?
2 Would you enjoy seeing a show like the one in the photo at a wildlife park? Why?/Why not?

3 Read the text, ignoring the gaps.

1 How did Steve Irwin die?
2 How did he become rich?
3 What business did he take over when his parents retired?

4 Match sentences A–H with gaps 1–7 in the text. There is one sentence that you do not need.

A But the 44-year-old, who is believed to have suffered an instant cardiac arrest, was pronounced dead by medical staff at about noon local time.
B It's a shame that audiences need that to be attracted to wildlife.
C Although Irwin was one of Australia's most successful exports, he provoked mixed feelings at home.
D A theme park famous around the world, it has more than 1,000 animals on 60 acres of bushland and employs 360 people.
E He appeared to have no fear.
F In spite of this, Irwin's death was reported widely in the press and on TV.
G Irrepressibly ebullient, he thrived on his death-defying encounters with wildlife.
H He simply could not understand what the fuss was about.

5 Answer the questions.

1 Why were people surprised that Irwin had been killed by a stingray?
2 How did he react when people criticised him for exposing his baby son to danger?
3 Why did many Australians have mixed feelings about Irwin?
4 Why did some people object to Irwin's television programmes?

6 Choose the correct verbs to complete these collocations from the text and the sentences in exercise 4.

1 **provoke / spark off** mixed feelings
2 **drop / shake off** an image
3 **take / make** a risk
4 **acquire / take** fame and fortune
5 **laugh off / laugh** an incident
6 **announce / pronounce** somebody dead
7 **take out / take over** a business
8 **administer / issue** a heart massage
9 **create / cause** pain

Steve Irwin

▶▶▶ **VOCABULARY BUILDER 5.2: VERB-NOUN COLLOCATIONS: WORKBOOK PAGE 104** ◀◀◀

7 Explain the meaning of these sentences.

1 Steve Irwin was a man in tune with his surroundings. (line 3)
2 Nothing fazed him. (line 9)
3 And it was, perhaps, that sense of invulnerability that killed him. (line 14)
4 Animals were in Irwin's blood. (line 31)
5 He was a natural showman. (line 57)
6 I get called an adrenaline junkie. (line 78)

8 SPEAKING Work in pairs. Discuss the questions. Justify your opinions.

1 Do you admire Steve Irwin?
2 Do you agree that TV has become 'gladiatorial and voyeuristic'?
3 Do you agree that 'some things in nature should be left alone'?

Unlike most Australians, who shrink from the tropical sun and shudder at the dangerous creatures that surround them, Steve Irwin was a man in tune with his surroundings. A true environmental warrior and lifelong animal rights advocate, he founded Wildlife Warriors Worldwide, which protects habitat and wildlife, sets up breeding and rescue programmes for endangered species, and leads scientific research to aid conservation.

Nothing fazed him – not the sharks or killer jellyfish, nor the man-eating crocodiles, nor the dozens of snakes and spiders capable of delivering a fatal bite. For Irwin, Australia's animals were 'like a magnet', and he acquired fame, and considerable fortune, by getting up close to them. [1] And it was, perhaps, that sense of invulnerability that killed him.

The warrior who wrestled crocodiles and handled pythons without a scratch was diving in the warm waters of Queensland's Great Barrier Reef when a stingray shot its poisonous barb into his heart. According to a witness, Irwin swam too close to it. Triangular-shaped stingrays, which glide through the water on their wide, flat bodies, are usually placid, lashing out with their long tails only when they feel threatened or are trodden on. Irwin was believed to be only the third person killed by a stingray in Australian waters.

Irwin, whose television show *Crocodile Hunter* made him an international celebrity and a superstar in America, was filming an underwater sequence for a documentary called *Ocean's Deadliest* at the remote Batt Reef. The crew of his boat called the emergency services and administered heart massage as they rushed to a nearby island to meet a rescue helicopter. [2]

Animals were in Irwin's blood. At the age of six he was given a four-metre python for his birthday. When he was eight, his father, Bob, a plumber with a passion for reptiles, moved the family from Melbourne to Queensland's Sunshine Coast, where they opened a small wildlife park. By the time Irwin was nine, he was catching crocodiles, and in his twenties he worked for the Queensland government as a crocodile trapper, removing problem animals from populated areas. In 1991, when his parents retired, he took over the business – originally called the Queensland Reptile and Fauna Park, and now known as Australia Zoo – and developed it into a major tourist attraction. [3]

Irwin told the ABC documentary: 'I've got animals so genetically inside me that there's no way I could actually be anything else.' Visitors came in droves to Australia Zoo to watch Irwin hover perilously close to untethered crocodiles, often leaping on to their backs. But in 2004 he went too far,

cradling his baby son, Bob, in one arm while feeding a large, snapping crocodile with the other, there was an uproar and Irwin apologised. He later insisted, however, that boy had been in no danger, and in later interviews laughed off the incident. [4] It was all about 'perceived danger' he said, claiming that 'in front of that crocodile I was in complete control, absolute and complete control.' One commentator blamed his death on the demands of an increasingly voyeuristic brand of television. But Irwin was only doing what had come naturally. He was a natural showman. [5]

The British television presenter and survival expert, Ray Mears, said his death proved that 'some things in nature should be left alone'. He said of Irwin: 'He clearly took a lot of risks, and television encouraged him to do that. [6] You leave dangerous animals alone because they will defend themselves.' Mears, too, condemned some wildlife programmes as 'voyeuristic', saying: 'Television has become very gladiatorial, and it's not healthy. The voyeurism we are seeing on television has a cost, and it's that cost Steve Irwin's family are paying now.' However, scientists who study stingrays say that Irwin was extremely unlucky. Unprovoked attacks are virtually unheard of, and although a stingray's venom will cause agonising pain, it is rarely fatal.

[7] Like Kylie Minogue, he was not taken entirely seriously in Australia, and appeared to be more valued abroad. Urban Aussies want to shake off the image embodied by the brash, blond Irwin, and to have their modern, multicultural nation portrayed overseas in a rather more sophisticated fashion. Whatever one thought of Irwin, his passion for life could not be denied, nor the 100 per cent enthusiasm that he brought to everything he did. 'I get called an adrenaline junkie every other minute, and I'm just fine with that,' he once remarked. On another occasion, he claimed never to have experienced 'fear of losing my life'.

I can use devices to avoid repetition.

1 🎧 2.04 Read and listen. What words have been missed out, or are understood, following the words in red in the dialogues?

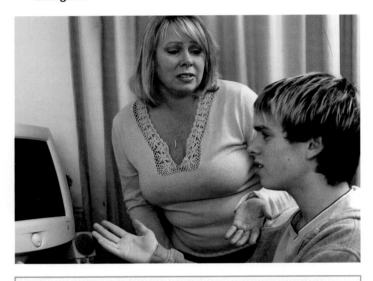

Mum	Harry, can you turn off the computer now, please?
Harry	I don't want to.
Mum	Have you done your homework yet?
Harry	No, I haven't. But I will when I've finished this email.
Fred	Have you drunk all the Coke?
Lucy	No, I haven't.
Fred	Well someone has. There were a couple of cans in the fridge this morning.
Lucy	Go and buy some more.
Fred	Why should I? I bought the last lot!
Dad	Did you remember to post that letter for me?
Sally	Er … No, I forgot.
Dad	Oh, Sally! You promised you would.
Sally	I know I did. I'm sorry!

LEARN THIS!

Ellipsis
We often leave words out in order to avoid repetition.
1 We can use *to* instead of a whole infinitive (a 'reduced infinitive'), or sometimes the whole infinitive is omitted.
I love reading sci-fi stories, but I didn't use to.
Stay for lunch if you want.
2 A main verb can be omitted after a modal or auxiliary verb.
He didn't phone me, but he should have.
3 In ellipsis the pronunciation of the auxiliary/modal verbs and *to* is usually *strong*.

▶▶▶ **GRAMMAR BUILDER 5.2: ELLIPSIS: PAGE 122** ◀◀◀

2 Read the *Learn this!* box, then complete the sentences using a reduced infinitive and a verb below in the correct form. If more than one answer is possible, explain your choice.

be able   hope   intend   not like   love   not mean   want   use to

1 'Do you want to join us for a bite to eat?'
  'Yes, I _____ .'
2 'You broke my new MP3 player!'
  'Sorry, I _____ .'
3 'Did you go for a stroll along the beach?'
  'No, I _____ , but I was feeling a bit under the weather.'
4 'I think you should apologise to Jean.'
  'I _____ .'
5 'Do you think you'll get the job?'
  'I _____ .'
6 'You could have asked Kate if she'd lend you her car.'
  'I know, but I _____ . I'm always asking her for favours.'
7 'I was hoping to come to your leaving do, but I'm afraid I _____ .'
8 'Dave doesn't run as much as he _____ .'

3 🎧 2.05 Complete the dialogues with appropriate auxiliary or modal verbs, or *like*. Sometimes you need a negative verb. Then listen and check.

Dad	You're not going out dressed like that!
Alice	Why ¹_____ I?
Dad	Because you'll freeze to death.
Alice	I ²_____ ! It isn't that cold. And anyway all my friends dress like this.
Dad	Maybe they ³_____ , but I insist that you put on something warmer.
Mum	Neil, will you tidy up in the bathroom, please?
Neil	I ⁴_____ .
Mum	You ⁵_____ . You've left your clothes in a heap on the floor.
Sandra	Who's pinched my hairdryer?
Cathy	I ⁶_____ . Maybe Ellie ⁷_____ .
Sandra	No, she ⁸_____ . She never uses one.
Cathy	If you ⁹_____ , you can borrow mine.

4 Prepare a dialogue in which a parent and a teenager argue about something. Avoid repetition by including a number of auxiliary verbs and reduced infinitives. Use one of the ideas below or choose your own.

1 an argument about tidiness
2 an argument about staying out late
3 an argument about schoolwork
4 an argument about the television

5 **SPEAKING** Work in pairs. Act out your dialogue to the class, paying attention to the pronunciation.

1 SPEAKING **Work in pairs. Discuss the questions.**

1 What does the graph tell us about military spending? What is your reaction to this information?

2 Look at the poster. How do the armed forces recruit people in your country?

3 What are the people in the photo demonstrating against? Are protests like these generally effective? Why?/Why not?

Global distribution of military expenditure

SPEAKING TIP

Giving a presentation

1 Present your strongest argument first.

2 Acknowledge the opposing view and then give a counter-argument or restate your own opinion.

3 When you are thinking what to say next, use fillers.

4 When you don't know the English for something, try to paraphrase.

5 Look at the examiner and speak loudly and clearly. Try to sound confident.

2 🎧 2.06 **Read the *Speaking tip* and the task below. Then listen to two students doing the task and answer the questions.**

1 To what extent do the speakers follow the advice?

2 Which arguments do you find the most persuasive? Why?

'To be a pacifist is to be a coward.' Do you agree or disagree? Present your opinion, giving arguments to support your view. Speak for a maximum of three minutes.

3 🎧 2.06 **Listen again. Add the phrases the speakers use for structuring their presentations to the chart below.**

> **Changing the subject**
> I'll now turn to …
> I'd now like to deal with …
> 1 _____   2 _____
>
> **Acknowledging an opposing view**
> I freely admit that …
> Others take a different view.
> 3 _____   4 _____
>
> **Dismissing an opposing view**
> I don't accept there's any merit in the argument that …
> I entirely reject the notion that …
> 5 _____   6 _____
>
> **Referring to something said earlier**
> Returning to (the issue of … /the point about …)
> To restate the main argument, …
> 7 _____   8 _____

4 **Complete the sentences with the correct form of the words below.**

defend   destroy   eradicate   have   spend   too much

1 _____ poverty through health and education would mean wars wouldn't be necessary.

2 Everyone should be able _____ their country.

3 _____ a single global superpower is safer than having two or three.

4 There are more important things for young people _____ their time on.

5 _____ power in the hands of a single state is a dangerous thing.

6 Even if all weapons _____, there would still be disease and poverty.

5 **Match the sentences in exercise 4 with the statements below. Which are arguments for the statements, and which are arguments against?**

a National Service should be compulsory.

b Every country should reduce military spending and spend the money instead on humanitarian causes.

c The USA poses the biggest threat to world peace.

6 **Work in pairs. Choose one of the statements in exercise 5. Decide if you agree or disagree and brainstorm two or three additional arguments to support your opinion. Include at least one opposing argument. Make notes.**

7 SPEAKING **Give your presentation to the class. Speak for a maximum of three minutes. Follow the advice in the *Speaking tip* and use some of the phrases in exercise 3.**

1 Explain this quotation about admiration. Do you agree with it? Why?/Why not?

We always love those who admire us, but we do not always love those whom we admire.

WRITING TIP

Writing an article
When writing an article, it is important to consider:
1 the target audience, i.e. who you are writing for.
2 the purpose of the article (e.g. to entertain, to persuade, to inform, etc).
3 the appropriate style (e.g. formal, informal, 'chatty' and personal; the use of headings, bullet points, etc.).

---

2 Read the *Writing tip* and the task below. What is the target audience? What is the purpose of the article? What style would be most appropriate?

Someone I admire
Write an article about someone you admire. It could be someone you know personally or a public figure.
• Include information about their life.
• Include information about their achievements.
• Explain why you admire them.
The three best articles will be published in the school magazine next month.

---

3 The opening of the article should grab the reader's attention and draw them in. Which of these openings works least well? Why?

a There are a number of people I admire, but one person stands out from all the others.

b Patience, wisdom and generosity are three qualities that I value greatly, and my friend Susan has all three in abundance.

c The person I admire most is my elder brother, Joseph. He's a really admirable person.

d If there's one person that embodies all that I admire in a human being, it's my Aunt Linda.

e What makes us admire people? Often it is because they have admirable qualities which we don't ourselves possess.

4 Read the article. Find passages where the writer has:
1 addressed the reader.
2 used a rhetorical question.
3 used: (a) a chatty, personal style (b) a more formal style.

Top of the list of people I greatly admire comes my great-grandfather, who, at the age of 97, is still living a full and active life. If you were to meet him, you wouldn't believe he's only three years short of a hundred.
Throughout his long life he has battled against adversity and misfortune. He lost both his parents before his twelfth birthday, and on top of that his elder brother died in the First World War. As a young man in the 1930s he was out of work for long periods and really struggled to support his young family. Then, just as things began to go better for him, he was called up to fight in the Second World War. He joined the RAF and was shot down over France in 1944. Not only was he badly injured, but he was also captured and spent the rest of the war in a prisoner-of-war camp. After the war, he opened a small garage, doing repairs and servicing, and selling second-hand cars, and through sheer hard work built it up into a successful business. However, the business ran into difficulties during a recession and he went bankrupt.
All this was long before I was born, of course. But what's he really like as a person? In the years that I have known him he has shown other great qualities besides the courage and determination which helped him through the difficult times. He's kind, willing to listen and offer a word of advice – but he never forces it on you. What's more, he's great fun to be with and very witty.
He's one of the wisest and most tolerant people I know, and I'm very lucky to have him as my great-grandfather.

5 An article needs a good title. Choose the best title for the article in exercise 4.
1 A long life
2 A lovely old man
3 Battling against adversity
4 My great-grandfather
5 Someone I admire

6 In the article, find two of the nouns below and three adjectives formed from the nouns below.

altruism   amiability   charm   courage   determination
devotion   generosity   honesty   intelligence   loyalty
patience   reliability   sensitivity   sincerity   tolerance
trustworthiness   wisdom   wit

7 Form adjectives from all the other nouns in the box.

▶▶▶ **VOCABULARY BUILDER 5.3: WORD FORMATION (1): WORKBOOK PAGE 105** ◀◀◀

8 **SPEAKING** Work in pairs. Make a list of five well-known people whom you admire. What are the qualities and achievements that you find admirable? Use the nouns and adjectives in exercises 6 and 7 to help you.

Article: decribing a person

I can write an article describing someone I admire.

1 Look at the pictures. What achievements are the people famous for? What difficulties did they have to overcome?

1 *Beethoven*

2 *Nelson Mandela*

3 *Emmeline Pankhurst*

2 Check the meaning of the words and phrases used to express addition in the *Learn this!* box. Which two would you only expect to see in a formal context? Find four more in the article on page 56 and put them in the correct place in the *Learn this!* box.

Linkers for addition

Preposition + noun	**Adverbs/adverbial phrases**
alongside	*besides, …*
along with	*furthermore*
apart from	*… into the bargain*
as well as	*moreover*
1 _____	2 _____
in addition to	*… to boot*
plus	3 _____

Preposition + gerund	**Paired conjunctions**
apart from	*both … and …*
as well as	4 _____
besides	
in addition to	

⟫⟫ VOCABULARY BUILDER 5.4: LINKERS (1): WORKBOOK PAGE 105 ⟪⟪

3 Complete the second sentence so that it means the same as the first.

1 Wendy is very determined and she's also very ambitious.
Besides _____ .
2 Henry travelled up the Amazon, and some of his friends went with him.
Henry _____ along with _____ .
3 Liam is a fine painter and he's a good pianist too.
Liam _____ to boot.
4 My mum has a full-time job and does all the housework.
My mum _____ as well as _____ .

5 Jake has got both a great sense of humour and great deal of charm.
In addition to _____ .
6 My grandmother looked after five children and she looked after her own sick mother.
My grandmother _____ plus _____ .
7 Pete owns a flat in London as well as a house in the country.
Apart from _____ .

4 Read the task. Plan an article, making notes for the sections below.

> **Heroes**
> Write an article about someone you admire because they have overcome adversity. It could be someone you know personally or a public figure.
> • Describe the problems they faced.
> • Describe the qualities they have that make them special.
> The three best articles will be published in the school magazine next month.

Opening paragraph: (Introduce the topic. Grab the reader's attention. Refer to the question, but do not copy it.)

Main part: (Adversities that they have overcome and the personal qualities that make them special – one or two paragraphs.)

Final paragraph: (Briefly sum up.)

5 Work in pairs.

1 Look at your partner's notes from exercise 4 and write down at least three questions which you'd like to ask about the person.
2 Ask your partner the questions you noted down.
3 Use your answers to your partner's questions to add more details to your article plan.

6 Think of a good title for your article.

7 Write a first draft of the article. Write between 200–250 words following your plan.

8 Check your work using the list below.

> **CHECK YOUR WORK**
> **Have you:**
> ☐ followed the plan correctly?
> ☐ written the correct number of words?
> ☐ grabbed the readers' attention in the first paragraph?
> ☐ used some linkers for addition?
> ☐ checked the spelling and grammar?

1 **Get ready to SPEAK** Work in pairs. Answer the questions.

1 Have you ever witnessed, or heard about, a road rage incident? What happened?

2 Do you ever row with anyone? What do you argue about?

2 Do the Speaking exam task.

SPEAKING exam task

Compare and contrast the photos then asnwer the questions.

1 Why are the people arguing, do you think?

2 Can rows be beneficial? Why?/Why not?

3 What's the best way of avoiding family rows?

3 Do the Use of English exam task.

USE OF ENGLISH exam task

Choose the best word or phrase (A–D) to complete each gap.

'Homework at root of many family arguments'

Homework can cause friction between parents and children, especially in middle-class families where concerns about a child's future can lead to a dangerous [1]_____ of pressure to succeed, according to a recent report by the Institute of Education, University of London. Homework can also create anxiety, boredom, fatigue and emotional exhaustion in children, who resent the encroachment on their free time, [2]_____ they think homework helps them do well at school. The resulting [3]_____ to the parent-child relationship may [4]_____ any educational advantage homework may [5]_____, the Institute claimed. The report found that problems can [6]_____ when parents try to help with homework, especially when they feel they [7]_____ the knowledge or the time. Parents may inhibit their children's effectiveness in doing homework by trying to control the homework environment – telling children when and where to do homework or trying to eliminate distractions – instead of helping them [8]_____ it to suit their learning styles, the body said. On the plus side, the report said, parental [9]_____ in homework has been shown [10]_____ the strongest predictor of better grades. Report author Dr Susan Hallam said: 'Parents have the most positive influence when they offer moral support, make appropriate resources available and discuss general issues. They should only actually help with homework when their children specifically ask them to.'

1 A atmosphere B mood C attitude D climate
2 A while B even though C supposing D if
3 A damage B injury C destruction D hurt
4 A exceed B overbalance C outweigh
   D compensate for
5 A bring B do C make D grow
6 A proceed B derive C rise D arise
7 A go without B miss C lack D are deprived of
8 A amend B adapt C refine D convert
9 A involvement B contribution C collaboration
   D connection
10 A being B having been C as being D to be

4 **Get ready to LISTEN** Do you know why the year 1066 is important in British history?

5 🎧 2.07 Do the Listening exam task.

LISTENING exam task

Listen to the radio programme. Decide whether the information in each sentence (1–7) is true (T), false (F) or not stated (NS).

	True	False	Not stated
1 Everyone in Britain knows what happened in 1066.	☐	☐	☐
2 In history lessons children have to learn too many dates.	☐	☐	☐
3 No country has invaded Britain since 1066.	☐	☐	☐
4 Some people think that the English Channel has defended the country from invasion.	☐	☐	☐
5 Other battles have changed history to the extent that Battle of Hastings did.	☐	☐	☐
6 The Norman system of government was superior to the Anglo-Saxon model.	☐	☐	☐
7 After 1066, the whole population of Britain was forced to speak French.	☐	☐	☐

THIS UNIT INCLUDES

Vocabulary ■ synonyms of *predict* ■ expressions for plans and predictions ■ adjective-adverb/verb-noun collocations ■ dependent prepositions (2) ■ register ■ collocations with *sleep* ■ synonyms of *prize* ■ idioms for expressing joy ■ concession and counter-argument ■ reporting verbs
Grammar ■ talking about the future ■ phrasal verbs: particles and their meanings ■ reporting structures
Speaking ■ talking about personal ambitions ■ talking about sleep and dreams ■ talking about the EU ■ photo comparison
Writing ■ a story

Dreams | 6

6A | **VOCABULARY AND LISTENING** Looking into the future

I can speculate and make predictions about the future.

1 **SPEAKING** Work in pairs. Describe the photo and answer the questions.

1 What job does the woman do?
2 Have you ever had your fortune told? If not, would you like to? Why?/Why not?
3 Why do people want to know their future?
4 Do you think it is possible to predict the future?
5 Do you know any famous prophecies? Did they come true?

>>> VOCABULARY BUILDER 6.1: SYNONYMS OF *PREDICT*: WORKBOOK PAGE 106 <<<

2 🎧 2.08 Listen to six teenagers answering the question: *Where do you see yourself in ten years' time?* Answer the questions. Give reasons for your answers.

1 Who has the most/least interesting ambitions?
2 Who is the most/least optimistic about fulfilling their ambitions?
3 Do you have similar ambitions to any of the speakers?

3 🎧 2.08 Complete the expressions with the words below. Then listen again and check.

come counting determined everything foreseeable
fulfil goal hopes likely myself position realise
sights succeed work

1 I think it's _____ that …
2 I can(not) see _____ (+ gerund)
3 I've set my _____ on (+ noun)
4 I'm not _____ on it.
5 Assuming that I _____ my ambition …
6 If my plans _____ to nothing, …
7 I'm _____ to (+ base form)
8 I'll give it _____ I've got.
9 _____ my dream (*of* + gerund)
10 I'm (not) pinning my _____ on (noun/gerund)

11 … achieve my _____ (*of* + gerund)
12 I hope I _____ in (+ gerund)
13 I may _____ towards that.
14 I don't see that happening in the _____ future.
15 I'll be in a better _____ to … (+ base form)

>>> GRAMMAR BUILDER 6.1: TALKING ABOUT THE FUTURE: PAGE 122 <<<

4 Where do you see yourself in ten years' time? Make notes under these headings.

Education	Job
Study what? Where?	What? Where?
Marriage and children	**House and home**
Yes or no? When? How many?	Where? What type?
Travel	**Money**
Where to?	How important?

5 **SPEAKING** Work in pairs. Make predictions about your partner's future.

6 Work in pairs. Look at each other's notes from exercise 4 and ask some questions about the predictions. Add your answers to your notes.

> Why did you write 'lead guitarist'?

7 Prepare to present your ideas using some of the expressions in exercise 3 and the box below.

> **Expressing doubt and uncertainty**
> It's difficult to say, really.
> I guess I'll …
> I (don't) suppose I'll … /I (don't) imagine I'll …
> I would(n't) say that …
> I doubt if I'll …
> It's unlikely that I'll …
> Assuming that …
> I may/might well …
> It depends whether/how/what, etc. …
> It's anyone's guess what/when/where, etc. …
> I could go in a number of directions.

8 **SPEAKING** Work with a different partner. Tell him or her about where you see yourself in ten years from now.

1 Discuss this question in pairs: How do dreams differ from real life?

2 Choose the best word (a–d) to complete each gap.

Have you ever ¹_____ why we dream? It seems such an easy question, but it is very difficult to answer. Most scientists agree that we don't yet know what purpose dreams ²_____. Given the amount of time we spend in a dreaming ³_____, this may at first seem baffling. However, it isn't really surprising when we consider that science is still ⁴_____ the exact purpose and function of sleep itself. Scientists have put forward a number of theories as to why we dream, but as yet no ⁵_____ consensus has emerged. Some experts are of the opinion that in all likelihood dreaming has no real purpose. They maintain that sleep probably has a biological function (allowing the body and brain to recuperate), but that dreaming is merely a mental ⁶_____, nothing but a sequence of images and feelings experienced ⁷_____ sleeping. Other scientists, on the other hand, believe that dreaming is essential to mental, emotional and physical well-being. They suggest that dreams are ⁸_____ triggered by the feelings we experience while we are awake, such as fear, anger or love. This is why dreams are more frequent and intense following powerful emotional experiences, especially stressful or traumatic ones. According to this theory, such dreams allow the mind to make sense of the emotional experiences, ⁹_____ suggests that they help us both to reduce the distress caused by the trauma, and to cope better if further traumatic or stressful events occur.

1 **a** wondered	**b** thought	**c** speculated	**d** reflected
2 **a** serve	**b** carry out	**c** complete	**d** do
3 **a** condition	**b** circumstance	**c** position	**d** state
4 **a** unwinding	**b** unravelling	**c** separating	**d** untying
5 **a** single	**b** sole	**c** singular	**d** solitary
6 **a** act	**b** activity	**c** action	**d** procedure
7 **a** on	**b** in	**c** during	**d** while
8 **a** somewhat	**b** somehow	**c** anyhow	**d** anyway
9 **a** this	**b** and	**c** that	**d** which

3 🎧 2.09 Listen to three people talking about dreams. Answer the questions in your own words.

1 How did Belinda's dream relate to her life?
2 In his dream, what makes Harry able to fly?
3 According to Christine, what function do dreams serve?

LEARN THIS!

Phrasal verbs: particles and their meanings
Particles often add a specific meaning to a phrasal verb. Most particles have more than one meaning.
back = 1 repeating   2 looking into the past
*The secretary read the letter **back** to her boss.*
*This building dates **back** to 1650.*
down = 1 record in writing   2 reducing
*I jotted **down** the phone number on a scrap of paper.*
*Wait till your coffee cools **down**.*
off = 1 departing   2 ending
*The thieves made **off** with £1 million in cash.*
*Sam broke **off** his engagement to Tilly.*
on = 1 continuing   2 attacking
*My boss droned **on** for ages at the meeting.*
*Pick **on** someone your own size!*
out = 1 disappearing   2 solving, searching
*Dinosaurs died **out** about 60 million years ago.*
*I could just make **out** a ship on the horizon.*
over = 1 visiting   2 considering, examining
*Let's pop **over** to Jamie's.*
*Always look **over** your work before you hand it in.*
up = 1 approach   2 improve
*Don't creep **up** on me like that!*
*I'm going to evening classes to brush **up** on my French.*

4 Study the *Learn this!* box. Then complete these sentences from the listening with the particles below. Which meanings in the *Learn this!* box do the particles convey, 1 or 2?

back down off on out over up

1 I remember the wolf coming _____ to the house.
2 I've never tried to work _____ what it means, though.
3 I throw myself forward and I take _____ .
4 So in order to carry _____ flying, I have to believe I can fly.
5 Gradually I calm _____ .
6 Mostly my dreams are just a rehash of events of the day, coming _____ in muddled form.
7 It's quite amusing sometimes to go _____ the dream in your own head.

➤➤ GRAMMAR BUILDER 6.2: PARTICLES AND THEIR MEANINGS: PAGE 123 ◀◀◀

5 SPEAKING Work with a partner. Discuss these questions. Try to use some phrasal verbs in your answers.

1 How often do you dream? Do you often remember your dreams? Do you have recurring dreams? What happens?
2 Do you think your dreams can tell you anything about your true state of mind? If so, what?
3 Do you believe that dreams can foretell the future? Why?/ Why not?
4 Have any of your dreams ever come true? If so, what happened?

The European Union

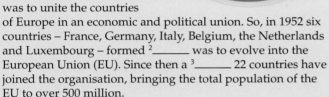

Origins and growth

In the aftermath of the Second World War, some political leaders in Western Europe believed that the only ¹_____ to avoid war and conflict in the future was to unite the countries of Europe in an economic and political union. So, in 1952 six countries – France, Germany, Italy, Belgium, the Netherlands and Luxembourg – formed ²_____ was to evolve into the European Union (EU). Since then a ³_____ 22 countries have joined the organisation, bringing the total population of the EU to over 500 million.

How does it work?

The EU is not a federation ⁴_____ the United States. The member states of the EU remain independent sovereign nations but they pool their sovereignty in certain areas of policy. Pooling sovereignty means, ⁵_____ practice, that the member states delegate some of their decision-making powers to shared institutions they have created, so that decisions ⁶_____ specific matters of joint interest can be made democratically at European level.

The three main decision-making institutions are:

- the *European Commission*, consisting of 28 commissioners, one chosen by each member state. The role of the Commission is to propose new legislation, but it cannot pass laws ⁷_____ itself.
- the *Council of the EU*, consisting of one government minister from each country. The Council is the EU's main decision-making body. It votes on legislation proposed by the Commission.
- the *European Parliament*, based in Brussels and Strasbourg, and consisting of 785 MEPs directly elected by the citizens of the EU. Elections are held ⁸_____ five years. Like the Council, the Parliament votes on and passes laws proposed by the Commission.

Controversy

The British have a very uneasy relationship with the EU. British Europhiles claim that the EU continues to bring tangible economic and political benefits to the UK, and that it has delivered peace and stability to Europe for over half a century. Eurosceptics, however, who are probably ⁹_____ a majority in the UK, are concerned about the direction the EU is taking. They believe that it is fundamentally undemocratic and unaccountable, and maintain that the real aim of the EU is to create an enormous federal state in which individual member states will exercise little control ¹⁰_____ their own affairs.

1 Test your knowledge of the EU. Try the quiz, then read the text and check your answers.

1 In which decade was the organisation that was to become the EU formed?
2 Can you name three of the six original members?
3 How many member states are there now?
4 In which two cities does the European Parliament meet?

2 Complete the text with appropriate words. Use one word only in each gap.

3 Read the text and explain in your own words:

1 what the founders of the EU hoped that it would achieve.
2 what 'pooling sovereignty' means.
3 how the European Commission, the Council of the EU and the European Parliament are made up, and what their roles are.
4 what Eurosceptics fear.

4 Find these nouns in the text and complete the collocations with the correct verbs.

1 _____ an organisation
2 _____ powers
3 _____ new legislation
4 _____ a law
5 _____ an election
6 _____ benefits
7 _____ peace and stability
8 _____ control

5 Complete these phrases from the text with prepositions.

1 evolve _____   2 consist _____   3 vote _____

▶▶▶ **VOCABULARY BUILDER 6.2: DEPENDENT PREPOSITIONS: WORKBOOK PAGE 106** ◀◀◀

6 🎧 2.10 Listen to four people talking about the EU. Match each speaker with one benefit (a–d) and one drawback (e–h).

Speaker 1 ☐ ☐   Speaker 3 ☐ ☐
Speaker 2 ☐ ☐   Speaker 4 ☐ ☐

Benefits of the EU

a The EU gives European countries a voice in world affairs.
b The EU has made it much easier to travel around Europe.
c The European single market is a real success.
d The EU provides economic aid to the poorer regions of Europe.

Drawbacks of the EU

e The EU should leave more decisions to national governments.
f The EU is over-bureaucratic and many of the laws it passes are unnecessary.
g The free movement of labour has created problems.
h The EU is undemocratic.

7 SPEAKING Discuss the statements in exercise 6 and decide if you agree or disagree with them. Justify your opinions.

>> Discuss the EU at http://www.debatingeurope.eu

I can understand and react to an article about the importance of sleep.

1 SPEAKING **Work in pairs. Describe the photos. Then ask and answer these questions.**

1 What time do you usually go to bed?
2 Do you have a computer or a TV in your bedroom?
3 Do you go straight to sleep? If not, what do you do?
4 Do you ever lie in at weekends? Until what time?

2 Read the text. Which explanation for teenagers not getting enough sleep does the writer favour?

1 Teenagers think they catch up with sleep at weekends.
2 Teenagers' bodies do not produce a hormone that makes them sleepy until the early hours of the morning.
3 Teenagers engage in late-night activities such as playing computer games and watching TV instead of going straight to sleep.

3 Answer the questions.

1 In what two ways can lack of sleep affect teenagers?
2 Why do some experts believe that activities such as playing computer games before bed are more likely to prevent teenagers from sleeping than reading a book?
3 What evidence does the writer produce to support his/ her view that it is normal for teenagers to go to sleep later than adults?

4 Scan the text and underline all the examples of the noun *sleep*. Look at the words *sleep* collocates with in the text. How many of the collocations can you find in the extract from the *Oxford Collocations Dictionary*?

---

sleep noun
1 condition of rest
ADJ. **deep** | **light** | **much-needed** ◇ *I'm off to bed for some much-needed ~.* | **adequate** | **REM**
VERB + SLEEP **drift into, drift off to, drop off to, fall back to** (*AmE*), **get to, go to** ◇ *She turned over and went back to ~.* | **cry yourself to** | **catch, get, snatch** ◇ *Close your eyes and get some ~ now.* ◇ *I snatched a few hours' ~ in the afternoon.* | **need** | **survive on** ◇ *They seem to survive on only a few hours' ~ a night.* | **induce, promote** ◇ *They use drugs to induce ~.* | **lull sb to, send sb to** ◇ *The quiet music soon sent her to ~.* | **drift in and out of** ◇ *He drifted in and out of ~ all night.* | **lose** (*often figurative*) ◇ *Don't lose ~ over it—we'll sort everything out in the morning.* | **disrupt, disturb, interrupt** | **catch up on** ◇ *I used Saturday to catch up on my ~.* | **feign** ◇ *I feigned ~ when the nurse came around.*
SLEEP + VERB **come** ◇ *Sleep came to her in snatches.* | **overcome sb, overtake sb** ◇ *Sleep finally overtook me.*
SLEEP + NOUN **cycle, pattern, schedule** (*esp. AmE*) | **deprivation, loss** | **disorder** | **apnoea/apnea** | **aid** (*esp. AmE*) ◇ *the nation's most commonly prescribed ~ aid*
PREP. **during ~** ◇ *a decreased heart rate during ~* | **in your ~** ◇ *He often walks and talks in his ~.*
PHRASES **a lack of ~** ◇ *I was suffering from a lack of ~.* | **a wink of ~** ◇ *I won't get a wink of ~ with that noise downstairs.*

2 period of sleep
ADJ. **long** | **little, short** | **dead, deep, heavy, sound** | **uninterrupted** | **good, restful** | **light** | **disturbed, exhausted, fitful, restless, troubled, uneasy** ◇ *I woke up early after a disturbed ~.* | **dreamless, peaceful** | **drunken, beauty** ◇ *Sorry, but I need my beauty ~.*
VERB + SLEEP **need** | **have** ◇ *Did you have a good ~?* | **be in** ◇ *I was in a deep ~ when the phone rang.* | **drift into, fall into, sink into** ◇ *I immediately fell into a dead ~.* | **awake (sb) from, awaken (sb) from, wake (sb) from** ◇ *He woke from a fitful ~ with a headache.*
PHRASES **a good, poor, etc. night's ~** ◇ *You'll feel better after a good night's ~.*

Let **sleeping teenagers** lie

1 Why is it that many teenagers have the energy to play computer games until late at night but can't find the energy to get out of bed in time for school? According to a new report, today's generation of children are in danger of getting so little
5 sleep that they are putting their mental and physical health at risk. Adults can easily survive on seven to eight hours' sleep a night, whereas teenagers require nine or ten hours. According to medical experts, one in five youngsters gets anything between two and five hours' sleep a night less than
10 their parents did at their age.

This raises serious questions about whether lack of sleep is affecting children's ability to concentrate at school. The connection between sleep deprivation and lapses in memory, impaired reaction time and poor concentration is
15 well established. Research has shown that losing as little as half an hour's sleep a night can have profound effects on how children perform the next day. A good night's sleep is also crucial for teenagers because it is while they are asleep that they release a hormone that is essential for their 'growth
20 spurt' (the period during teenage years when the body grows at a rapid rate). It's true that they can to some extent catch up on sleep at weekends, but that won't help them when they are dropping off to sleep in class on a Friday afternoon.

So why aren't teenagers getting enough sleep? Some experts
25 suggest the presence of televisions, computers and mobile phones in children's bedrooms may be to blame. Instead of reading a book at bedtime, children are going to their rooms and playing computer games, surfing the web, texting and messaging, or watching television. As these new childhood
30 pre-sleep activities have become more widespread, so more traditional ones such as reading have declined. Dr Luci Wiggs, a research fellow at Oxford University's Section of Child and Adolescent Psychiatry said, 'One of the problems
35 with these pre-sleep activities is that they are unstructured, i.e. they do not have clearly defined start
40 and end times.' She went on, 'This is the first generation of children to face such a plethora of
45 alternatives to going to sleep and the long-

term consequences in terms of physical and mental health for both the child and their family can only be guessed at. What we do know is that impaired sleep quality or quantity
50 may compromise children's physical health, academic achievements and mental health.'

Research has shown that teenagers have different sleep patterns from younger children and adults. A timing mechanism in the brain regulates our bodily functions over a
55 24-hour period. At night, the heart rate falls, blood pressure is lowered and urine ceases to be produced. When the sun rises, the body begins to wake up. One important change that occurs at night time is increased levels of the 'darkness hormone' melatonin, which helps us to fall asleep. Most
60 adults start to produce melatonin at about 10 p.m. When teenagers were studied in a sleep laboratory, researchers discovered that they only began to produce the hormone at 1 a.m. It is possible that this delay in melatonin production is caused by the behaviour of teenagers. Playing with
65 electronic gadgets late at night stimulates the brain and exposes the teenagers to bright lights which could cause the later release of melatonin. A more likely explanation, however, is that the hormonal upheaval of puberty is pushing the melatonin release back, in which case teenagers are
70 being kept awake by their bodies – they simply can't help their peculiar sleeping behaviour. Although it isn't impossible for adolescents to go to sleep before 11 p.m., or even to be alert in the morning, their bodies make it difficult for them, and in some cases nearly impossible. This is
75 borne out by studies conducted in the USA, where some schools have delayed the start of their classes to give their teenagers some extra time in bed. Many teachers reported that students were more alert and less moody. One school even noticed a significant improvement in the educational
80 performance of its students.

Issues surrounding sleep – who needs how much and when – are usually given short shrift in efforts to improve student achievement. But modern brain researchers say it is time that more schools woke up to the biological facts and started
85 lessons at a time better suited to their teenage students.

5 Use the examples in the dictionary entry to help you identify which collocations have meanings 1–5.

1 worry about something with the result that you aren't able to sleep
2 get a little sleep in a short available time, usually during the day
3 while you are sleeping (two phrases)
4 make somebody go to sleep
5 pretend to be asleep

6 Complete the sentences with collocations of *sleep* from the dictionary. Sometimes more than one answer is possible.

1 The moment her head touched the pillow she _____ into a deep sleep.
2 Teenagers have different sleep _____ from adults.
3 After splitting up with her boyfriend, she went home and _____ herself to sleep.
4 I'm going to get an early night. I need to _____ on my sleep.
5 He drank a whole bottle of wine and fell into a _____ sleep.
6 I woke at 3 a.m. and couldn't _____ to sleep for ages. Sleep finally _____ me at about five o'clock.

7 Match these words with the more formal equivalents in red in the text.

1 need (v)	5 happen
2 a big impact	6 a very large number
3 control (v)	7 stop
4 carry out	

>>> **VOCABULARY BUILDER 6.3: REGISTER: WORKBOOK PAGE 106** <<<

8 SPEAKING Work in pairs. Answer the questions. Give reasons for your answers.

1 Do you think you get enough sleep?
2 Do you sometimes feel tired and unable to concentrate at school? Why is that?
3 Would you prefer it if school started and finished later?
4 What would be the drawbacks of starting school later?

1 Read the text. Have you ever had an 'anxiety dream' like this?

I had the strangest dream the other night. I was having breakfast and my mum reminded me that the school exams started that day. She asked me if I had done enough revision and I told her the exams weren't for another three weeks, and promised to revise for them. But when I got to school, I found that my classmates had already started the English Literature exam. I apologised for being late. The teacher instructed me to sit down and start writing, but when I opened the exam paper, I couldn't answer any of the questions. I claimed not to have read any of the books, but the teacher insisted that I should do the exam. It was at that point that I woke up.

2 What do you think were the original words spoken by the people in the dream?

⟫⟫ GRAMMAR BUILDER 6.3: REPORTING STRUCTURES: PAGE 124 ⟪⟪

3 Report the sentences using the verbs below.

beg ~~claim~~ congratulate insist promise recommend threaten warn

1 'I've never had a nightmare,' he said.
   He claimed never to have had a nightmare.
2 'I think you should go to that restaurant. It's really good,' said Ben to Lee.
3 'Please, please don't wear those old jeans,' said Jo to Ian.
4 'If you don't stop talking, I'll give you a detention,' said Mr Medway to his class.
5 'Don't swim too far out to sea as the currents are quite strong,' said Jo to Tom.
6 'Well done for passing your driving test,' said Sue to Chris.
7 'I'll never lie to you again,' said Steve to Vanessa.
8 'You must eat your vegetables,' said Liam to his daughter.

4 Choose the correct alternatives. Then change the sentences to direct speech.

1 My dad **suggested** / **advised** me to get an early night.
2 Harry **refused** / **denied** that he had cheated in the exam.
3 Dave **asked** / **insisted** that I should help him.
4 Kate **agreed** / **proposed** to buy a new car.
5 Fred **ordered** / **reminded** his son that he had to turn off the computer.
6 Robbie **blamed** / **accused** his brother for the accident.
7 The robbers **admitted** / **agreed** to steal the gold bullion from the security van.

5 Rewrite the sentences in exercise 4 using the verbs you did not use.

My dad suggested that I should get an early night.

> **LEARN THIS!**
> 1 We often use adverbs with reporting verbs to convey the tone or emotional content of the original words.
> *'I've had enough of your insolence!'*
> *He shouted angrily that he'd had enough of her insolence.*
> 2 We can report speech without giving the precise words that were spoken.
> *'Fancy seeing you here!' said James.*
> *James expressed his surprise at seeing me there.*

6 🎧 2.11 Listen to the sentences and add an adverb below to convey the emotions of the speaker.

bitterly callously defiantly resignedly sarcastically sharply sympathetically

1 'Unfortunately, there's nothing we can do about it,' she said _____ .
2 'You've never really loved me, have you?' she said _____ .
3 'That was really clever, wasn't it?' said Sarah _____ .
4 'You can't stop me from seeing whoever I like!' said Sam _____ .
5 'Mind your own business!' said Frank _____ .
6 'It's not my problem. Sort it out yourself,' said John _____ .
7 'You must be feeling terrible. If there's anything I can do, just let me know,' said Christine _____ .

7 🎧 2.12 Listen to eight extracts and match them with a–h.

a She expressed her gratitude for … ☐
b She boasted of her ability to … ☐
c She enquired after her grandfather's … ☐
d She expressed her sincere apologies for … ☐
e She complimented him on … ☐
f She declined the invitation to … ☐
g She confirmed her willingness to … ☐
h She told him off for being … ☐

8 🎧 2.12 Listen again and complete each report a–h above in a suitable way.

9 **SPEAKING** Work in pairs. Tell your partner about 1–8 below. Use reporting verbs and adverbs that convey the tone and emotional content.

1 something your parents forbade you to do
2 something you complimented somebody on
3 something you apologised for
4 an invitation you declined
5 something you were blamed for
6 something you reminded somebody to do
7 something you expressed surprise at
8 something you refused to do

1 SPEAKING Find one of these items in the photos. Explain the difference in meaning between the six words.

award honour medal prize reward trophy

2 SPEAKING Have you, or anyone you know, ever won any of the things in exercise 1? What was it for? How did you/they feel?

3 🎧 2.13 Listen to four people talking about achievements. Match the speakers with four of the people below. How did they feel (a) when they won the award or prize and (b) now?

1 a sportsperson   4 a scientist
2 a film star   5 an explorer
3 a politician   6 a lottery winner

Speaker 1 ☐   Speaker 3 ☐
Speaker 2 ☐   Speaker 4 ☐

4 🎧 2.13 Match 1–8 with a–h to complete the expressions. Then listen again and check.

1 I was over   a our luck.
2 I couldn't believe   b to bits.
3 It was a   c for joy.
4 I felt as if I was walking   d of the world.
5 It is such   e dream come true.
6 I was thrilled   f on air.
7 I'm on top   g the moon.
8 They are jumping   h an honour.

5 Work in pairs. Read the task. Compare and contrast the photos using the prompts below. Use the expressions in exercise 4, and in exercise 6 on page 21, to help you.

1 Where are the people and what they have won?
2 How do you think they are feeling?
3 How similar are their achievements?

> These photos show people who have won something. Compare and contrast the photos. Say what you think motivated them, what they did to achieve success, and how it might affect their lives.

6 🎧 2.14 Listen to a student answering the second part of the task. Do you agree with her opinions? Give reasons.

7 Which of these phrases for concession and counter-argument does the speaker use? Which are adverbs and which are conjunctions?

Concession and counter-argument
although even though all the same and yet
granted even so having said that in spite of this
it's true that mind you much as nevertheless
nonetheless though yet

8 Rewrite the sentences using the words in brackets. Sometimes you will need to make two sentences into one, and vice versa.

1 I'd like to be rich. Nevertheless, I'm not prepared to waste my money on lottery tickets. (much as)
2 He hardly did any revision for his exams and yet he managed to pass. (even though)
3 Much as I admire his achievements, he's neglected his family in his quest for success. (although)
4 Although she's worked really hard, she's never really got the recognition she deserves. (nonetheless)
5 Even though she's widely acknowledged to be the best actress of her generation, she's never won an Oscar. (yet)
6 The winning goal may have been lucky, but they deserved to win the match. (though)

⟫ **VOCABULARY BUILDER 6.4: CONCESSION AND COUNTER-ARGUMENT: WORKBOOK PAGE 107** ⟪

9 SPEAKING Turn to page 151 and do the exam task.

1 **SPEAKING** Work in pairs or small groups. Think of a book or film that you all like and discuss what makes it a good story.

2 Read this extract from a story. Does it exemplify any of the features of a good story that you identified in exercise 1?

I was awoken from a lovely deep sleep by the sound of someone knocking loudly at the door.

'Who can that be?' I muttered to myself. The alarm clock said three minutes past two.

I fumbled around for my dressing gown and went cautiously down the stairs to answer the door.

A strange old man was standing on the doorstep. His face was hidden in a tall, black hood.

'Who are you? What do you want?' I asked nervously.

'Come with me. I've got something to show you,' he whispered in a husky voice. I hesitated, then closed the door quietly behind me.

I awoke in a cold sweat and sat bolt upright in bed. My heart was pounding furiously. Gradually it dawned on me that I had been dreaming. I looked at the clock. It said three minutes past two. I turned over and closed my eyes. There was a knock on the door ...

3 Underline the adjectives, adverbs and adverb phrases in the story.

4 Find three pairs of adjectives in the story. Complete the *Learn this!* box with *age, colour, opinion, size*.

LEARN THIS!

Order of adjectives
Before a noun, adjectives usually come in this order:
¹_____ ²_____ ³_____ shape ⁴_____ origin material
Numbers usually come before adjectives.

5 Correct the mistakes in adjective order in these phrases.
1 an old wonderful Italian painting
2 two leather enormous black suitcases
3 a Siamese grey stupid fat cat
4 a square modern small house
5 a linen cream beautiful suit

6 Rewrite the sentences using the adverbs and adverb phrases in brackets. You may need to change the punctuation. Sometimes more than one answer is correct.
1 We used to go skiing. (at this time of year / often / in France / in the past)
2 I go for long rides. (still / along the river / now and then / on my own)
3 I couldn't have done it. (so quickly / certainly / without your help)
4 It's raining. (heavily / today / quite)
5 Your letter arrived. (here / yesterday morning / oddly enough / only)
6 He didn't understand what you said. (just now / fully / clearly)

7 Put the adverbs on the right into this extract from a story, on the same line as they appear. You may need to change the punctuation. Sometimes more than one answer is correct.

Gemma marched into the café.	angrily
Where was Ryan and why hadn't he	
phoned? She hoped he had got her text	earlier
reminding him to meet her.	here
She would wait for him and no	for 15 minutes
more. She walked to the far side of	moodily
the café and threw her bag onto	in a fit of pique
the table furthest from the door.	
She got herself a coffee, sat down and	
took her phone out to check	again
for messages. Nothing. Sighing,	loudly
she tried his number again, but it went	
onto voicemail. She didn't	straight, like before
leave a message. She felt very	suddenly
upset. It had all been going wrong.	lately
Ryan was not himself, but what	at the moment
was the matter, and why wouldn't	
he talk about it? She had finished	ever, just
her coffee and was getting up to	wearily
go, when in he walked.	

▶▶▶ **GRAMMAR BUILDER 6.4: ADVERBS AND ADJECTIVES: PAGE 125** ◀◀◀

8 🎧 2.15 Check the meaning of the reporting verbs below and find two of them in the story in exercise 2. Then listen and match each verb with the direct speech.

gasp groan mutter shriek sigh whine whisper yell

▶▶▶ **VOCABULARY BUILDER 6.5: PUNCTUATING REPORTED SPEECH: WORKBOOK PAGE 107** ◀◀◀

9 **SPEAKING** Work in pairs or small groups. Discuss how the story in exercise 2 might continue. Write the second half of the story in 100 words. Include some direct speech and use some adverbs and pairs of adjectives to make your writing more interesting.

WRITING TASK Story-writing

I can write a story.

1 You are going to write a story (200–250 words) about a dream, ending with the words, 'I woke up. It had all been a dream.' The outline of the story is told in the pictures, but the end of the dream is missing. Work in pairs. Read the outline and discuss what the characters are like and how the dream ends.

> **WRITING TIP**
>
> Make your writing more interesting by using:
> - a variety of adverbs and adverb phrases.
> - a variety of adjectives.
> - direct speech, with a variety of reporting verbs and adverbs.

2 Read the *Writing tip*, then write the first paragraph of your story. Use the first picture and the sentences below it, and these questions to help you.

What kind of book was it? How often do you read in bed? Were you feeling sleepy?

3 Write the second paragraph of your story, using the second picture, the sentences below it and these questions to help you.

What does the window overlook? What was the weather like? How did you feel? Did you call out?

4 Write the third paragraph of your story, again using the sentences and these questions to help you. Use direct speech for the conversation.

Was your brother already awake? How did he react? Had he heard the noise too? Did he try to reassure you? Who suggested going outside?

5 Write the final paragraph of your story, again using the sentences and the question. Add the ending you thought of in exercise 1. Finish with the words, 'I woke up. It had all been a dream.'

6 Count the words. If there are fewer than 200, add some more detail, events or direct speech. If you have written more than 250 words, look for unnecessary repetition, or cut some detail or events.

7 Now write a final copy of your story.

> **CHECK YOUR WORK**
>
> **Have you:**
> - [ ] used adverbs and adverb phrases?
> - [ ] used a variety of reporting verbs and correct punctuation with direct speech?
> - [ ] used a variety of adjectives and put them in the correct order?
> - [ ] checked the spelling and grammar?
> - [ ] written the correct number of words?

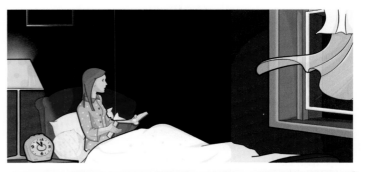

1 I was reading in bed. It was late. I heard a strange noise outside.

2 I got up and looked out of the window. I couldn't see what was making the noise.

3 I went to my brother's room. We discussed what to do.

4 We went outside. The door closed behind us.
What happens next?

Vocabulary

1 Complete the sentences with the correct form of the verbs below. The answers may be active or passive.

break grind inflict make put up

1 Scientists _____ a breakthrough in their quest for a cure for cancer recently.
2 The stalemate _____ last night by the offer of a ten per cent pay rise.
3 Negotiations between unions and the management _____ to a halt yesterday.
4 Over a thousand casualties _____ upon the civil population so far in the conflict.
5 Residents _____ resistance to the new parking laws introduced by the city council last week.

Mark: _____ /5

2 Write the noun form of these adjectives.

1 wise
2 altruistic
3 courageous
4 sincere
5 amiable

Mark: _____ /5

3 Choose the correct words.

1 Paula has set her **goals** / **sights** on winning the gold medal in the Olympics.
2 Igor hopes to get the job, but he's not **realising** / **counting** on it.
3 I can't see myself getting married in the **foreseeable** / **likely** future.
4 Do you think he'll ever **succeed** / **fulfil** his ambition of playing for Real Madrid?
5 They're not pinning their **hopes** / **dreams** on victory, but they're going to give it everything they've got.

Mark: _____ /5

4 Complete the sentences with the verbs below and punctuate them correctly.

gasp mutter sigh whisper yell

1 He _____ to her you look gorgeous
2 Slow down her husband _____ we're going to crash
3 I suppose so she _____
4 Look at your leg _____ Grace I think it's broken
5 Why doesn't he just get to the point _____ Dan

Mark: _____ /5

Grammar

5 Rewrite the sentences using the construction *for ... to ...* .

It's time that we admitted defeat.
It's time for us to admit defeat.

1 It's important that athletes should train hard.
2 The aim is that we should learn English in six months.
3 In the past, women wearing trousers was scandalous.
4 The manager is unhappy about staff taking time off work.
5 It is vital you read the instructions before switching on.

Mark: _____ /5

6 Choose the correct form of ellipsis. Sometimes more than one answer is correct.

1 I apologise for hurting your feelings,
   a I didn't.   **b** I didn't mean.   **c** I didn't mean to.
2 You can park in the garage
   a if you want.   **b** if you want to.   **c** if you want it.
3 She's really tight-fisted now, but
   a she didn't use.   **b** she didn't use to.   **c** she didn't use to be.
4 We didn't win the match, but
   a we could.   **b** we could have.   **c** we were able.
5 She's worried. Her boyfriend said he'd call, but
   a he hasn't.   **b** he wouldn't.   **c** he wasn't.

Mark: _____ /5

7 Complete the sentences with the particles below.

back off on out up

1 My mother is hunting _____ a costume for the party.
2 She has to smarten _____ if she wants to be promoted.
3 A colleague rounded _____ her unexpectedly in the meeting.
4 They hadn't understood, so she went _____ over the rules.
5 We wanted to see our visitors _____ properly, so we accompanied them to the airport.

Mark: _____ /5

8 Report the sentences using the verbs below.

blame claim remind suggest threaten warn

'Don't forget to empty the bin,' Jim's mother told him.
Jim's mother reminded him to empty the bin.

1 'I think we should consult an expert,' said Amy.
2 'I've never cried at the cinema,' said Harriet.
3 'My iPod's broken and it's your fault!' said Mia to Ryan.
4 'If you don't pay, I'll sell the photos,' she said.
5 'Don't take the motorway as there's been an accident,' he told him.

Mark: _____ /5

Total: _____ /40

Listening

1 In pairs, think about what has happened to Edgars so far. What problems is he currently facing? How should he tackle them, in your opinion?

2 🎧 2.16 Listen and choose the correct answers.

1 Edgars won't formally complain about being offered the job and then rejected because
   A it was probably a misunderstanding anyway.
   B he doesn't have any proof.
   C he doesn't have the money to pursue a complaint.
   D he doesn't have the same rights as British employees.

2 What is Edgars's reaction to Tomas's comments about dreams?
   A He thinks Tomas may be right.
   B He finds it hard to understand what Tomas is saying.
   C He pretends to agree at first, but then disagrees.
   D He's sceptical about Tomas's comments.

3 Tomas invites Edgars to
   A go out with him and his sister.
   B have dinner with him at his sister's house.
   C join him and his sister for dinner.
   D have dinner with him, his brother and his sister.

4 Edgars is speechless when Rita arrives because
   A he recognises her from his dream.
   B she fulfils all his romantic dreams.
   C he realises that they've already met.
   D he's pretending to be amazed.

Speaking

3 Think about your own dreams for the future. Make notes about (a) three personal ambitions and (b) three hopes for the world in general.

4 In groups of three or four give a short presentation to the group about your dreams using your notes from exercise 3.

Reading

5 Read the text quickly. Explain the connection between the text and the photo.

6 Answer these questions about the text.

1 Using current technology, what can scientists tell about a person's thoughts by looking at brain scans?
2 What might a more advanced version of this technology allow them to do in the future?
3 What ethical issues would arise if this technology were successfully developed?
4 What safeguards does Professor Gallant suggest to prevent misuse of the technology?

Minority Report

Scientists have developed a mind-reading technique which could one day allow them to take pictures of memories and dreams. By comparing brain activity scans, they were able to correctly predict which of 120 pictures someone was focusing on in 90 per cent of cases. The technique could one day form the basis of a machine to project the imagination on to a screen.

Professor Jack Gallant led the Californian research team. Writing in the journal *Nature*, he said: 'It may soon be possible to reconstruct a picture of a person's visual experience from measurements of brain activity alone. Imagine a general brain-reading device that could reconstruct a picture of a person's visual experience at any moment in time.'

Two scientists volunteered to look at 1,750 images while data was recorded from their brains and linked mathematically to the 'points' that make up a 3D thought image. This link between brain activity and image was then used to identify which images were seen by each volunteer from a new set of 120, just by looking at their brain scans.

The research evokes sci-fi film *Minority Report*, where police in the future read people's minds and arrest them for 'thought crimes'. But such a situation is a long way off, as the technique currently only works on viewed images, not imagined ones, and it takes hours for the scanners to take the brain images.

Professor Gallant said: 'It is possible that decoding brain activity could have serious ethical and privacy implications in 30 to 50 years. We believe strongly that no one should be subjected to any form of brain-reading involuntarily, covertly, or without complete informed consent.'

Writing

7 Read the question in the box and make notes for an essay. Use the paragraph plan below.

> What would be the possible uses and misuses of a machine that could read people's thoughts and dreams? Do you think it would be a good or bad thing, on balance?

Paragraph 1 Introduction   **Paragraph 3** Possible misuses
Paragraph 2 Possible uses   **Paragraph 4** Conclusion

8 Write an essay of 200–250 words, following your plan from exercise 7.

1 Work in pairs. What do you know about former US President Abraham Lincoln? Share your ideas with the class.

2 Do the Reading exam task.

READING exam task

Read the text. Complete the text with the phrase (A–K) that best fits each gap. There is one phrase you do not need.

A famous dream

Although Abraham Lincoln is today one of America's best-loved presidents, that was not always so. During the American Civil War he was hated by Southerners for abolishing slavery, and ¹_____ that he fully expected to be murdered by his political opponents, and had resigned himself to his fate. According to a close friend of his, three days prior to his assassination, Lincoln recounted a dream he'd had to his wife and a few acquaintances, ²_____ . In the dream, he was lying in bed in the White House in Washington, and there seemed to be a death-like stillness around him. Then he began to hear quiet sobbing, ³_____ . He got out of bed and wandered downstairs. There the silence was broken by the same pitiful sobbing, but he couldn't see who was making the noise. He went from room to room but they were all deserted, ⁴_____ . It was light in all the rooms and every object was familiar to him; but where, Lincoln wondered, were all the people ⁵_____ ? He was both puzzled and alarmed. What could be the meaning of all this? Determined to find the cause, he kept on walking ⁶_____ , which he entered. There he met with a sickening surprise. Before him was a platform, ⁷_____ . Around it were stationed soldiers who were acting as guards; and there was a crowd of people, some gazing mournfully upon the coffin, others crying bitterly. 'Who has died in the White House?' Lincoln demanded of one of the soldiers. 'The President,' came the answer. 'He was killed by an assassin.' Then there was a loud exclamation of grief from the crowd, ⁸_____ .
Some people have ascribed a powerful meaning to his dream, claiming that ⁹_____ . Others point out that, given the fact that he fully expected that someone would try to assassinate him, ¹⁰_____ .

A although the same mournful sounds of distress met him as he walked along
B as if a number of people were crying
C in which he foresaw his own death
D it is hardly surprising that he dreamt of his own death
E Lincoln knew that he was about to die
F on which rested a coffin
G such was their antipathy towards him
H he had had the dream before

I until he arrived at the East Room
J which awoke him from his dream
K who were grieving as if their hearts would break

3 Do the Use of English exam task.

USE OF ENGLISH exam task

Complete the second sentence so that it means the same as the first. Use two to five words including the word given in brackets. Do not change the form of word given.

1 'I didn't steal the money!' said William. (denied)
William _____ the money.
2 'Don't forget to write thank-you letters for your presents,' said Mandy to her daughter. (reminded)
Mandy _____ thank-you letters for her presents.
3 'I'll pay for the meal,' said Jake. (insisted)
Jake _____ for the meal.
4 'I'll send you to your room if you speak to me like that again,' said George to his son. (threatened)
George _____ to his room if he spoke to him like that again.
5 'You broke my MP3 player!' said Sally to Tom. (accused)
Sally _____ her MP3 player.
6 'I won't tell anyone what you've told me,' said Fred. (promised)
Fred _____ what I'd told him.
7 'Thank you so much for everything you've done,' said Martha. (gratitude)
Martha _____ everything I'd done.
8 'I'm definitely going to apply for the job,' said Ben. (intention)
Ben confirmed _____ for the job.

4 Do the speaking exam task.

SPEAKING exam task

Compare and contrast the photos of two 'dream' homes. What might the owners of these homes be like and which photo more closely matches your idea of a 'dream' home?

THIS UNIT INCLUDES

Vocabulary ■ informal language ■ phrasal verbs with *run* and *walk* ■ synonyms of *journey* and *walk* ■ phrases for 'softening' ideas ■ nouns related to phrasal verbs ■ noun suffixes ■ easily confused words ■ linkers: other people's expectations ■ benefits and drawbacks ■ cause, purpose and result ■ formal language
Grammar ■ *-ing* forms after preparatory *it* ■ emphasis
Speaking ■ talking about travel ■ presentation: tourist destinations ■ talking about immigration ■ presentation: the benefits of tourism
Writing ■ a letter of complaint

Journeys 7

7A VOCABULARY AND LISTENING Travelling about

I can talk about different kinds of travel and journey.

1 **SPEAKING** Work in pairs. Describe the photos. Would you enjoy these types of journey or trip? Give reasons.

2 Discuss the difference in meaning between these words. Use your dictionary to help you.

1 a break   6 an outing
2 an expedition 7 a pilgrimage
3 an excursion   8 a trip
4 a journey   9 a voyage
5 a tour   10 travels

3 🎧 2.17 Listen. What are the four speakers describing? Match each speaker with a word from exercise 2.

Speaker 1 ☐ Speaker 2 ☐ Speaker 3 ☐ Speaker 4 ☐

4 🎧 2.17 Listen again. What informal equivalents did the speakers use instead of these words?

Speaker 1   **Speaker 3**
1 complain   7 dirty
2 very crowded   8 food
3 make sb pay too much 9 spend

Speaker 2   **Speaker 4**
4 nervous   10 hotel or restaurant
5 exhausted   11 rain heavily
6 sleep   12 sell

➤➤➤ **VOCABULARY BUILDER 7.1: INFORMAL LANGUAGE: WORKBOOK PAGE 107** ◀◀◀

5 Match the verbs and particles to make phrasal verbs related to travel. They are all from the listening.

1 stop   a round
2 show sb   b up
3 touch   c off (at)
4 get   d away
5 hold   e down

6 Complete the sentences with phrasal verbs from exercise 5 and below.

check into   drop off   pick up   put up   see off   stop by
stop over

1 The guy who _____ the palace had some fascinating stories about the history of the place.
2 This evening the taxi _____ you _____ in the town centre and _____ you _____ at the hotel.
3 My uncle's returning home to the States tomorrow. I'm going to the airport to _____ him _____ .
4 My plane _____ and I didn't arrive until after midnight, so I _____ a hotel near the airport.
5 Do _____ in if you're ever in London. We can easily _____ you _____ .
6 Last summer we _____ in Greece on our way to Israel.

➤➤➤ **VOCABULARY BUILDER 7.2: PHRASAL VERBS WITH *RUN* AND *WALK*: WORKBOOK PAGE 108** ◀◀◀

7 Make notes about a memorable journey, trip, excursion, etc. that you have made. Use some of the words from exercises 2, 4 and 5, and try to include some informal words and phrases.

1 Where did you go?
2 What happened?
3 Why was it memorable?

8 **SPEAKING** Work in pairs and tell your partner about it.

➤➤➤ **VOCABULARY BUILDER 7.3: SYNONYMS FOR *WALK*: WORKBOOK PAGE 108** ◀◀◀

I can talk about the reasons people go on holiday.

1 Look at the chart. Do any of the statistics surprise you? Why?

World's Top Ten Tourist Destinations

Number of visitors (millions)

1 France	79.5		6 Turkey	29.3
2 USA	62.3		7 UK	29.2
3 China	57.6		8 Germany	28.4
4 Spain	56.7		9 Malaysia	24.7
5 Italy	46.1		10 Mexico	23.4

2 Match the photos with four of the countries in the chart. What do you know about the places in the photos? Would you like to visit them? Give reasons.

3 🎧 2.18 Listen to three people talking about where they would like to visit and why. Match three or four of the reasons below (1–10) to each speaker.

Speaker 1 _____ Speaker 2 _____ Speaker 3 _____

1 architecture
2 atmosphere
3 cultural activities
4 food
5 history
6 landscape
7 to improve language skills
8 to meet people
9 outdoor activities
10 personal challenge

LEARN THIS!

-ing form with preparatory *it*

It can be used as a preparatory subject or object for an *-ing* form, especially in informal style.

It was amazing walking along the Great Wall.
It's fun travelling with friends.
It's no good just staying in hotels.
I'd find it strange being on my own in a foreign country.
It'd be tiring travelling non-stop to the south of Italy.

In this structure with *worth*, the object of the *-ing* form can become the subject of the sentence.

It's well worth visiting Paris.
Paris is well worth visiting.

---

4 Read the information in the *Learn this!* box, then complete the sentences from the listening with the *-ing* form of the verbs below.

attempt backpack kip lug pay see trek

1 For me it'd be a place well worth _____ a visit because I'm really interested in doing outdoor activities.
2 It's always fascinating _____ how other people live.
3 I'd find it really exhilarating _____ through the mountains at high altitude.
4 It's hard work _____ all your equipment with you.
5 Obviously it'd be crazy _____ to get to every country inside a month.
6 I actually think it would be fun _____ on my own, a real adventure.
7 It's a bit of a pain _____ on the train, but I'll survive I'm sure.

⟫⟫ GRAMMAR BUILDER 7.1: *-ING* FORMS AFTER PREPARATORY *IT*, NOUNS AND ADJECTIVES: PAGE 125 ⟪⟪

SPEAKING TIP

In informal speech you can soften ideas or make them less precise by using the following words and phrases.

a bit (of a)   in a way   in one way or another
just kind of   sort of   or something along those lines
or that kind of thing   or some(thing) like that
or whatever

I just kind of want to visit somewhere really remote.
(=In a way, I'd sort of prefer to go on a package holiday or that kind of thing.)

---

5 🎧 2.18 Read the *Speaking tip*. Which of the phrases did the speakers use in the listening? Listen again and check your answers to exercises 4 and 5.

6 Read these sentences aloud, adding some phrases from the speaking tip.

1 Paris, Rome and Madrid are good places to visit.
2 I'd like to travel round the world.
3 Tom wants to backpack or hitchhike round Europe.
4 We're planning to visit the Seychelles or the Maldives.
5 Thailand has to be top of my list of holiday destinations.

7 Work in groups of three. Decide on three places (e.g. a country, a city, a tourist site) that you would like to visit. Make notes on why you would like to visit those places, using the ideas in exercise 3 to help you.

8 SPEAKING Present your ideas to the class. Try to use some of the structures in the *Learn this!* box and the phrases in the *Speaking tip*.

9 Take a class vote on the most popular destination.

1 SPEAKING Work in pairs. When, approximately, did the groups of people on the map invade Britain? Mark your answers on the map. The invasions are numbered in chronological order.

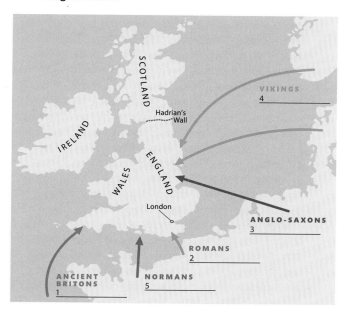

2 What legacy did the invaders leave behind? Match the photos to four of the groups on the map.

3 🎧 2.19 Listen and check your answers to exercises 1 and 2.

4 🎧 2.19 Listen again and explain why these statements must be false.

1 Foreign influences on the British identity began in the nineteenth century.
2 In the distant past people couldn't migrate to Britain unless they came by sea.

3 Julius Caesar led a successful invasion of Britain.
4 The Anglo-Saxon invaders lived peacefully alongside the existing population of Britain.
5 Despite many frequent attempts by the Danish to invade Britain, they never gained control.
6 The existing population welcomed the Norman invaders.

5 Write the compound nouns related to these phrasal verbs. They are all in the listening.

1 come out *outcome*
2 rise up
3 take over
4 pull out
5 fall down
6 make up

6 Complete the sentences with nouns formed from the verbs in brackets combined with a preposition below. (Sometimes the verb comes first, sometimes the preposition.)

back off out out over up

1 There was an _____ in the number of people fleeing the country. (surge)
2 Following the _____ of war, the Britons launched an attack on the Romans. (break)
3 The Celtic languages made a _____ following the departure of the Romans. (come)
4 The Normans ruled Britain following the _____ of the Anglo-Saxon nobility. (throw)
5 There was a _____ between the defenders and the invading forces. Neither could gain the upper hand. (stand)
6 Following the Norman invasion, the _____ for the Anglo-Saxon people was bleak. (look)

⟫⟫ VOCABULARY BUILDER 7.4: NOUNS RELATED TO PHRASAL VERBS: WORKBOOK PAGE 108 ⟪⟪

7 Make nouns from these words. They are all in the listening.

1 succeed (= *follow*)
2 migrate
3 attempt
4 invade
5 know
6 conquer
7 resist
8 supreme

⟫⟫ VOCABULARY BUILDER 7.5: WORD FORMATION (2): WORKBOOK PAGE 109 ⟪⟪

8 SPEAKING Work in groups. Discuss the questions.

1 Who were the earliest settlers in your country?
2 Were there any subsequent invasions? Who by? When? Was there much resistance?
3 What legacy did the settlers and invaders leave, if any? (e.g. cultural, linguistic, political, etc.)
4 When was the last uprising in your country? What was it about?
5 Has there been an upsurge of migration in the past five years? If so, why do you think that has been the case?

1 SPEAKING Work in pairs. Answer the questions.

1 Do you know any stories or films in which the characters travel through time?

2 Do you think it will ever be possible to travel through time? Why?/Why not?

2 Read the text. Which sentence best sums up the opinion of the writer?

1 Time travel runs counter to common sense and must therefore be impossible.

2 Time travel may one day be possible because the laws of science do not rule it out.

3 Time travel is impossible because of the inherent paradoxes.

3 Match headings 1–6 with paragraphs A–F.

1 The impossibility of time travel

2 Limitations

3 Can we trust our common sense?

4 Versions of reality

5 A schoolboy error

6 A writer comes to the aid of the scientists

Time travel for beginners

A ☐ Just over 100 years ago, in 1895, H. G. Wells's classic story *The Time Machine* was first published. As befits the subject matter, that was the 'minus tenth' anniversary of the first publication, in 1905, of Albert Einstein's special
5 theory of relativity. It was Einstein, as every schoolchild knows, who first described time as 'the fourth dimension' – and every schoolchild is wrong. As a matter of fact it was Wells who wrote in *The Time Machine* that 'there is no difference between Time and any of the three dimensions of
10 Space, except that our consciousness moves along it.'

B ☐ Ever since then, writers have been fascinated by time travel, and especially by the paradoxes that seem to confront any genuine time traveller (something that Wells neglected to investigate). The classic example is
15 the so-called 'granny paradox', where a time traveller inadvertently causes the death of his granny when she was a little girl, so that the traveller's mother, and therefore the traveller himself, were never born. In which case, he did not go back in time to kill his relative, and so on.
20 A less gruesome example was entertainingly provided by the science-fiction writer Robert Heinlein in his story *By His Bootstraps*. The protagonist stumbles across a time-travel device brought back to the present by a visitor from the distant future. He steals the device and travels forward
25 in time. He constantly worries about being found by the old man from whom he stole the time machine – until one day, many years later, he realises that he himself is now the old man, and carefully arranges for his younger self to 'find' and 'steal' the time machine.

30 **C** ☐ As these paradoxes show us, the possibility of our being able to travel through time is clearly irrational and runs counter to common sense. The problem is that common sense is not always the most reliable means of assessing scientific theories. To take Einstein's own
35 theories again, it is hardly common sense that objects get both heavier and shorter the faster they move, or that moving clocks run slow. Yet both of these predictions of relativity theory have been borne out many times in experiments. In fact, when you look closely at the general
40 theory of relativity – the best theory of time and space we have – it turns out that there is nothing in it to rule out the possibility of time travel. The theory implies that time travel may be exceedingly difficult, but not impossible.

D ☐ Perhaps inevitably, it was through science fiction
45 that serious scientists finally convinced themselves that time travel could be made to work by a sufficiently advanced civilisation. What happened was this. Carl Sagan, a well-known astronomer, had written a novel in which his characters travelled through a black hole from
50 a point near the Earth to a point near the star Vega.

Although he was aware that he was bending the accepted rules of physics, this was, after all, fiction. Nevertheless, as a scientist himself, Sagan wanted the science in his novel to be as accurate as possible, so he asked Kip
55 Thorne, an established expert in gravitational theory, to check it out and advise on how it might be improved. After looking closely at the fictional equations, Thorne realised that such a passage through space–time from one black hole to another (a 'wormhole') actually could exist
60 within the framework of Einstein's theory. Sagan gratefully accepted Thorne's modification to his fictional 'star gate', and the wormhole duly featured in the novel, *Contact*, published in 1985.

[E] The star gate, however, still only acted as a
65 shortcut through space. Scientists soon realised that, theoretically, a wormhole could just as well link two different times as two different places. While it is hard to see how any civilisation could build a wormhole time machine from scratch, it is much easier to envisage that
70 a naturally occurring wormhole might be adapted to suit the time-travelling needs of a sufficiently advanced civilisation. Sufficiently advanced, that is, to be able to travel through space by conventional means, and locate and manipulate black holes. Even then, there's one snag.
75 It seems you can't use a time machine to go back in time to a point before which the time machine was built. You can go anywhere in the future, and come back to where you started, but no further. Which rather neatly explains why no time travellers from our future have yet visited us
80 – because the time machine still hasn't been invented!

[F] So, where does that leave the paradoxes, and common sense? Actually, there is a way out of all the difficulties, but you may not like it. It involves another favourite idea from science fiction: parallel worlds. These
85 are the 'alternative histories', which are envisaged as in some sense lying 'alongside' our version of reality. According to the theory, each of these parallel worlds is just as real as our own, and there is an alternative history for every possible outcome of every decision ever made.
90 Alternative histories branch out from decision points, bifurcating endlessly like the branches and twigs of an infinite tree. Bizarre though it sounds, this idea is taken seriously by a handful of scientists. And it certainly fixes all the time travel paradoxes. According to the theory of
95 parallel worlds, if you go back in time and prevent your own birth it doesn't matter, because by that decision you create a new branch of reality, in which you were never born. When you go forward in time, you move up the new branch and find that you never did exist, in that reality;
100 but since you were born and built your time machine in the reality next door, there is no paradox. Hard to believe? Certainly. Counter to common sense? Of course. But the plain fact is that all of this bizarre behaviour is at the very least permitted by the laws of physics, and in some
105 cases required by those laws. I wonder what H. G. Wells would have made of it all.

4 Are the sentences true (T) or false (F)? In which paragraph(s) did you find the evidence?

1 Most scientists dismiss the idea of different worlds co-existing alongside one another.
2 It won't be possible to travel through time until we are able to find and control black holes.
3 H.G. Wells demonstrated the problems thrown up by the concept of time travel.
4 The possibility of taking a short-cut through space led scientists to realise that time travel may be theoretically possible.
5 Einstein's theories are validated both in scientific experiments and by common sense.

5 Read paragraphs B and F again and explain in your own words:

1 the 'granny paradox'.
2 the theory of parallel worlds.

6 Find one word from each pair in the text. Then translate the pairs of words into your language.

1 classic / classical (line 2)
2 unreasonable / irrational (line 31)
3 possibility / opportunity (line 42)
4 imply / infer (line 42)
5 excessively / exceedingly (line 43)
6 borne / born (line 98)

>>> VOCABULARY BUILDER 7.6: EASILY CONFUSED WORDS: WORKBOOK PAGE 109 <<<

LEARN THIS!

Linkers that refer to the other person's expectations
as a matter of fact (paragraph A)
in fact (paragraph C)
actually (paragraphs D and F
the plain fact is (paragraph F)
to tell the truth

7 Read the *Learn this!* box. Find four of the linkers in the text and then match all five linkers with their uses.

1 used when admitting something
2 used to show a contrast between the truth and what the other person believes
3 used for talking about a fact that some people do not accept or may not like to hear
4 used to give extra details about something
5 used to add a comment, of interest to the other person

>>> VOCABULARY BUILDER 7.7: LINKERS (2): WORKBOOK PAGE 110 <<<

8 SPEAKING Work in pairs. Discuss the questions.

1 If you could travel back in time, when and where would you travel to? Give reasons.
2 How might it change your view of the world?
3 Would you try to change anything in the past? What? Why?

I can use a variety of structures to add emphasis.

Fly-drive commuting

For decades scientists have dreamed of building a car that can also fly, but it's only in the past few years, with the development of light-weight construction materials and highly efficient engines, that the dream has become a reality. I recently visited the headquarters of a company called Terrafugia in Massachusetts. 'What you are going to see,' said the young man who showed me around, 'will revolutionise the way we travel around.' He led me into a hangar. Before me stood the 'Transition', brainchild of a group of young graduates from the Massachusetts Institute of Technology (MIT). It was while they were studying at MIT that they came up with the idea, but not until they'd left college did they build the prototype. You can drive the Transition to the airport, extend its wings, take off, fly up to 800 km and land at another airstrip. Then, having folded up the wings, you can complete the journey to your destination by road. But not only is it very

versatile, it's also fairly economical, travelling 13 km per litre of unleaded petrol in the air and 17 km on the ground. The Transition has attracted a huge amount of general interest, but the question is, is there a market? What may put a lot of people off is the price-tag: $148,000. The company doesn't anticipate huge sales in the first year or so, but it does believe that it's only a matter of time before hybrid car–planes replace conventional cars.

1 Read the text. What is unusual about the vehicle?

2 Read the *Learn this!* box and underline nine examples in the text of ways of adding emphasis. What is being emphasised in each sentence in the *Learn this!* box?

LEARN THIS!

Adding emphasis

1 Cleft sentences
I don't understand how the Transition can take off.
≫ *What I don't understand is how the Transition can take off.*
The cost may put a lot of people off.
≫ *It's the cost that may put a lot of people off.*

2 Fronting phrases
  a negative and limiting expressions
  I've rarely been so impressed by a new invention.
  ≫ *Rarely have I been so impressed by a new invention.*
  b adverbial expressions of place
  The pilot sat in the cockpit.
  ≫ *In the cockpit sat the pilot.*
  c Phrases such as *The problem/trouble/truth/fact/question is, …*

3 Use of *do/does/did* for emotive or contrastive emphasis
The Transition looks elegant!
≫ *The Transition does look elegant!*
I don't like the colour, but I like the design.
≫ *I don't like the colour, but I do like the design.*

≫≫≫ GRAMMAR BUILDER 7.2: EMPHASIS: PAGE 126 ≪≪≪

3 Read paragraphs A, C, D and F of the text on pages 74 and 75 and find examples of ways of adding emphasis.

4 Rewrite the sentences to make them more emphatic, using the techniques in the *Learn this!* box. More than one answer is sometimes possible. Compare your answers with a partner and explain any differences.
I don't like the design. *It's the design I don't like.*
1 I don't have a car, but I have a bicycle.
2 I've never read such a thought-provoking book.
3 I don't like his attitude to women.
4 I can't afford a new car. That's the problem.
5 A man in a yellow jacket came round the corner.

5 🎧 2.20 Listen. How do the speakers make the following sentences more emphatic?
1 What are you doing?   5 Why did you do that?
2 I know I'm wrong.   6 Take a seat.
3 The weather's nice today.   7 You're wearing a nice tie.
4 You've done well.

6 Make the following sentences more emphatic. Say them out loud, paying attention to the stress and intonation.
1 Where have you been?
2 You should apologise to me, not to him.
3 He scored a fantastic goal.
4 Help yourself to more potatoes.
5 I was just dozing off when Jack burst in.

7 **SPEAKING** Complete the sentences in an appropriate way, using an emphatic structure. Compare your answers with your partner.
1 What really bothers me is …
2 Rarely have I seen …
3 It's not just me that …
4 What I've set my sights on is …
5 I don't …, but I do …

1 SPEAKING Look at the photos and the graph. What aspects of foreign travel do they show?

Millions **Number of passengers flying from UK airports**

250
200
150
100
50
0

1953 1962 1971 1980 1989 1998 2005 2007 2008 2009 2010 2011

2 🎧 2.21 Listen to two people answering the question below. Which of their opinions and supporting arguments do you find most persuasive?

Should people be encouraged to travel abroad on holiday, or discouraged?

3 🎧 2.21 Complete the first gap in these sentences from the listening exercise using the words below. If there is a second gap, use a preposition. Then listen again and check.

consequences   due   leads   mean   purpose   resulted
the reason   this reason

1 A vast increase in the number of flights over recent years has _____ _____ increased carbon emissions.
2 An increase in the number of visitors inevitably _____ _____ expansion and development.
3 The local environment was _____ _____ the resort's popularity in the first place.
4 More hotels and more restaurants inevitably _____ more strain on the local infrastructure.
5 The _____ _____ more flights will be increased climate change.
6 For _____ , I think it's particularly important for people to travel.
7 Climate change is partly _____ _____ carbon emissions from planes.
8 The _____ _____ travel is to learn about other cultures.

⟫⟫ **VOCABULARY BUILDER 7.8: EXPRESSING CAUSE, PURPOSE AND RESULT: WORKBOOK PAGE 110** ⟪⟪

4 Match 1–10 to a–j to make complete sentences. Look at the collocations in bold.

1 Increased carbon emissions have clearly **had a detrimental**
2 Climate change, then, is a **major**
3 Tourism can **have a negative**
4 Big hotels spring up along the coast, usually **to the**
5 The increased demand for water, for example, can **pose**
6 I don't think **the benefits** to local people **outweigh**
7 Local people **benefit**
8 When the purpose of travel is to learn about other cultures, it's clearly **of mutual**
9 I don't think we can avoid **doing**
10 We should endeavour to minimise **the damage**

a **from** the money that tourists spend while they are on holiday.
b **effect on** the earth's atmosphere.
c **a threat to** rivers and lakes.
d **benefit to** the tourist and the local people.
e **the damage** that tourism does.
f **detriment of** the local environment
g **we cause** to the environment.
h **concern,** but by no means the only one.
i **harm** altogether.
j **impact on** the physical environment.

5 Complete the phrases for generalising with the words below.

broadly   by   in   in   on   to

Generalising

1 _____ the whole
2 _____ a great extent
3 _____ general
4 _____ and large
5 _____ most cases
6 _____ speaking

6 Read the task below. Make notes about your opinion and arguments that support it. Include at least one opposing argument. Think about the environment, economic benefits/ drawbacks, quality of life for your compatriots, and the image of your country abroad.

> To what extent does tourism benefit your country? Should more tourism be encouraged? Give reasons for your opinions.

7 SPEAKING Prepare a presentation of no more than three minutes using some of the phrases and collocations from exercises 3, 4 and 5. Then give your presentation to the class.

I can write a letter of complaint.

1 SPEAKING **Describe the photos. What do you think the customer is saying? What do you think the call centre assistant is saying? Use the ideas below to help you.**

faulty goods   overcharging   poor workmanship
slow/poor service   wrongly priced goods

2 SPEAKING **Answer the questions.**

1 Have you ever wanted to complain about something you bought? Why?
2 Did you actually complain? If not, why not? If so, what happened?

3 **Read the letter of complaint. Choose the most formal expressions to complete it.**

4 **Answer the questions about the letter.**

1 Where does the writer put (a) her own address?
(b) the recipient's address? (c) the date?
2 If the writer knew the name of the recipient, how would she (a) greet the person? (b) sign off?

5 **Find linkers in the letter with the following functions. How many more linkers can you add to the lists?**

1 making a contrast (find two)
2 ordering points (find two)
3 making additional points (find two)
4 generalising (find one)

6 **Match words 1–6 with their more formal equivalents below.**

address   conform with   numerous   purchase
respond   seek

1 match	3 reply	5 many
2 ask for	4 buy	6 deal with

7 **Complete the sentences using the formal words from exercise 6 in their correct form.**

1 Despite _____ calls to your office, up to now no one _____ my complaints.
2 I am writing to complain about a CD player that I _____ from your shop.
3 As the holiday did not _____ the description in the brochure, I shall _____ legal advice from my solicitor.
4 Should you fail to _____ to my letter, I shall have no option but to initiate court proceedings.

▶▶▶ **VOCABULARY BUILDER 7.9: FORMAL LANGUAGE: WORKBOOK PAGE 110** ◀◀◀

---

33 Charles Road
Morecambe
Lancashire LA34 5GH
24th August 2009

Customer Services Dept.
Sunny Day Holidays
PO Box 342
Birmingham B89 6GH

Dear Sir or Madam,
Booking reference: SD3467PH-7
I have just ¹**got back / returned** from a holiday organised by your travel company and ²**I'm writing / I am writing** to complain in the strongest terms about ³**a number of / quite a few** things.

⁴**First of all / To start with**, on your website ⁵**you say the hotel is / the hotel is described as being** 'a short walk from the beach', ⁶**but actually / whereas in fact** it took us nearly fifteen minutes to get there, walking briskly. ⁷**What is more, / On top of that**, the beach itself was dirty and there were a number of submerged rocks near the shore ⁸**which made swimming hazardous / which meant it was dangerous to swim.**

My second complaint concerns Sunny Day's representative in the resort. ⁹**On our arrival, we were informed by your representative / When we got there your rep told us** that the excursions ¹⁰**we'd / which we had** pre-booked had been cancelled and that we would have to ¹¹**make our own arrangements / sort it out ourselves** if we wanted to see the local sights. ¹²**To make matters worse, / Even worse**, she ¹³**made no apology for this / didn't say sorry** and was generally brusque and unhelpful.

Finally, I should like to ¹⁴**draw your attention to / point out** the quality of the food at the hotel. On the whole, breakfast and lunch were ¹⁵**fine / great**. However, dinner was of a very poor standard and ¹⁶**we were not offered / they didn't offer us** a choice of main dishes.

All this has spoilt what should have been a wonderful holiday, ¹⁷**and I would therefore like a partial refund / so I want some money back**. I suggest fifty per cent of the cost of the holiday.

I look forward to hearing from you.

Yours faithfully,

Helen Woodward

Helen Woodward

WRITING TASK Letter of complaint

I can write a letter of complaint.

1 **SPEAKING** Work in pairs. Look at the holiday photos. What complaints might the holidaymaker make to the travel company? Use the ideas below to help you.

bad plumbing   bland, inedible food
last minute change to the date of departure
polluted beach   unbearably long delays at the airport
unexpected additional fees and surcharges
view over a construction site

2 Read the task, the advertisement and notes.

> You have just returned from a short holiday in London and are very disappointed. Write a letter of 200–250 words to the customer services department of the company complaining about the holiday and the way in which the advertisement misled you.

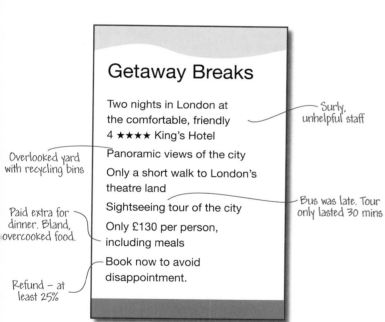

Getaway Breaks

Two nights in London at the comfortable, friendly 4 ★★★★ King's Hotel — *Surly, unhelpful staff*

Overlooked yard with recycling bins — Panoramic views of the city

Only a short walk to London's theatre land

Sightseeing tour of the city — *Bus was late. Tour only lasted 30 mins*

Paid extra for dinner. Bland, overcooked food. — Only £130 per person, including meals

Book now to avoid disappointment.

Refund – at least 25%

3 Turn the notes from exercise 2 and some of the complaints in exercise 1 into full sentences using the phrases below.

1 I was disappointed that/to (find) …
2 It is really unacceptable that …
3 The brochure claimed that … However, …
4 I was appalled that/by …
5 What I found totally unacceptable was …
6 To our horror, …
7 Seldom have I …
8 One major problem was …

4 Write the first paragraph of your letter. Say why you are writing.

5 Write the middle section of your letter. Put each major complaint in a separate paragraph. Use some of the sentences from exercise 3.

6 Write the final paragraph of your letter. Say what you expect the company to do. Finish with an appropriate set phrase.

7 Once you have written a rough draft, check your work using the checklist below. Then write a final copy of the letter.

CHECK YOUR WORK

Have you:
- [ ] included all the necessary information?
- [ ] laid out your letter correctly?
- [ ] started and finished the letter correctly?
- [ ] used formal language, and linking words?
- [ ] checked the spelling and grammar?
- [ ] written the correct number of words?

1 Get ready to SPEAK What reasons do people have for suddenly leaving home and starting a new life abroad?

2 Make sentences about the photos using the words in the box.

load (v)   possessions   precariously balanced   ramp
removal van   stack (v)   strap (n)

3 Do the Speaking exam task.

SPEAKING exam task

Compare and contrast the photos. Answer the questions about each photo.

1 Why are the people moving, do you think?
2 Where do you think they are going?
3 How are their experiences different?

EXAM TIP

Completing a text with appropriate words
- Most of the missing words in this type of task will be 'grammar words' (articles, auxiliary verbs, pronouns, prepositions, etc.).
- Do not write more than one word in each gap.

4 Do the Use of English exam task.

USE OF ENGLISH exam task

Complete the text. Write one word only in each gap.

For such a small seabird, the sooty shearwater has an ambitious take ¹_____ the world. ²_____ its diminutive size, it thinks nothing of flying from New Zealand to Alaska ³_____ pursuit of an endless summer.

For years, ornithologists have known that sooty shearwaters breed off the coasts of New Zealand and Chile in the southern hemisphere, and then cross the equator to the rich summer feeding grounds of the North Pacific, ⁴_____ stretch from California to Japan. Now a study has shown that this epic feat ⁵_____ performed over a single breeding season, with individual birds travelling as far ⁶_____ 62, 400 km in just one year.

It is the longest migration route undertaken by individual animals that has been recorded by scientists, according ⁷_____ Scott Shaffer, a research biologist at the University of California, Santa Cruz, who led the team behind the study. 'The ⁸_____ bird species known that ⁹_____ rival the migrations of the sooty shearwater would be the arctic tern, which breeds in the Arctic and migrates to Antarctica,' Dr Shaffer said. 'But we don't know ¹⁰_____ they do that in a single season, because nobody's ever tracked them.'

5 Get ready to LISTEN Read the sentences in the Listening exam task. What do you think the listening is about?

6 🎧 2.22 Do the Listening exam task.

LISTENING exam task

Listen to part of a radio programme. Choose the correct option(s) to complete the sentences. At least one of the options is always correct, and sometimes both options may be correct.

1 Humpback whales
   A travel further in one go than any other animal.
   B are born in warm waters off the coast of Central America.
2 The markings on the whales' tails enabled the researchers to
   A identify the same whale in entirely different locations.
   B identify which calves belonged to which mothers.
3 Baby humpback whales
   A spend the first year of their lives in warm water.
   B sometimes travel thousands of kilometres from the breeding ground soon after they are born.
4 The researchers employed a satellite
   A to establish how warm the water is where the baby whales are born.
   B to track the whales' journey across the equator.
5 One result of the research is that scientists now know
   A which type of whales migrates the furthest.
   B why humpback whales travelled north across the equator.

THIS UNIT INCLUDES

Vocabulary ▪ clothes and styles ▪ two-part adjectives ▪ colloquial language ▪ food related words and phrases ▪ phrases for describing statistics, graphs, charts and trends ▪ phrases for giving estimates ▪ periphrasis and euphemism • connotation
Grammar ▪ *would* ▪ modal verbs
Speaking ▪ talking about attitudes to food ▪ talking about youth culture ▪ stimulus based-discussion
Writing ▪ a report

8A VOCABULARY AND LISTENING Fashion

I can talk about clothes and fashion.

1 SPEAKING Discuss this quotation by English eccentric Quentin Crisp. What does it mean? Do you agree? Are there other reasons for wanting to be fashionable?

> *Fashion is what you adopt when you don't know who you are.*

2 SPEAKING Look at the photos. Do you think these people look fashionable or unfashionable? Which clothes do you like most and least?

3 Read the *Speaking tip*. Work in pairs. Match as many of the words below as possible with the photographs in exercise 2.

General
chic dishevelled elegant neat scruffy shabby smart stylish trendy unkempt well-dressed

Specific
garments: bandana corset cravat waistcoat
parts of garments: buckle button collar cuff laces
designs, materials, etc.: check denim fishnet ripped stripy studded tartan
hair: bob dreadlocks extensions goatee plaits stubble
accessories: bangle chain piercing

4 SPEAKING Describe one photo from exercise 2. Follow the structure suggested in the *Speaking tip*.

5 🎧 3.01 Listen to four teenagers talking about clothes. Are the sentences true (T) or false (F), or is the answer not stated (NS)?

1 **Speaker 1** talks about a boy from school and recalls that casual clothes were his thing.
2 **Speaker 2** was made to wear an outfit that, if it had been up to her, she wouldn't have been seen dead in.
3 **Speaker 3** thinks that the style of clothing worn by Chandler in *Friends* quite suits his brother.
4 **Speaker 4** complains about having to wear clothes with logos on the front.

6 🎧 3.01 Complete these two-part adjectives with the words below. Try to remember which nouns they describe. Then listen again and check.

fitting length neck piece sleeved tight toed up

1 three-_____ 5 loose-_____
2 full-_____ 6 long-_____
3 open-_____ 7 skin-_____
4 V-_____ 8 zip-_____

▶▶▶ **VOCABULARY BUILDER 8.1: CLOTHES IDIOMS: WORKBOOK PAGE 111** ◀◀◀

7 SPEAKING Work in pairs. Tell your partner whether you agree or disagree with these statements, and why.

1 Women are more interested in fashion than men.
2 Some clothes only suit young people.
3 You need a lot of money to always look fashionable.
4 Some clothes do not look good on anybody and should never be worn.

SPEAKING TIP

When describing a photo, it is often helpful to structure your description in this way:

general ⟶ specific ⟶ speculative

For example, if describing a person's appearance, start by saying whether they look smart, casual, etc. Then describe their appearance in detail. Then speculate about who they might be, where they might be going, etc.

1 SPEAKING You are going to read part of an article called *Meat for vegetarians*. What kind of meat do you think it could be? Discuss your ideas in pairs.

2 Quickly read the article and find the answer to exercise 1.

Meat for vegetarians

It is the ultimate conundrum for vegetarians who think that meat is murder: a revolution in processed food that will see fresh meat grown from animal cells without a single cow, sheep or pig being killed. Researchers have published details in a biotechnology journal describing a new technique which they hailed as the answer to the world's food shortage. Lumps of meat would be cultured in laboratory vats rather than carved from livestock reared on a farm.

According to researchers, meat grown in laboratories would be more environmentally friendly and could be tailored to be healthier than farm-reared meat by controlling its nutrient content and screening it for food-borne diseases. Vegetarians might also be tempted because the cells needed to grow chunks of meat can be taken without harming the donor animal.

Experiments for NASA, the US space agency, have already shown that morsels of edible fish can be grown in petri dishes, though no one has yet eaten the food. Now researchers have taken the prospect of 'cultured meat' a step further by working out how to produce it on an industrial scale. They envisage muscle cells growing on huge sheets that would be regularly stretched to exercise the cells as they grow. Once enough cells had grown, they would be scraped off and shaped into processed meat products such as chicken nuggets.

3 Find examples of *would* in the text in exercise 2. How would the meaning be slightly different if these were changed to *will*?

4 SPEAKING In pairs, discuss these questions about the text. Give reasons for your answers.
1 Would you eat 'cultured meat'?
2 Do you think many vegetarians would eat it?
3 Do you think the mass production of 'cultured meat' would be a good or bad thing for the world?
4 In general, do you think it is good to try new and unusual kinds of food?

5 🎧 3.02 Listen to four people talking about their attitudes to food. Does each speaker eat a wider or narrower range of food now than in the past? Why?

6 🎧 3.02 Complete these excerpts from the listening with the words below. Then listen again and check.

craved   foodie   fuel   gorge   lived   menu   tooth   touched   treat

1 It was a real _____, going to the local take away.
2 Lots of things are off the _____.
3 As teenagers, we _____ nothing else.
4 I pretty much _____ on chocolate and sweets.
5 I hardly _____ a piece of fruit.
6 My friends reckon I _____ on chocolate.
7 I just don't have a sweet _____.
8 I suppose I treat food as _____.
9 My sister's a real _____.

7 Study the following excerpts and match the uses of *would* to types 1–5 in the *Learn this!* box. Which example is difficult to match? Explain the meaning of that example.
1 I would have been about fourteen at the time.
2 I wouldn't eat swordfish, for example.
3 I'd say there are very few foods that are safe to eat!
4 My dad wouldn't let us have sugar when we were kids.
5 But he would say that, wouldn't he?
6 She'd insist that we try it, though.
7 I would guess she's hoping to make a career out of it.
8 I would love to sample their everyday dishes.

We can use *would*
1 with verbs like *say* and *think* to make a statement less definite.
2 to talk about habitual actions in the past.
3 to talk about willingness (or unwillingness) to do something in the past or in the hypothetical future.
4 with verbs like *love*, *like* and *rather* when talking about preferences.
5 to make a logical deduction (similar to *must*).

⟫ GRAMMAR BUILDER 8.1: *WOULD*: PAGE 127 ⟪

8 Rewrite these sentences using *would*.
1 My dad always used to cook lunch on Sundays.
2 I'm not prepared to eat genetically modified food.
3 He's trying to lose weight, probably.
4 Spending a year travelling has broadened her tastes in food, probably.
5 My mother refused to buy South African fruit because of apartheid.

9 SPEAKING Work in pairs. Ask and answer the questions.
1 Do you consider food to be fuel, or are you a bit of a 'foodie'? Justify your answer.
2 How have your tastes changed over the years?
3 If you had to live entirely on three different dishes, what would they be?

I can talk about youth culture and fashions.

1 SPEAKING Work in pairs. Describe what the people in the photo are wearing. Do some young people dress like this in your country?

2 Look quickly through the text *Our gang*. Which of the five styles does the photo in exercise 1 show?

3 For questions 1–10, choose from the five styles (A–E).

Which gang

1 is interested in creating music? ☐

2 always dresses immaculately? ☐

3 is interested in 'green' issues? ☐

4 often wears very high shoes? ☐

5 tends not to mix with the opposite sex? ☐

6 prefers the cinema to the television? ☐

7 has a keen sense of business? ☐

8 enjoys provoking negative reactions? ☐

9 often wears distinctive make-up? ☐

10 is more interested in fun than reflection? ☐

4 Match eight of the colloquial words in red in the text with definitions 1–8. Then write similar definitions for the other six. Use the context to help you and a dictionary, if necessary.

1 wannabe (adj) having an ambition to be something

2 _____ (v) avoiding work/school

3 _____ (adj) very tight

4 _____ (phr v) seeing or watching (a show, etc.)

5 _____ (adj) dirty, not smart

6 _____ (adj) knowledgeable, well-informed

7 _____ (phr v) accept gratefully

8 _____ (n) a group of friends

5 Compare your six definitions from exercise 4 with your classmates. Do you agree on the meanings?

6 Work in pairs or groups.

1 Decide on a distinctive style that is common among young people where you live. Invent a name for it, if it does not have one.

2 Make notes about the style using the same subheadings as the ones in *Our gang*.

3 Write a text about the style similar to the ones in *Our gang*. Use colloquial language where possible.

Our gang

A Hippie

Who they are They may care about the environment but this crew are less alienated than their early 1990s counterparts. They don't reject the modern world – they embrace it to change it.
Where you find them Noses buried in ecology books; organising online petitions.
What their look is Sweatshirts from Howies; dreadlocks or undercuts.
What they listen to Jungle-folk band Vampire Weekend; drum'n'bass DJ Mechanical Organic.

B URBANITE

Who they are Street kids, but not as you know them – imagine mini-entrepreneurs who are ridiculously clued-up on art, fashion and, of course, music.
Where you find them In the day, spot them skiving in their local record shop, looking for rare 1990s tracks to remix. Later, it's everyone over to a mate's place to hear his latest demo.
What their look is Hoodies from Supreme or Bathing Ape; limited-edition trainers.
What they listen to Dubstep, a heavier, more meaningful branch of hip-hop.

C Neo Indie

Who they are Instead of ruthless introspection, life for neo-indie kids is about pushing each other home in trolleys and then posting the photos online.
Where you find them Travelling around town in single-sex packs; queuing for tickets to see bands.
What their look is Whatever it is – Topshop and American Apparel, mostly – it must be perfect.
What they listen to Their favourite band, of course. We Smoke Fags and The Enemy are hot.

D NU GRAVE

Who they are Goths, but flamboyant ones. They love to be different and lap up the attention they get from shocked relatives.
Where you find them Find them at nu-grave nights in grungy venues like Korsan Bar in east London.
What their look is They take inspiration from the darker side of high fashion. Add wet-look hair, black lips, patent-leather trench coats and 20 cm platforms.
What they listen to Good-looking young nu-grave bands such as The Horrors and Ipso Facto.

E FAUX PUNK

Who they are Art students and wannabe actors who live for creativity, love and their friends. Do not mistake them for real punks.
Where you find them Watching bands at the Dot to Dot festival in Nottingham; reading underground 'zines such as the PiX; taking in films by Gregg Araki or Gus Van Sant; actively not watching telly.
What their look is Like old punks, but much better-looking. Yellow DMs; super-skinny jeans; McQ vests; biker jackets.
What they listen to Good-looking, well-dressed bands such as Gallows and Late of the Pier.

1 SPEAKING **Read the newspaper cutting and answer the questions.**

1 What are nano-particles and what potential benefits do they have in relation to food?

2 Why are some people concerned about nano-particles in food?

104 products on shelves already contain toxic nano-particles, warns Friends of the Earth

Potentially toxic chemicals are being incorporated into food, packaging, health supplements and other products by stealth, it is claimed. Manufacturers boast that nano-particles, which are thousands of times thinner than a human hair, can deliver drugs or vitamins more effectively, kill harmful bugs in food or create self-cleaning windows. But scientists, consumer groups and green campaigners fear the technology is being introduced into the diet, body and environment without proper safety checks.

2 **Look quickly through the text on page 85. Match paragraphs 2–6 with five of the headings below.**

Create your own flavours   Healthier and more exciting food
Products available now   Public protests   Tiny toxins
Unknown dangers

Paragraph 1   Introduction
Paragraph 2   _____
Paragraph 3   _____
Paragraph 4   _____
Paragraph 5   _____
Paragraph 6   _____

3 **Read the text and choose the best answers.**

1 What does Willy Wonka's magical chewing gum have in common with types of nano-food in development?
  a They both contain an exciting mix of tastes.
  b Both are appealing to young children.
  c They both allow the consumer to choose the flavours.
  d They're both made in a factory.

2 Which elements of 'programmable food' would consumers be able to determine by zapping it?
  a colour, consistency and nutritional value
  b temperature, colour and taste
  c taste, nutritional value and colour
  d texture, taste and colour

3 Unlike ordinary packaging, 'smart' packaging
  a keeps food fresh permanently.
  b prevents any oxygen from reaching the food.
  c has yet to arrive on supermarket shelves.
  d can monitor the condition of the food it contains.

4 Technology developed to keep cooking oil fresh could help the world's poorest people by
  a increasing their consumption of nutrients.
  b preventing fish from going off too quickly.
  c alerting them when water supplies become contaminated.
  d enabling them to purify water more easily.

5 At its most advanced, nano-technology might enable consumers to
  a experience previously undreamed-of combinations of tastes.
  b make any food they can think of without the need for conventional ingredients.
  c have a much higher level of protein in their diet.
  d avoid foods they dislike altogether.

6 In the opinion of the scientist David Bennett, how will the public react to nano-food?
  a They'll give it a cautious welcome.
  b They'll be too concerned about the dangers to welcome it.
  c They'll eventually be won over by all the potential benefits.
  d They'll want to decide whether the potential benefits outweigh the dangers.

7 How is the size of nano-particles relevant to their potential dangers?
  a Most substances are toxic at nano-scales.
  b They are too small for scientists to track their position.
  c Once they're inside the body, they behave like viruses.
  d Their microscopic size allows them to pass through the body's usual defences.

4 **Find these words in the text.**

Paragraph 1 two sweet dishes and two savoury dishes
Paragraph 2 four adjectives that describe food or drink
Paragraph 3 two things that can spoil food and make it inedible
Paragraph 4 three of the elements that most food contains (such as carbohydrate…)
Paragraph 5 four words which mean *danger*
Paragraph 6 four organs of the human body

5 **Work in pairs. Write as many words as you can under these headings in three minutes. Which pair has the most words?**

1 sweet dishes   3 adjectives that describe food or drink
2 savoury dishes   4 elements that food contains

6 SPEAKING **Work in pairs. Discuss the questions.**

1 Would you be willing to eat food which contained nano-particles? Why?/Why not?

2 Do you think research into nano-food should be banned? Why?/Why not?

▶▶▶ VOCABULARY BUILDER 8.2: TALKING ABOUT FOOD: WORKBOOK PAGE 111 ◀◀◀

Nano-food

1 Willy Wonka is the father of nano-food. The great chocolate-factory owner, you'll remember, invented a chewing gum that was a full three-course dinner. 'It will be the end of all kitchens and cooking,' he told the children on his tour – and produced a prototype sample of Wonka's Magic Chewing Gum. One strip of this would deliver tomato soup, roast beef with roast potatoes and blueberry pie and ice cream – in the right order.

2 Far-fetched? The processed-food giant Kraft and a group of research laboratories are busy working towards 'programmable food'. One product they are working on is a colourless, tasteless drink that you, the consumer, will design after you've bought it. You'll decide what colour and flavour you'd like the drink to be, and what nutrients it will have in it, once you get home. You'll zap the product with a correctly-tuned microwave transmitter – presumably Kraft will sell you that, too. This will activate nano-capsules – each one about 2,000 times smaller than the width of a hair – containing the necessary chemicals for your choice of drink: green-hued, blackcurrant-flavoured with a touch of caffeine and omega-3, say. They will dissolve while all the other possible ingredients will pass unused through your body, in their nano-capsules.

3 The end of cooking? Probably not. But nano-food and nano-food packaging are on their way because the food industry has spotted the chance for huge profits: according to analysts, the business will soon be worth $20 billion annually. You'll first meet nanotechnology in food packaging.

Most people have heard about the 'smart' food packaging that will warn when oxygen has got inside, or if food is going off – research on that is complete and the products are arriving. Samsung has fridges on the market in Asia and America that use nano-silver to kill bacteria. Also available in American supermarkets is cooking oil that, in theory, can be kept fresh for ever – thanks to nano-engineered molecules which lock onto contaminants. These could also simplify the process of cleaning drinking water – potentially hugely important for the developing world. In Australia, you can buy bread that contains undetectable nano-capsules of omega-3, a valuable nutrient found naturally in oily fish like salmon.

4 Food manufacturers including Unilever and Nestlé plan to use nano-encapsulation to improve shelf life and engineer taste sensations in fat-based foods like chocolates, ice creams and spreads. There could be huge reductions in fat and salt in processed foods. Unilever believes it can reduce the fat content of ice cream from fifteen per cent to one per cent. In the future, atomic-level encapsulation techniques will get more sophisticated. A chef might decide that some flavours in his dish would only be released to the eater a certain number of seconds or minutes after chewing, or when they sip a glass of wine. Further ahead, the industry is looking at food that is pre-engineered to cater for your tastes, your dislikes and your allergies – or just built from scratch. Ultimately, it might be possible to create any meal you want at the push of a button, using nothing but plant proteins.

5 But Dr David Bennett, a veteran biochemist now working on a European Commission project on the ethics of 'nanobiotechnology', believes the public will almost certainly reject nano-food because of the perceived perils. 'Very little risk assessment has been done on this area, even on some products already entering the market'. What's to be afraid of, from a technology that offers so much – healthier food, fewer, better-targeted chemicals, less waste, 'smart' (and thus less) packaging, and even the promise of a technological solution to the problem of the one billion people who don't get enough to eat? 'Matter has different behaviour at nano-scales,' says Dr Kees Eijkel from the Dutch Twente University. 'That means different hazards are associated with it. We don't know what these are.' For example, some metals will kill bacteria at nano-scale – hence the interest in using them in food packaging – but what will happen if they get off the packaging and into us? Could they be a threat to our health? No one seems to know.

6 The size question is central to these concerns. Nano-particles that are under 100 nano-metres wide – less than the size of a virus – have unique abilities. They can cross the body's natural barriers, entering into cells or through the liver into the bloodstream or even through the cell wall surrounding the brain. 'I'd like to drink a glass of water and know that the contents are going into my stomach and not into my lungs,' says Dr Qasim Chaudhry of the British government's Central Science Laboratory. 'We are giving very toxic chemicals the ability to cross cell membranes, to go where they've never gone before. Where will they end up? It has been shown that free nano-particles inhaled can go straight to the brain. There are lots of concerns. We have to ask – do the benefits outweigh the risks?'

1 SPEAKING Look at the newspaper cutting and explain the wordplay in the headline. What do you think the sandwich might contain?

How does the £110 sandwich taste? In a word: rich

It's not a gimmick, says chef who created it.

2 Read opinions 1–7 about the £110 sandwich. Decide which modal or modals fit each gap. Try to explain why the other(s) do not fit.

1 'It _____ be a publicity stunt by the restaurant.'
   a can   b must   c should

2 'A sandwich _____ be worth £110, however amazing.'
   a can't   b mustn't   c couldn't

3 'People _____ spend so much on a sandwich when there's poverty and hunger in the world.'
   a shouldn't   b ought not to   c don't have to

4 'If you think it's a waste of money, you _____ buy it.'
   a needn't   b mustn't   c don't have to

5 'If you have that much money to spend, you _____ buy a sandwich for £3 and give £107 to charity.'
   a have to   b ought to   c should

6 'The moral is: You _____ believe everything you read in the newspapers!'
   a mustn't   b don't have to   c needn't

7 'A lot of people _____ work for a whole day or more to earn £110!'
   a must   b have to   c should

3 Look at your answers to exercise 2. Decide which modals we use to talk about 1–7.

1 what we believe is right (_____ or _____)
2 what we believe is wrong (_____ or _____)
3 what we can deduce is definitely true (_____)
4 what we can deduce is definitely not true (_____ or _____)
5 what we are obliged to do (_____)
6 what we are not obliged to do (_____ or _____)
7 what we are obliged or strongly advised not to do (_____)

>>> GRAMMAR BUILDER 8.2: *MODALS*: PAGE 127 <<<

4 Look at the photo of a dessert that costs $25,000 and talk about it using these phrases.

It must be…
It couldn't be…
You'd have to…
People should/ shouldn't… because…

5 🎧 3.03 Listen to a conversation about the dessert. Who would like to try it: the man or the woman?

6 🎧 3.03 Read the sentences from the conversation. Decide which modal makes better sense in the context. Then listen again and check.

1 They **may / must** have sold hundreds.
2 You **might / may** have told me you were going to New York next week!
3 You **could / should** take him out for a meal.
4 We **may / might** have been arrested.
5 You **might / should** have a better evening this time.
6 It **couldn't / might** not be any worse!
7 You **could / may** give me a lift to the airport!
8 Well, if you **might / should** try it, let me know!

7 Explain how the meaning of each sentence in exercise 6 would change if the other modal were chosen.

8 Work in pairs. Decide whether the sentences are natural English or not. Improve the sentences which are not.

1 This dessert is amazing. You really must try it!
2 The food there is always terrific, but the service could be a bit slow sometimes.
3 'Could I try your pizza?' 'Yes, you could. Go ahead!'
4 Customers may only consume drinks purchased on the premises.
5 My credit card bill is astronomical! I guess I ought not to have spent so much on eating out!
6 It's only another 30 kilometres. We should be there in time for dinner.
7 I prefer eating out now that people mustn't smoke anywhere inside a restaurant.
8 Because my sister works in a restaurant, she must work late every night.

9 SPEAKING Work in pairs. Discuss the question.

Is it morally wrong for people to pay that much for a restaurant dish, even if they can afford it? Why?/Why not?

1 Work in pairs. Match the charts (1–4) with their names and their descriptions (a–d) below.

bar chart   graph   pie chart   table

1 _____ ideal for ☐   3 _____ ideal for ☐
2 _____ ideal for ☐   4 _____ ideal for ☐

a displaying statistics which total 100%
b showing how a situation has changed over time
c visually comparing two related sets of statistics
d presenting a variety of statistical information in a clear but non-diagrammatic form

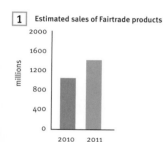
1 Estimated sales of Fairtrade products

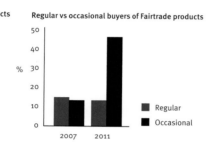
Regular vs occasional buyers of Fairtrade products

2 In an average week, how often do you eat at a fast-food outlet?

never 27%
once 43%
every day 7%
twice 15%
3 times or more 8%

3 Sales of organic food

4 Healthy eating

	Avoiding fat	Avoiding sugars	Eating a lot of vegetables
Teenagers	25%	17%	53%
65s and over	49%	44%	77%

2 🎧 3.04 Listen to four people talking about different charts. For each speaker, identify what the general topic of the chart they are speaking about is.

Speaker 1 _____   Speaker 3 _____
Speaker 2 _____   Speaker 4 _____

3 🎧 3.04 Listen again. Tick the expression (a or b) that the speakers use. (Both are valid expressions.)

1 a For me, the most interesting aspect is …
  b What strikes me as most interesting is …
2 a … a sharp rise in the total number of …
  b … a significant increase in the total number of …
3 a … a very large proportion of people …
  b … the vast majority of people …
4 a The chart tells us that …
  b According to the chart, …
5 a … more or less the same number of people …
  b … roughly equal numbers of people …
6 a … seeing it in this form really brings home to you …
  b … the way it is presented helps to emphasise …
7 a There's a strong tendency to reject … /embrace …
  b There's a definite trend away from … /towards …
8 a … the rate has remained quite stable …
  b … the rate has not fluctuated very much …
9 a There has been a slight increase/decrease in …
  b … has increased/decreased marginally.
10 a The significance of this is that …
  b This is significant because …

4 Explain the following expressions. Use language from exercise 3 where appropriate.

Rates of obesity have:
1 rocketed   5 plateaued
2 crept up   6 slumped
3 plummeted   7 tailed off
4 multiplied   8 stabilised

5 Complete the sentence below using expressions below in position a or b. Which expression could go in either position? What other words could you use to mean the same?

Fast food consumption has risen (a) _____ 10 per cent (b) _____ .

give or take a per cent   in round numbers   in the region of
more or less   or thereabouts   something like

SPEAKING TIP

When you are talking about charts and statistics, do not simply report the information they contain. Give a personal reaction too. What is surprising or important about the information?

6 Read the *Speaking tip*. Which expressions from exercise 3 can be used to give a personal reaction?

7 SPEAKING Talk about the information contained in the charts in exercise 1. Use expressions from exercises 3, 4 and 5 where possible.

8 SPEAKING Turn to page 152 and do the exam task.

I can write a report.

Introduction

The aim of this report is to give an insight into the wide range of live music that is available in this area, and to single out one venue which I would particularly recommend visiting.

Large venues

There are two live music venues of a reasonable size: the Apollo and the Hippodrome. These attract headline acts from all parts of the UK, and occasionally from overseas too. The Apollo has recently been refurbished and is clean, well-run and well-appointed. To my mind, however, it is a little on the sterile side. The Hippodrome is the polar opposite: dark, grungy and chaotically-managed – and it could certainly do with better air-conditioning. But what it lacks in slickness, it makes up for in character!

Smaller venues

If it's internationally-renowned performers you're looking for, the Cave isn't the venue for you. However, as a showcase for local talent, it's garnering quite a reputation among serious music fans in the area. Tickets are reasonably priced, with concessions for students and the unemployed. The room is a little cosy, to say the least, but that adds to the atmosphere! That said, it does have a tendency to be very crowded on Saturday nights, perhaps unpleasantly so. Stage One is somewhat larger than the Cave, with an advertised capacity of 350 as opposed to the Cave's 250. They tend to attract slightly better-known acts, but at £25–30 a throw, tickets aren't exactly cheap, and when bought over the phone incur an additional booking fee of £2.50 per ticket.

Recommendation

If you only have time to visit one venue, I would recommend _____ . Its programme includes the best bands in the UK and while it may not be the most polished gig you've ever seen, it should be a memorable evening.

1 **SPEAKING** Compare and contrast the photos. Which gig would you rather be at? Give reasons.

2 Read the report about live music venues in the writer's area. Answer the questions.
   1 Is the report written in formal or relatively informal language? Give examples to support your answer.
   2 Who do you think the intended audience for the report might be? Give reasons.
   3 Which venue does the writer recommend? Complete the gap in the report.

3 Find words or phrases in the text which mean the opposite of 1–8.
   1 unknown acts
   2 badly-managed
   3 poorly-equipped
   4 clean
   5 overpriced
   6 empty
   7 unrehearsed
   8 forgettable

WRITING TIP

In order to soften a negative comment, we often use **periphrasis** (using more words than necessary) or **euphemism** (replacing negative or offensive words with something less direct).
Periphrasis: *This venue is a little on the shabby side.* (instead of *This venue is shabby.*)
Euphemism: *The floor could do with a clean.* (instead of *The floor is dirty.*)

4 Read the *Writing tip*. Then find examples of periphrasis and euphemism in the text with the meanings below.
   1 It's sterile.
   2 It needs better air-conditioning.
   3 It isn't slick, but it has character.
   4 The Cave doesn't have internationally-renowned performers.
   5 The room is small.
   6 It's very crowded on Saturday nights.
   7 Tickets are expensive.
   8 The gig won't be polished, but the evening should be memorable.

5 Soften these negative comments using periphrasis or euphemism.
   1 The band isn't very successful.
   2 The drummer isn't skilful, but he's enthusiastic.
   3 The song isn't very original, but it's catchy.
   4 The singer's voice is unattractive.
   5 The singer sometimes goes out of tune.
   6 The stage is too small.
   7 The sound system sometimes doesn't work.
   8 The room is too hot.

6 **SPEAKING** Discuss the questions as a class.
   1 What are the advantages and disadvantages of listening to live music, rather than recorded music?
   2 Which performers would you most like to see performing live? Give reasons.

1 SPEAKING Work in pairs. Compare and contrast the restaurants in the photos. Which would you prefer to eat at, and why?

2 Read these two descriptions of the same restaurant meal. Which is more positive about the experience?

A Lunch was a relaxed affair. I began with a light starter of garlic prawns. This was followed by 'Creole Gumbo', a novel combination of pork, chicken and seafood which came with a side dish of succulent vegetables. For dessert, I opted for the mango sorbet, which was particularly sweet.

B Lunch was a long and drawn-out affair. I began with a meagre starter of garlic prawns. This was followed by 'Creole Gumbo', an odd concoction of pork, chicken and seafood which came with a side dish of soggy vegetables. For dessert, I opted for the mango sorbet, which was particularly sickly.

> **WRITING TIP**
>
> Words with the same core meaning can have very different **connotations**: these give us information about the writer's attitude.

3 Read the *Writing tip*. Find words in the texts in exercise 2 which share the same core meaning but have different connotations.

4 Find pairs of words with similar core meaning below. Decide:

a whether each pair is most likely to be used when describing a restaurant's food, staff or interior.

b which word in each pair has a more positive connotation.

~~attentive~~ bustling cloying cramped crowded
deserted formal hearty heavy hurried
insubstantial intimate ~~intrusive~~ laid back light
sloppy sour stiff swift sweet tangy uncrowded

attentive – intrusive   describing staff   'attentive' is more positive

5 In pairs, think of words which have the same core meaning as the words below, but a less negative connotation. Use a dictionary if necessary.

1 bossy – assertive
2 stubborn
3 tactless
4 out-dated
5 scrawny
6 arrogant
7 flippant
8 abnormal

> **WRITING TIP**
>
> A report should be laid out in the clearest possible form. Unlike other forms of writing, it is fine to use subheadings in a report.

6 Read the *Writing tip*. Then, in pairs, read the task and decide what headings to use for sections 2 and 3 of the plan below. Divide the venues according to size, style of food, price, or your own idea.

> *A group of foreign students are visiting your town for a week. Write a report giving information about the range of cafés and restaurants. Include at least one personal recommendation.*

1 Introduction (the aim of the report)
2 _____ (first type of venue)
3 _____ (second type of venue)
4 Recommendation

7 SPEAKING Work in pairs. Talk about cafés and restaurants you know (or invent them if you don't know any). Add notes to the plan in exercise 6. Decide which venue to recommend.

8 Working individually, write a report of 200–250 words following your plan from exercise 6. Remember to write in an appropriate style for your audience. Include at least one example of periphrasis or euphemism.

9 Check your work using the list below.

> **CHECK YOUR WORK**
>
> **Have you:**
> ☐ followed the plan?
> ☐ written the correct number of words?
> ☐ included at least one example of periphrasis or euphemism?
> ☐ used words with positive/negative connotations?
> ☐ used correct grammar and vocabulary?

Vocabulary

1 Complete the sentences with phrasal verbs formed from a verb in A and a particle in B. Use active or passive.

A check drop get hold show stop
B around away into off over up

Harry was checking into the hotel when I arrived.

1 We aren't having a holiday this summer, but I'm sure we _____ to somewhere nice in the autumn.
2 They arrived two hours late because they _____ in the rush hour traffic leaving London.
3 Emma's taxi was late _____ her _____ at the station, so she nearly missed her train.
4 During our flight to Australia last year we _____ in Singapore for four hours.
5 She _____ the exhibition by the artist himself.

Mark: ____ /5

2 Complete the sentences using a noun related to the phrasal verb in brackets.

1 There has been an _____ of flu. (break out)
2 There was a peasant _____ in 1917. (rise up)
3 The _____ has caused many job losses. (take over)
4 The scandal led to the president's _____. (fall down)
5 Boy band Take That made a _____ in 2006. (come back)

Mark: ____ /5

3 Complete the sentences with compound adjectives formed from the words in brackets.

1 It didn't look as if it would rain, so she put on her _____ - _____ (toe) sandals.
2 My brother is cultivating his trendy image by wearing _____ - _____ (skin) T-shirts wherever he goes.
3 There was a cold breeze and Jess wished she had worn a _____ - _____ (sleeve) top instead of a T-shirt.
4 Since she's been pregnant, my sister feels more comfortable in _____ - _____ (fit) garments.
5 Josh wanted to make a good impression, so he wore a _____ - _____ (three) suit to the interview.

Mark: ____ /5

4 Give the sentences a more negative connotation by replacing the underlined words with the words below.

cloying cramped crowded ~~heavy~~ sloppy

1 They were served a heavy breakfast. heavy
2 We were served a <u>sweet</u> dessert.
3 The streets are <u>bustling</u> with shoppers.
4 The tavern had an <u>intimate</u> atmosphere.
5 The waiters have quite a <u>laid-back</u> attitude.

Mark: ____ /5

Grammar

5 Rewrite the sentence with extra emphasis using the words in brackets.

I was first attracted to his smile. (it)
It was his smile that I was first attracted to.

1 We need to know when their flight is due. (what)
2 The new head teacher is charming, and she's very professional too. (only)
3 He earns too little to support himself. (truth)
4 Your new haircut looks nice. (does)
5 I don't understand why he's upset. (what)
6 You told everyone my secret. (it)
7 We're lost. (fact)
8 I rarely stopped to think about her feelings. (did)

Mark: ____ /8

6 Tick the verbs which can complete the sentences correctly. (Sometimes both are correct.)

1 They were going to call this morning, so he ____ about the job by now.
   a would know   b should know
2 I'm amazed that she ____ you like that.
   a would treat   b should treat
3 They took some extra blankets in case they ____ cold.
   a would get   b should get
4 We ____ to express our thanks by inviting you both to dinner.
   a would like   b should like
5 It's essential that everyone ____ on time.
   a would arrive   b should arrive

Mark: ____ /5

7 Complete the sentences with the modal verbs below and the correct form of the verbs in brackets.

can't may not might must needn't
ought not to should

1 Candidates _____ (leave) the room until the examination is over.
2 Jane's dad is furious with her for having a party while he was away. He says she _____ (ask) him first.
3 You _____ (joke) if you think I'm going to lend you the money for my birthday present!
4 People _____ (put) used batteries in their household rubbish.
5 He _____ (tell) me he wouldn't be home for lunch!
6 There's plenty of time so we _____ (hurry).
7 You _____ (see) Tom yesterday. He's in China.

Mark: ____ /7

Total: ____ /40

Speaking

1 Choose a capital city that you would like to visit. Think about why and make notes.

2 Work in groups. Present your ideas to the other members of your group.

Reading

3 Read the text. For questions 1–4, choose the best answer.

Dublin ● ● ● ● ● ● ● ● ●

Low-slung, grey and solid, Ireland's premier city can look surprisingly dark and gloomy at first glance. Its appearance – the result of its 19th-century architecture of Irish stone and granite – is deceptive. The town itself is anything but gloomy, and it's not the stodgy, old-fashioned city of the late 20th century. Behind all those sturdy columns and beneath all that grey is the real, modern, Euro-Dublin – an affluent place filled with trendy coffee shops, organic juice bars, pricey five-star restaurants and expensive designer boutiques. The European money that has flooded in over the last decade changed many things in Ireland, but it altered Dublin most of all, catapulting this historic town from the early 20th century, where it had lingered too long, into the 21st, where it now revels in its own success.

Gone are the days when many visitors to Ireland chose to skip Dublin altogether. Nowadays, a weekend in Dublin is one of the hottest city breaks in Europe, as people pile into its old pubs and modern bars, shop in its thriving markets and malls, and relax in its trendy cafés. Because of all of this, Dublin's population has swollen to 1.5 million; more than a third of the Irish population lives in this city, which, while good news for the economy, has residual side effects of overcrowding, high property prices, and gridlocked traffic. It has also helped make Dublin one of the world's most youthful cities, with an estimated 50% of the population under 25 years old.

It is a contrary, amusing, complex small city, and my advice to those who haven't been here in a while, or who have never been here is this: the first thing you should do is leave your preconceptions behind. Then you can see this historic, modern, flawed, charming, and entertaining city for what it really is.

1 Dublin's physical appearance is misleading because it makes the city

   A seem poorer than it really is.

   B seem colder than it really is.

   C seem less lively and up-to-date than it really is.

   D look grander and wealthier than it really is.

2 What has been the effect of European funding on Dublin?

   A The city has become very expensive.

   B The city has changed faster than the rest of Ireland.

   C The city no longer has a strong sense of history.

   D The city has rebuilt many of its derelict buildings.

3 The fact that Dublin's population has grown rapidly

   A is good news for people under 25.

   B has had positive and negative consequences.

   C has damaged the economy of other regions.

   D has meant some people can't find housing.

4 The writer advises visitors to Dublin to

   A see both the old and the new parts of the city.

   B ignore whatever they previously thought about the city.

   C ignore the city's bad points.

   D find out about the history of the city before they arrive.

Listening

4 🎧 3.05 **Edgars, Tomas and Rita are on holiday in Dublin. Listen and identify the three locations for the dialogue.**

5 🎧 3.05 **Listen again. Complete each sentence with a single word.**

1 Edgars says that the hotel reservation was made _____ .

2 Edgars complains that his room looks really _____ .

3 One bad thing about the hotel restaurant is that they are made to _____ .

4 By the time the food arrives, Rita no longer feels _____ .

5 Regarding his new business, Edgars feels _____ .

6 Rita would prefer to have their next meal in the _____ .

Writing

6 Imagine you are Edgars, Rita or Tomas. Make a note of three different things you were unhappy with at the hotel in Dublin. Invent details or use information from the dialogue.

7 Write a letter of complaint to the hotel. Say:

   • what you are complaining about and why.

   • what you would like the hotel to do about it.

1 [Get ready to LISTEN] What are the advantages and disadvantages of bottled water, as opposed to tap water? Which do you prefer to drink?

EXAM TIP

If you miss an answer during the first listening, don't worry about it. Move on to the next sentence. When you listen again, focus on the missing answers.

2 🎧 3.06 Do the Listening exam task.

LISTENING exam task

Listen to the radio programme and complete each sentence with up to four words.

1 About one in five restaurant customers order bottled water because they don't want to _____ .
2 It takes 162 grams of oil to make one _____ .
3 When discarded plastic bottles reach the ocean, they become a _____ .
4 The Eastern Garbage Patch is a particularly polluted area of _____ .
5 Plastic breaks down into pieces which can be smaller than _____ .
6 In order to reach its customers, about a quarter of all bottled water has to _____ .
7 Waterhouse, a new restaurant in London, is unusual because it won't _____ .
8 Bottled water has had so much bad publicity that eventually people who drink it could look like _____ .

3 Look quickly through the text in the Use of English exam task about Claridge's, a luxury hotel in London. Find the most expensive and the cheapest water available.

4 Do the Use of English exam task.

USE OF ENGLISH exam task

Read the text and decide which word or phrase (A–D) best fits each gap.

Water for £50 a litre

Claridge's has taken luxury to a new [1]_____ by offering its guests more than 30 [2]_____ of water – with prices stretching to as much as £50 a litre. The opulent hotel in the heart of London has [3]_____ an extensive menu with water from places as far flung as Norway, Patagonia, New Zealand and Hawaii. Customers are given advice on which water is best [4]_____ to what occasion. For those suffering from exhaustion or trying to get over jet lag, OGO spring water from the Netherlands contains 35 times more oxygen than [5]_____ water [6]_____ the drinker. The most expensive on the menu is 420 Volcanic, spring water from New Zealand, which can be bought for £21 for 42 cl – the equivalent of £50 a litre. Its low mineral content and 'smooth sensation on the palate' come from its journey from the [7]_____ at the bottom of an extinct volcano through 200 metres of volcanic rock. Fiuggi from Italy has [8]_____ been admired: Michelangelo wrote about its restorative effects in 1554 and it is said to be very popular with the Vatican. [9]_____ included on the list is Mahalo Deep Sea Water, from Hawaii, which is £21 for 75 cl. Originally a fresh water iceberg, the ice melted thousands of years ago and sank to the bottom of the ocean floor because of its different temperature and salinity. It is now [10]_____ to the surface through a 1,000 metre pipeline. But among all the grandeur there is one option which is free of charge – a glass of 'old-fashioned London tap water'.

1 A height   B peak   C summit   D rate
2 A varieties   B differences   C variations   D options
3 A revised   B advised   C comprised   D devised
4 A appropriate B suited   C suitable   D linked
5 A common   B typical   C ordinary   D natural
6 A revitalising B revitalised   C is revitalised
  D to revitalise
7 A source   B foundation   C basis
  D beginning
8 A much   B thoroughly   C once   D long
9 A Futhermore, B Also   C Plus,
  D Moreover
10 A dragged   B hauled   C pulled   D pumped

THIS UNIT INCLUDES

Vocabulary ▪ gossip and secrets ▪ giving and withholding information ▪ colloquial omissions ▪ literal and figurative language ▪ vague language
Grammar ▪ passive structures ▪ the causative ▪ participle phrases
Speaking ▪ talking about gossip and secrets ▪ talking about spy stories ▪ talking about conspiracy theories ▪ drawing conclusions
Writing ▪ an opinion essay

9A | VOCABULARY AND LISTENING Gossip

I can understand and use the language of news and gossip.

1 SPEAKING Work in pairs. Describe what the people in the photos are doing. Why do you think they might be doing it? How might you explain their expressions? Use the words below to help you.

confide (in somebody)   drop a bombshell
eavesdrop (on a conversation)   gossip (n & v)   indiscreet
outraged   rumours   scandal   scandalised   scandalous

2 🎧 3.07 Listen to three people gossiping over the phone. Complete each sentence with the information you hear, using up to four words.

1 Kate tells Gerry that Harry has got _____ .
2 She urges Gerry not to tell anyone because Harry hasn't yet _____ .
3 She claims only to have told Gerry the secret because he is _____ .
4 Brian tells Jake about secret plans to _____ .
5 He suspects that some of the people involved in the deal will _____ .
6 Julia tells Karen about two friends who started a relationship at a _____ .
7 She reveals that Sue is very keen to keep the relationship secret from her _____ .
8 She expects the secret will eventually come out when the couple _____ .

3 🎧 3.07 Choose the correct word in these expressions. Then listen again and check.

1 Have you heard the **latest / newest**?
2 I'm telling you this in the **firmest / strictest** confidence.
3 If **word / truth** gets out, it'll cause…
4 Harry's the **heart / soul** of discretion.
5 He hasn't **breathed / whispered** a word to anybody.
6 I know it won't go any **longer / further**.
7 I managed to **glean / clean** some information.
8 It's **fully / highly** confidential at the moment.
9 Don't **quote / repeat** me on this, but…
10 I've got some really **fruity / juicy** gossip for you.
11 It's all very **hush-hush / hush up**.
12 They won't be able to keep it under **hats / wraps** for ever.

4 Rewrite these sentences using expressions from exercise 3. More than one answer may be possible.

1 Don't tell anyone who you heard this from, but I think my brother is getting married.
2 I discovered a few interesting titbits about her private life, but I won't tell a soul. My lips are sealed!
3 Her plans for next year are top secret.
4 For the time being, they're withholding the identity of their new manager.
5 I'll tell you my secret because I know you aren't a gossip.
6 She told me one really fascinating secret about Tony. If it ever becomes common knowledge, he'll be furious!

5 SPEAKING Work in pairs. Discuss the questions. Then compare your ideas with the class.

1 What kinds of topic often form the basis of gossip?
2 Why are so many people interested in gossip?
3 In what ways could gossip be damaging?
4 What would be the advantages and disadvantages of being friends with a gossip?

▶▶▶ **VOCABULARY BUILDER 9.1: GIVING AND WITHHOLDING INFORMATION: WORKBOOK PAGE 111** ◀◀◀

1 SPEAKING Have you ever failed to keep a secret? If so, what were the consequences?

2 Complete the text with the verbs below.

betray boost crop drop fall feign get give
go hold prise turn

How to keep a secret

- Just don't tell anyone! Avoid the subject as much as you can. Should it ¹_____ up in conversation for whatever reason, ²_____ ignorance.
- Never ³_____ hints in company that you know a secret but can't say what it is. This is like a red rag to a bull. The people you are with will try to ⁴_____ the information out of you and you probably won't be able to ⁵_____ out.
- If you feel yourself weakening, ⁶_____ your motivation by focusing on why it's so important to keep the information secret. Is it to avoid ruining a surprise? Or to protect a friend's reputation?
- Whenever you're tempted to ⁷_____ a friend's secret, remind yourself of the long-term damage that this could do to your friendship. At the same time, tell yourself that being trustworthy is a wonderful trait to have.
- Don't ⁸_____ into the trap of thinking you can tell just one other person provided you insist that it should ⁹_____ no further – it always does! And sooner or later, your lack of discretion will ¹⁰_____ back to your friend.
- If you know you're bad at keeping secrets, don't encourage people to share them with you – or at least ¹¹_____ them some warning of your track record!

WARNING! Sometimes it is better to pass on a secret, if you suspect the person who told you may be in trouble. A secret can ¹²_____ out to be a cry for help.

3 SPEAKING Work in pairs. Decide whether you agree or disagree with the advice in exercise 2. Can you add any more advice?

LOOK OUT!
It's often more natural to use a phrase (verb + noun) instead of a single-word verb, especially in informal language.
talk → have a talk   decide → make a decision

4 Read the *Look out!* box. Then rewrite the sentences using phrases instead of the underlined verbs.
1 I'd love to <u>shop</u> with you this afternoon, but I need to <u>revise</u>.
2 <u>Think</u> about what I've said and <u>call</u> me later.
3 I've <u>concluded</u> that what I really need is to <u>rest</u>.
4 I <u>looked</u> at her painting and <u>complimented</u> her.
5 I <u>hinted</u> that I'd like to be paid, but I didn't want to <u>offend</u> by asking.

LEARN THIS!
Colloquial omissions
In informal, spoken English, we often omit unstressed words at the beginning of the sentence (pronouns, articles, etc.) provided the meaning is clear. For example:
Can't talk now!   (*I can't talk now.*)
Speak later.   (*We'll speak later.*)
Need a lift?   (*Do you need a lift?*)
A negative form is sometimes replaced by *not*.
Not a cloud in the sky.   (*There isn't a cloud in the sky.*)

>>> GRAMMAR BUILDER 9.1: COLLOQUIAL OMISSIONS: PAGE 128 <<<

5 Read the information in the *Learn this!* box. Then cross out any words in the dialogue that you think could be omitted in normal, colloquial speech. (You may have to make other minor changes as a result.)

Sam	Are you on your way home?
Colin	No. I'm just hanging around.
Sam	Do you fancy a coffee?
Colin	Sure.
Sam	It's my turn to pay.
Colin	Thanks. So, how are you?
Sam	I'm good. How are you?
Colin	I can't grumble. Have you heard any good gossip recently?
Sam	I have, as it happens.
Colin	Well, go on then. Spill the beans!
Sam	Well, apparently Ben and Molly have split up.
Colin	You're kidding! Really?
Sam	But they haven't told people yet. So don't say a word to anyone!
Colin	I understand.
Sam	Do you promise?
Colin	Yes!
Sam	OK. Would you like another coffee?
Colin	No, thanks. I'd better make a move.
Sam	OK. I'll see you later.
Colin	Sure. It was nice talking to you.

6 🎧 3.08 Listen to the dialogue and compare what you hear with your answer to exercise 5.

7 SPEAKING Work in pairs. Role-play a dialogue using the outline below. Include some colloquial omissions.
A: You meet your old friend B in a café and start chatting. B asks about a mutual friend, and you hint that you know a secret. You are unwilling to share it at first, but B persuades you. You make B promise that it won't go any further.
B: You meet A in a café and start chatting. You ask about a mutual friend, and A seems to know a secret about that friend but is unwilling to share it. You persuade A to let on.

1 SPEAKING Work in pairs. How much do you know about the writer Joseph Conrad? Can you name:

1 the country he was born in?
2 the country he adopted as his home?
3 any of his works?

2 🎧 3.09 Listen to the information about Conrad. Find the answers to question 1.

3 🎧 3.09 Listen again. Are the sentences true (T) or false (F), or is the answer not stated (NS)?

1 The themes of Conrad's works are very relevant to the problems of the modern world.
2 Conrad lived in London and later in a village.
3 Special postage stamps were issued to commemorate the 150th anniversary of Conrad's birth.
4 Conrad's friends never really regarded him as English.
5 Conrad's contemporaries accused him of racism.

4 Read the opening to the novel *The Secret Agent* by Joseph Conrad. How does it convey the fact that Mr Verloc is a secret agent of some kind? Is it:

a by describing the shadowy characters who frequent his shop?
b by mentioning the political propaganda displayed in his shop window?
c by implying that the shop is a front for some other clandestine activity?

5 Read the *Reading tip*. Then find these phrases in the extract. What exactly do they imply? Choose a or b.

1 *nominally in charge of his brother-in-law*
a His brother-in-law was the one who really ran the shop.
b His brother-in-law was incapable of running the shop.

2 *his ostensible business*
a The shop was not his real business.
b He was ashamed that the shop was his business.

3 *a square box of a place*
a The shop was an attractive building.
b The shop was an ugly building.

4 *for the sake of the customers*
a His customers were ashamed to be seen there.
b His customers were really spies.

5 *who hung about the window for a time*
a The young men had nothing else to do.
b The young men needed time to summon up courage.

6 *with impudent virulence*
a The customers disliked the loud bell.
b The customers rang the bell loudly on purpose.

> **READING TIP**
>
> Literary texts often imply information without explicitly stating it. To get the most out of a text, you should be sensitive to this. Certain phrases can convey information indirectly, as can the repeated use of similar words.

6 Does the text imply that Mr Verloc's life is glamorous or not very glamorous? Find several adjectives in the text to support your answer.

¹ Mr Verloc, going out in the morning, left his shop nominally in charge of his brother-in-law. It could be done, because there was very little business at any time, and practically none at all before
⁵ the evening. Mr Verloc cared but little about his ostensible business. And, moreover, his wife was in charge of his brother-in-law.

The shop was small, and so was the house. It was one of those grimy brick houses which
¹⁰ existed in large quantities before the era of reconstruction dawned upon London. The shop was a square box of a place, with the front glazed in small panes. In the daytime the door remained closed; in the evening it stood discreetly but suspiciously ajar.

The window contained photographs of more or less undressed dancing
¹⁵ girls; nondescript packages in wrappers like patent medicines; closed yellow paper envelopes, very flimsy, and marked two-and-six in heavy black figures; a few numbers of ancient French comic publications hung across a string as if to dry; a dingy blue china bowl, a casket of black wood, bottles of marking ink and rubber stamps; a few books, with titles hinting at impropriety; a few
²⁰ apparently old copies of obscure newspapers, badly printed, with titles like *The Torch*, *The Gong* - rousing titles. And the two gas jets inside the panes were always turned low, either for economy's sake or for the sake of the customers.

These customers were either very young men, who hung about the
²⁵ window for a time before slipping in suddenly; or men of a more mature age, but looking generally as if they were not in funds. Some of that last kind had the collars of their overcoats turned right up to their moustaches, and traces of mud on the bottom of their nether garments, which had the appearance of being much worn and not very valuable. And the legs inside them did not, as
³⁰ a general rule, seem of much account either. With their hands plunged deep in the side pockets of their coats, they dodged in sideways, one shoulder first, as if afraid to start the bell going.

The bell, hung on the door by means of a curved ribbon of steel, was difficult to circumvent. It was hopelessly cracked; but of an evening, at the slightest
³⁵ provocation, it clattered behind the customer with impudent virulence.

7 SPEAKING Discuss the questions with the class.

1 Why do you think people are interested in stories about spies and secret agents?
2 Do you like this genre of fiction? Why?/Why not?
3 Do you know any writers from your own country who write spy stories or mysteries?

1 SPEAKING **Work in pairs. Discuss the conspiracy theories. Have you heard any of them before? Do you believe any of them?**

1 The US military has known for years that UFOs exist but is hiding the truth from the public.
2 The 1969 Apollo moon landing did not really happen – it was filmed in a TV studio on earth.
3 Elvis Presley did not really die – he faked his own death because he was tired of being famous.
4 The HIV/AIDS virus was created by scientists.
5 The US government were behind the bombing of the World Trade Center on 11 September 2001.
6 Princess Diana, who died in Paris in 1997, was murdered on the orders of the British royal family.

2 Read the article, ignoring the gaps. Which of the conspiracy theories in exercise 1 are mentioned?

CONSPIRACY
are they out

1 In 2003, a former government minister in the UK called Michael Meacher claimed that the US Government had known all about the September 11 attacks but let them happen to justify grabbing control of the world's oil
5 supplies. That such a bizarre conspiracy theory broke out from Internet chatrooms, grabbed the mind of a former minister and was splashed across the media reflects the growing popularity of conspiracy theories. [1] 🔲

Although Mr Meacher admitted that he got much
10 of his information from websites, he made his claim in the respected British newspaper *The Guardian*. The newspaper later published letters from readers relieved that the truth had come out. David Aaronovitch, a *Guardian* columnist, expressed alarm that his newspaper
15 had given credibility to such 'rubbish'.

According to David Alexander, author of *Conspiracies and Cover-Ups – What the Government Isn't Telling You*, 'There's been a tremendous increase in conspiracy theories about September 11.' In 1998, Rich Buhler, an
20 American radio show host, set up *Truthorfiction.com* to track and prove or disprove hoaxes, urban myths and conspiracy theories. [2] 🔲 Mr Buhler said: 'The Internet has proven a valuable tool for conspiracy theorists – they exchange ideas and fuel the stories. They have a much
25 larger canvas than before. There's an impression that whatever is written is more reliable than what is said. When it is written down, as it is on the Internet, it comes packaged as truth.'

Yet there are other reasons why conspiracy theories
30 are gaining currency – in particular the complexity of our rapidly changing world. 'A conspiracy theory becomes more compelling when reality makes less sense, when life is beset by problems, when the established order suddenly changes – even something as simple as losing
35 a job. If people can't absorb what's going on, conspiracy theories help us to make sense,' Mr Alexander said. [3] 🔲 'If people just knew a little more, they would know the thing is false,' he said.

People are becoming further removed from seats
40 of political and industrial power. Patrick Leman, a

THEORISTS: to get you?

psychologist at Royal Holloway College, London, who has been studying why conspiracy theories are so appealing, said: 'Conspiracy theories feed into a feeling of disconnection with government. People don't like gaps
45 in their accounts; they have a need to believe them. They invent fantastical things that protect them from the real world.' In one experiment, he showed people footage of a fictional president who was shot at, and provided fictional newspaper articles. 4 ☐ He concluded: 'People think that
50 a big event must have a big cause, but often things are caused by mistake or accident, not conspiracy.'

Thousands of people die in Europe every year in car accidents resulting from fast driving and too much alcohol. But when Diana, Princess of Wales died, many could not
55 accept that such an important event could have such a simple cause. Many believed that she was assassinated by the secret services to stop her marrying a Muslim. In Australia there were 161 suspected drownings between 1961 and 1985 in which the bodies were never found.
60 But when Harold Holt, the Prime Minister, disappeared when swimming in 1967, conspiracy theories ran wild. 5 ☐

Such is the public appetite for conspiracy theories, there is money to be made. Bart Sibrel makes money selling his video claiming that the first moon landing was a
65 fake.

There is no simple way to determine the truth of a conspiracy theory. 'The danger lies in buying overarching explanations of complex events. That having been said, there's danger in being too complacent and buying
70 into pat explanations of extraordinary occurrences,' Mr Alexander said. In other words, scepticism can go too far. When stories began to circulate about the Bilderberg Group, a secretive grouping of the world's political and business elite, most people dismissed it as just a
75 conspiracy theory. 6 ☐

Mr Alexander says that the growth of conspiracy theories is not something just to laugh at. 'It's dangerous if your belief system makes you see the world in a way that's unreal. Conspiracy theories can affect a whole society and
80 make the society mad.'

3 Match sentences a–g with gaps 1–6 in the text. There is one sentence that you do not need.

a His organisation now gets 1,000 such stories a week.
b People were more likely to believe that there was a conspiracy behind it if he was killed than if he was uninjured.
c And yet, it really does exist: members agree not to reveal the contents of their discussions, and the minutes of the meetings are not published for 50 years.
d Observers of the phenomenon, more pronounced in America than here, say that their increasing prevalence is destabilising vulnerable individuals and undermining society.
e That is how conspiracy theories gain momentum, even though there is no real evidence to support them.
f One held that he had been spying for the Chinese, and was spirited away by a Chinese submarine.
g A limited understanding of the world makes conspiracy theories seem more plausible.

4 Rephrase the underlined parts of these excerpts from the article in your own words.

1 A bizarre conspiracy theory was splashed across the media.
2 They … fuel the stories.
3 When it is written down … it comes packaged as truth.
4 There are other reasons why conspiracy theories are gaining currency.
5 People are becoming further removed from seats of political and industrial power.
6 When Harold Holt disappeared, conspiracy theories ran wild.
7 Such is the public appetite for conspiracy theories, there is money to be made.
8 There's danger in buying into pat explanations.

▶▶▶ VOCABULARY BUILDER 9.2: LITERAL AND FIGURATIVE LANGUAGE: WORKBOOK PAGE 112 ◀◀◀

5 SPEAKING Give an example of:

1 a story that has been splashed across the media very recently.
2 something which, in your opinion, is fuelled by the Internet.
3 something which is packaged as truth, but in your opinion is not.
4 an idea which is gaining currency in your country.
5 one of the main seats of power in your country.
6 a rumour which has run wild in your school but which may not be true.
7 something which there seems to be a growing public appetite for in your country.
8 something which you personally refuse to buy into.

6 SPEAKING Discuss the questions with the class.

1 Describe any conspiracy theories that are specific to your own country.
2 Why do so many conspiracy theories involve the USA?
3 Are conspiracy theories harmless or damaging? Give reasons.

1 Complete the article with appropriate passive forms of the verbs below. What is your opinion of the way Joyce Hatto and her husband behaved?

bomb   consider   copy   describe   hail   inform   issue
make   pass off   perform   record   reduce   show
uncover

Classical pianist Joyce Hatto was born in London in 1928 and remembers practising the piano as a teenager while London ¹_____ in the Second World War. As a performer in London during the 1950s and 60s, she ²_____ to be proficient but not outstanding and she more or less retired from professional music in the 1970s. She had her piano moved from London to a small house in the country, and there she lived with her husband, William Barrington-Coupe, a recording engineer. Over the next thirty years, she performed at home, and these performances – 104 of them in total – ³_____ by her husband and then ⁴_____ on his own record label, Concert Artists. They caused a sensation. Her performances ⁵_____ by music critics as some of the finest recordings that ⁶_____ ever _____ and Hatto ⁷_____ as 'the greatest instrumentalist that almost nobody has heard of'.

But in 2007 a music magazine discovered that one of the recordings ⁸_____ electronically from another artist's CD. Since then, further frauds have emerged. At least five of the pieces ⁹_____ in fact _____ by other artists, and more fakes ¹⁰_____ on a daily basis. It seems likely that in due course, all 104 pieces ¹¹_____ not to be genuine. Only yesterday, classical pianist David Owen Norris ¹²_____ that his 1988 solo piano recording of Elgar's *Symphony No 1 in A flat major* ¹³_____ as Hatto's work. 'I'm just very sad,' he said. 'I think it's pathetic really that somebody should ¹⁴_____ to this.'

▶▶▶ GRAMMAR BUILDER 9.2: THE PASSIVE: PAGE 128 ◀◀◀

Use of the passive
The choice between active and passive voice is often made for stylistic reasons, because we want a certain word to be the subject of the sentence in order to fit with the topic and flow of the text. Compare:
Clara Butt gave the first performance of Elgar's Sea Pictures. (in a text about the singer Clara Butt)
The first performance of Elgar's Sea Pictures was given by Clara Butt. (in a text about Elgar's music)

2 Read the *Learn this!* box. Then decide which of the underlined clauses in the text below would be better in the passive and rewrite them. Give reasons.

Joyce Hatto and her husband left London in the 1970s after doctors had diagnosed Joyce with cancer. Away from the public gaze, they worked together on recordings of some of the finest classical pieces that anybody had ever composed. But it soon became clear that her disease was hampering Joyce's efforts to produce outstanding recordings. William made the first electronic alterations in order to cover up her cries of pain. Although William knew that it was wrong, a desire to protect his wife's musical reputation triggered his dishonest actions. He simply wanted people to give her the acclaim which her disease had denied her. Was that so wrong? Although people never took Joyce's recordings seriously again, perhaps we should admire her courage, and her husband's love after all.

3 Does the text in exercise 2 change your opinion of Joyce Hatto and her husband? Why?/Why not?

Participle phrases
Remember that we can sometimes use a phrase beginning with a past participle (a participle phrase) in place of a passive construction. Compare:
The fraud was exposed by a music magazine and it became international news.
Exposed by a music magazine, the fraud became international news.

4 Read the *Learn this!* box. Then rewrite the following text using an appropriate mixture of active and passive constructions and participle phrases.

Millions in the USA watched the cookery show *Dinner: Impossible*. British chef Robert Irvine presented it. The Queen had knighted Irvine and she had given him a castle in Scotland – or so he claimed. Officials investigated Irvine when a business venture failed and they exposed him as a fraud. Irvine has finally admitted the truth. Now, angry creditors are pursuing Irvine and the TV channel has removed his fictitious biography from its website.

1 SPEAKING Work in pairs. Think of three different situations in which somebody might want to make themselves invisible, or very difficult to see. Then compare your ideas with the class.

2 SPEAKING Work in pairs. Compare and contrast the two photos. Answer the questions.

1 Why do you think each person is attempting to hide?
2 How successful do you think their attempts are?
3 In what ways do the photos emphasise the differences between the town and the country?
4 In what other situations might it be useful not to be visible?

3 🎧 3.10 Listen to two students talking about the photos in exercise 2. How different are their ideas from your own?

4 🎧 3.10 Read the phrases for drawing conclusions and clauses a–m. Think about which clauses belong together logically. Then listen again and match the clauses with gaps 1–13.

Drawing conclusions
Judging by the fact that ¹ ☐ I'd say that ² ☐
The fact that ³ ☐ would suggest that ⁴ ☐
⁵ ☐ so obviously ⁶ ☐
It's clear from the fact that ⁷ ☐ that ⁸ ☐
This would point to the fact that ⁹ ☐
¹⁰ ☐ which leads me to think that ¹¹ ☐
I take it that ¹² ☐
For that reason, I assume that ¹³ ☐

a He's sitting behind a bush,
b he's planning to be there for some time.
c the photo was taken in a forest or some such place.
d this could be Tokyo or some other large city in Japan.
e he's bothered to bring such a large piece of equipment
f he's some kind of photographer or cameraman.
g she's pulled the top part up in order to hide.
h there are bushes, long grass, and a river.
i she's in a back street rather than on a main road.
j the picture was set up, so to speak.
k he's got a camera
l The people look Japanese to me,
m he wants to blend in with his surroundings.

5 Use the prompts to make sentences. Include phrases for drawing conclusions from exercise 4.

1 there's a microphone ⟶ it's a video camera
2 he has a grey beard ⟶ he's quite old
3 he's chosen this career ⟶ he likes being alone
4 the boy is turning around ⟶ he's seen the woman
5 it doesn't look much like a real vending machine ⟶ it's just a joke

SPEAKING TIP

Vague language
Words like *thing* and *stuff* are useful when it isn't possible to be more precise about what you see. You can also use phrases like *some kind of* and *some… or other*.

6 Read the *Speaking tip*. Find examples of vague language in clauses a–m in exercise 4. Then use the same language to make these sentences more vague.

1 He's wearing a coat made of feathers.
2 The photo was taken in Brazil.
3 He's bored.
4 She works as a private investigator.
5 She's in her thirties.
6 She wants to blend into the background.

7 SPEAKING Turn to page 152 and do the exam task. Use phrases from exercise 4 for drawing conclusions and include vague language from exercise 6.

1 **SPEAKING** Discuss the quotation by academic Noam Chomsky. Is it an argument against or in favour of censorship? Do you agree?

> *If we don't believe in freedom of expression for people we despise, we don't believe in it at all.*

2 Read the essay. What is the writer's basic answer to the question in the title?

Should freedom of speech always be defended?

The first amendment to the American Constitution defends every citizen's right to free speech, and most democracies around the world pride themselves on a lack of state censorship. Indeed, the fact that newspapers and TV news stations report stories which are highly critical of the government is seen as one of the signs of a healthy democracy. But how far should this lack of censorship extend? Is it possible to have a society which places absolutely no controls on information?

Freedom of speech is usually regarded as one of the cornerstones of democracy. It is essential that the content of newspapers, for example, is decided by the newspaper editors and not by politicians or police. If politicians were allowed to determine what should or should not be printed, they would be able to suppress any information which did not put them in a good light. Corruption would increase and there would be no way of exposing politicians' wrongdoings. Moreover, it goes without saying that ordinary citizens in a democracy should be allowed to voice their personal opinions without fear of intimidation.

Having said that, it is clear that total freedom of speech is impossible, or at least extremely risky. This is because sometimes it is necessary to limit freedom of speech in order to protect individual members of society or society as a whole. An example of this would be the laws against libel. These prohibit you from making damaging and untrue statements about somebody. Without this protection, people's lives could be ruined by false accusations.

It is widely accepted that some information needs to be kept secret for reasons of national security or crime prevention. If a newspaper was allowed to print details of a secret anti-terrorist operation, there might be catastrophic results.

To sum up, I would say that freedom of speech should be defended in the majority of cases. However, there will always be situations in which this freedom would have negative consequences. In those instances, I believe that it is necessary to sacrifice freedom in order to protect people's lives.

WRITING TIP

Passive structures with verbs like *regard*, *consider* and *believe* make statements appear less personal and are therefore often appropriate in an essay. The plain statement: 'Censorship is undesirable.' could be rephrased in these ways:
Censorship is usually regarded as undesirable.
Censorship is generally considered (to be) undesirable.
Censorship is often seen as undesirable.
It is widely accepted that censorship is undesirable.
It is often said that censorship is undesirable.
It is generally believed that censorship is undesirable.

3 Read the *Writing tip*. How many times is this type of passive structure used in the model text? Choose one other sentence which could be rephrased in this way and rewrite it.

>>> GRAMMAR BUILDER 9.3: PASSIVE STRUCTURES WITH *CONSIDER, BELIEVE*, ETC.: PAGE 129 <<<

4 Match 1–6 with a–f to form common collocations. Check your answers by finding them in the essay in exercise 2.

1	free	a	opinions
2	state	b	security
3	personal	c	speech
4	false	d	results
5	national	e	censorship
6	catastrophic	f	accusations

5 Complete the sentences with the collocations in exercise 4.

1 It was felt that revealing the government's nuclear plans could jeopardise _____ _____ .
2 Whatever her _____ _____ may be, she never criticises her employer in public.
3 Attempts to close down the website have been portrayed as an attack on _____ _____ .
4 Allowing people to stir up racial hatred could have _____ _____ in a multiracial society.
5 In some countries, _____ _____ prevents newspapers from printing the truth.
6 The minister claimed that he was entirely innocent and had been the victim of _____ _____ .

6 **SPEAKING** Discuss whether it is more important, in your opinion, to protect freedom of speech or to protect people from false accusations. Give reasons.

1 SPEAKING Work in pairs. Discuss the proposition. Do you agree or disagree? Give reasons.

The Internet should be more tightly controlled by governments.

2 Read the start of four newspaper articles about Internet controls. Do they change your opinion about the proposition in exercise 1? Why?/Why not?

Cyber Bullying led to Teen's Suicide 1

The parents of a 13-year-old girl who believe their daughter's suicide was the result of a cruel cyber hoax are pushing for measures to protect other children online.

Terror websites could be blocked in EU crackdown 2

Access to websites that provide information on how to make bombs could be blocked by security forces in an attempt to crack down on terrorists.

Online anorexia sites shut down amid claims they glorify starvation

Microsoft abruptly closed 3 down four pro-anorexia websites in Spain yesterday after a complaint that they were endangering the lives of teenage girls.

Bank details being sold over the Internet for just £1 4

Lists of credit card numbers, names and addresses are being traded across the Internet by criminals involved in ID fraud, it is claimed today.

3 SPEAKING Work in pairs. Decide whether the following things should or should not be allowed on the Internet. Then compare your ideas with the class.

1 stories about famous people which may be untrue
2 unauthorised photos and video clips of ordinary people
3 instructions for writing computer viruses
4 unauthorised video footage of rock concerts
5 negative opinions about the government
6 adverts for untested medicines

4 Plan an opinion essay about the proposition in exercise 1. Make notes for paragraphs 2–4. Use ideas from exercises 1 and 3.

Paragraph 1 Introduction
Paragraph 2 Points in support of the opposite opinion
Paragraph 3 Points in support of your opinion
Paragraph 4 Further points in support of your opinion
Paragraph 5 Conclusion

> **WRITING TIP**
>
> One way of writing the introduction to an opinion essay is to describe the current situation as you see it and then restate the question in your own words.

5 Read the *Writing tip*, then look at the Introduction to the model essay on page 100. Which sentences describe the current situation? Which sentences rephrase the question in different words?

6 Work in pairs. Write the introduction to your essay using the phrases below to help you.

Describing the current situation
Over the past few decades, the Internet…
We have now reached a point where…
Newspapers are full of stories about…
In some countries… while in others…

Restating the question
The key question is…
What it comes down to is…
What needs to be decided is…
Many people are starting to wonder whether…

7 Compare your introduction with another pair's introduction. Share ideas to improve your work.

8 Working individually, write paragraphs 2–5 of your essay following your plan. Write 200–250 words in total.

9 Check your work using the list below.

> **CHECK YOUR WORK**
>
> **Have you:**
> ☐ followed the essay plan correctly?
> ☐ written the correct number of words?
> ☐ included passive phrases for distancing your opinions?
> ☐ checked the spelling and grammar?

1 Describe the photograph. What is the role of the two people in the photo? What does the machine do? Use the words below to help you.

blood pressure   deceit   deception   detect   detection
lie detector   pulse   sweat

2 🎧 3.11 Do the Listening exam task.

LISTENING exam task

Listen to a radio programme. Choose the best answers (A–D).

1 During an experiment into the development of deception in children
  A almost all of the three-year-olds lied.
  B about half of all the children lied.
  C all of the five-year-olds lied.
  D all of the three-year-olds and half of the five-year-olds lied.

2 According to research, what proportion of everyday lies are not identified as lies?
  A four out of five   C more than eighty per cent
  B a third   D eight percent

3 Research into how well people can detect lies has shown that
  A people can only tell if close family members are lying.
  B men are better than women at detecting lies.
  C young people are the best at detecting lies.
  D only a small number of people can identify lies consistently.

4 Psychologist Paul Ekman has demonstrated that
  A judges and psychiatrists lie just as much as robbers.
  B it's easier to detect a lie when you watch it on video.
  C it's hard to detect a lie when you are part of a group.
  D experts are no better than ordinary people at detecting lies.

5 Research by Professor Charles Bond suggests that people fail to detect lies because
  A they don't look into the eyes of the person speaking.
  B they are looking for the wrong signs.
  C they don't notice changes in body language.
  D people from different countries have very different body language.

3 Read the text quickly, ignoring any extra words. Why was an inability to lie a big problem for this criminal?

4 Do the Use of English exam task.

USE OF ENGLISH exam task

Some lines of the text are correct and some contain an extra word which should not be there. Cross out the extra words and tick the lines which are correct.

0	It may be tough for Alejandro Martinez to ~~be~~	
00	clear himself of charges that he robbed a Las	✓
1	Vegas pizza parlour after he allegedly leaving	___
2	behind a crucial piece of evidence. According to	___
3	prosecutors, the 23-year-old Martinez entered the	___
4	parlour, ordered a pie and requested for a job	___
5	application. 'The cashier immediately gave him an	___
6	application and a pen, so that he started filling it	___
7	out,' said Clark County Prosecutor Frank Coumou.	___
8	'Then, when he thought the moment was right, he	___
9	lifted his shirt, exposed the butt of a firearm, and had	___
10	told her to give him all of the money.'	___
11	Having stuffed over the $200 in his pocket, Martinez	___
12	rushed out to a waiting car, authorities say. But a	___
13	witness was followed the gunman and wrote down	___
14	the number plate. An easy trace of that number that	___
15	led to police straight to Martinez, whom they found	___
16	sitting at home. None of that has not made it easy	___
17	for the lawyer who he has been given the job of	___
18	defending Martinez. But the evidence that left behind	___
19	could render his job almost as impossible. When	___
20	police returned to the pizza parlour after the arrest,	___
21	they found Martinez's job application still was on the	___
22	counter. He had dutifully filled in with his real name	___
23	and address. 'I'd chalk it up to either inexperience	___
24	or plain stupidity,' he said Prosecutor Coumou.	___

5 **Get ready to SPEAK** Work in pairs. Decide in what circumstances, if any, you might be tempted to lie about:

  1 somebody's appearance.   3 your age.
  2 feeling unwell.   4 your emotions.

6 Do the Speaking exam task.

SPEAKING exam task

Read the following statement. Do you agree or disagree with it? Discuss the issue with your partner, responding to any counter-arguments they have.

If you want to succeed in life you should become a good liar.

THIS UNIT INCLUDES
Vocabulary ▪ synonyms for *end* ▪ the environment ▪ adverbs of degree ▪ adjectives to describe films (connotation) ▪ verb-noun collocations ▪ negative prefixes and suffixes ▪ stylistically appropriate language
Grammar ▪ *whatever, whoever,* etc. ▪ complex sentences ▪ prepositions in relative clauses ▪ impersonal structures for introducing opinions
Speaking ▪ role-play ▪ talking about threats to the planet ▪ talking about films and their endings ▪ communication strategies
Writing ▪ an opinion essay

Endings 10

10A VOCABULARY AND LISTENING Farewell

I can say farewell in a variety of contexts and situations.

1 SPEAKING Describe the photos of people saying goodbye to each other. What do you think they are feeling? What might they be saying?

2 Read the quotation from *Romeo and Juliet* by William Shakespeare. Explain its meaning.

Good-night, good-night! Parting is such sweet sorrow,

That I shall say good-night till it be morrow.

3 🎧 3.12 Listen to nine extracts and match them with descriptions a–j. One description is not needed.

1 ☐ 2 ☐ 3 ☐ 4 ☐ 5 ☐ 6 ☐ 7 ☐ 8 ☐ 9 ☐

a a job interview
b a radio interview
c a talent show
d a radio advertisement
e an announcement
f a news bulletin
g a speech
h a chat between friends
i a documentary
j a business meeting

4 🎧 3.12 Complete the sentences with the correct form of the verbs below. Use a dictionary to help you. Then listen again and check.

cease   close   culminate   conclude   wind up   wrap up

1 It is likely that many of these languages will _____ to exist over the next century or so.
2 This research _____ in the discovery of the gene responsible for a rare form of bone cancer.
3 Ryan Jones _____ it _____ for City with a goal in extra time.
4 And now I'd just like to _____ this rather long speech by thanking the bridesmaids for looking after Karen.
5 The party doesn't _____ till eleven.
6 The phone lines are now open and they _____ at nine o'clock.

5 Read the usage note from *The Oxford Learner's Thesaurus*. Which of the four verbs *cannot* be used to complete the sentences?

> **NOTE** **END, STOP, FINISH** OR **CONCLUDE?** **End** can be used for things that end in space as well as things that end in time: *The road ends here.* **End, finish** and **conclude** are used especially about things that you do not expect to start again after they have ended: *The war ended in 1945, after almost six years of fighting.* ◇ *The concert should finish by 10 o'clock.* ◇ *She concluded her speech with a quotation from Shakespeare.* **Finish** and **conclude**, in particular, suggest that sth has come to an end because it has been completed. **Finish** is used more to talk about *when* sth ends; **conclude** is used more to talk about *how* sth ends. **Stop** is used about things that may or will start again, or that cannot ever be 'completed': *The rain stopped just long enough for us to have a quick walk in the park.*

1 The river _____ in a long narrow lake.
2 The party didn't _____ until the early hours of the morning.
3 The police have _____ their investigation into the murder.
4 Will you please _____ interrupting me?
5 The sales conference _____ with a speech by the managing director.

6 Work in pairs.
- Prepare one of the following situations. Make notes.
- Start the situation a minute or two before the dialogue would end.
- End by parting from each other.

1 a job interview
2 a conversation with a friend at a party
3 an interview with a famous person
4 a business meeting

7 SPEAKING Act out your roleplay in front of the class.

⟫⟫⟫ **VOCABULARY BUILDER 10.1: SYNONYMS AND ANTONYMS: WORKBOOK PAGE 112** ⟪⟪⟪

1 Complete the facts about the environment using the words below.

carbon dioxide   degrade   equivalent   exported
extinction   impact   occurred   polar ice caps
raw material   resident   rubbish   tailbacks

Environmental facts

1 In the UK, twenty million tonnes of food are imported, and twelve million tonnes _____ , every year.
2 On average every person in the UK throws away their own body weight in _____ every three months.
3 Internationally, one in six species of mammal faces _____ .
4 On average, each UK _____ uses 55,000 litres of water every year.
5 Across the European Union at any one time, there are _____ stretching along 64,000 kilometres of road.
6 The ten warmest years in the last 130 have all _____ since 1978.
7 It takes around 450 years for a plastic bottle to _____ .
8 Aviation generates nearly as much _____ in one year as the total population of Africa.
9 An area of tropical rainforest _____ to sixteen football pitches is destroyed every single minute.
10 For every tonne of waste we produce in our homes, it is estimated that five tonnes of waste has already been created at the manufacturing stage, and twenty tonnes at the point where the _____ was extracted.
11 40% of the _____ have melted over the past 50 years.
12 The _____ of the average US citizen on the environment is approximately three times that of the average Italian, thirteen times that of the average Brazilian, 140 times that of the average Bangladeshi, and 250 times that of the average sub-Saharan African.

2 SPEAKING Work in pairs. Do any of these facts disturb you? Are many people concerned? Why?/ Why not? Agree on which three facts alarm you most. Give reasons.

3 🎧 3.13 Listen to three people talking about different global threats that we face. Who is least optimistic about the threat? Who is most optimistic?

4 Match the verbs and nouns to make collocations used by the speakers.

1	address	a	climate change
2	combat	b	vaccines
3	assess	c	weapons
4	stockpile	d	a threat
5	decommission	e	measures
6	bring in	f	a risk

LEARN THIS!

whatever, whoever, wherever, etc.
We use *whatever, whoever,* etc. to say 'it doesn't matter what, who, etc. because the result will be the same'.
Whatever we do, global warming is here to stay.
Whoever thinks we can ignore the problem is seriously mistaken.
Whichever country you live in, you'll be affected by climate change.
We'll never prevent sea-levels rising, however hard we try.
In some clauses we can omit the verb *be*.
However difficult (it is), we have to act now.

▶▶▶ GRAMMAR BUILDER 10.1: *WHATEVER, WHOEVER,* ETC.: PAGE 129 ◀◀◀

5 🎧 3.13 Read the *Learn this!* box. Then rephrase these ideas as they were expressed by the speakers, using *whatever, whoever, wherever,* etc. Then listen and check your answers to exercises 4 and 5.

1 It doesn't matter which way you look at it, global warming is a very real threat.
2 Everybody should do their bit and make an effort, even if it's really small.
3 Any time the media hear about an outbreak of bird flu, they always blow it out of proportion.
4 It doesn't matter how much the government scientists try to reassure us, nobody really believes them.
5 Realistically I don't think there's any chance at all of that happening in the foreseeable future.
6 It doesn't matter what we do with our own nuclear weapons, we have to prevent other countries from developing their own.

6 SPEAKING Work in pairs or small groups. Decide what, in your opinion, is the gravest threat facing either your country, your continent or the world. Choose one of the threats below, or come up with your own. Present your ideas to the class.

alien invasion   disease and starvation
excessive consumption   global terrorism
global viruses   global warming   natural disasters
nuclear war   population explosion   the drugs trade

1 SPEAKING **Look at the list of films. Have you seen any of them? Do you remember the ending? Use the words and phrases below to help you describe the ending.**

a great last shot   an upbeat finale   bleak
could see it coming   dramatically coherent
end with a twist   feel-good ending   long, drawn-out
mystifying conclusion   unsatisfying

1 *Shrek*
2 *Spider-Man 3*
3 *Pirates of the Caribbean: At World's End*
4 *Enchanted*
5 *The Sixth Sense*
6 *2001: A Space Odyssey*
7 *Carrie*
8 *Before Sunset*
9 *Love Actually*

2 🎧 3.14 **Listen to a film critic talking about the endings of the films in exercise 1. What is his opinion of them? Write: + (good), – (bad) or ? (doesn't know yet) next to the film title.**

3 🎧 3.14 **Listen again. Are the sentences true (T) or false (F), or is the answer not stated (NS)?**

1 Unsatisfying endings to Hollywood films are often the result of fear.
2 Film studios often use special effects because they can't come up with a good ending.
3 The film *Titanic* confirms Hollywood's view of what audiences want.
4 The only good thing about *The Sixth Sense* was the ending.
5 Nobody has succeeded in solving the riddle at the end *2001: A Space Odyssey*.
6 It is a shame that almost every horror movie follows the example set by *Carrie*.
7 The critic liked *Before Sunset* because the audience is left not knowing if the lovers get back together at the end.
8 The critic hates all films in which the lovers kiss at the end.

4 **Explain these sentences from the listening exercise in your own words.**

1 By the final reel, inspiration is often replaced by rote.
2 Special effects have become the crutch of lazy dramatists.
3 (The closing shot of *The Third Man* is) a shot that has echoed through movie history.
4 When someone does come up with an original ending, everyone apes it.

5 **Look at the list of adjectives that could be used to describe the ending of a film. Decide whether each one has a positive, negative or neutral connotation. Use a dictionary to help you.**

ambiguous   baffling   clichéd   feel-good   hackneyed
heart-rending   incongruous   intriguing   nonsensical
overblown   sentimental   shocking   spectacular
subtle   touching   thought-provoking   unexpected
unsatisfying   vague

6 **Complete the sentences with a suitable adjective from exercise 5. Several answers may be possible. Compare your answers with a partner.**

1 The final scene is really _____ – I was crying so much I could hardly see the screen!
2 The ending is completely _____ – you tend to assume that the hero is going to win, not die!
3 There's a very _____ twist at the end of the film, which I couldn't get out of my mind for days.
4 Unfortunately, the film's finale is totally _____ , with loud, frantic music and huge special effects.
5 The film deals with tragic events, so I found the happy 'Hollywood' ending totally _____ .
6 Thankfully, the director avoided the obvious endings and opted for something far more _____ .

7 SPEAKING **Complete the sentences with your own ideas. Then compare sentences with your partner, justifying your opinions. Does he or she know the film and agree about the ending?**

1 The film with the most touching ending I've ever seen is …
2 The film with the most spectacular ending I've ever seen is …
3 The film with the most baffling ending I've ever seen is …
4 The film with the most unexpected ending I've ever seen is …

8 SPEAKING **Work in pairs. Discuss the questions.**

1 Why do you think American films tend to have more happy endings than European films?
2 Is there a kind of ending that you particularly like or dislike in films?
3 Which film that you've seen recently had the most effective ending, in your opinion? Why?
4 Which film had the worst ending, in your opinion? Why?

⟫⟫ **VOCABULARY BUILDER 10.2: ADVERBS OF DEGREE: WORKBOOK PAGE 112** ⟪⟪

1 SPEAKING Work in pairs. Look at the photo of a patient care bay and the title of the text. What do you think is inside the metal cylinders?

2 Read the first two paragraphs of the text and find the answer to question 1. Explain in your own words what 'cryonics' is.

Would you die of boredom if you lived for ever?

1 Lined up in neat rows, their stainless steel sides gleaming, the huge metal cylinders stored in a nondescript office building give little clue as to their gruesome contents. On each vessel there is a sticker bearing the name and logo of a company called Alcor. Only the
5 small print beneath hints at what its work might be. 'Life Extension Foundation Since 1972,' it reads, offering a website address for those visitors who join the twice-weekly tours of Alcor's headquarters in Scottsdale, Arizona, and who might want to find out more about its highly unusual services.

10 Alcor is in the business of cryonics. For a fee of approximately $200,000 – depending on your age and health – it will dispatch a trained response team when you die to drain your blood and deep freeze your body in one of those huge vacuum flasks of liquid nitrogen. The theory is that the firm's employees will thaw you
15 out and revive you at some point in the future when science has advanced enough to cure you of whatever it was you died of. And although the total number of people across the world who have signed up for freezing is still little more than 1,000, Alcor says its membership has increased rapidly recently.

20 This may be explained by the growing conviction among scientists that mankind is closer than ever to achieving what until now has seemed the stuff of our wildest dreams or worst nightmares, depending on your perspective. They think it may well be possible to extend human life way beyond its current span – enabling us to live
25 many hundreds of years and perhaps even for ever.

The problem with all attempts to find the secret to longer life over the centuries has been that the human body somehow seems programmed to die. Although we generally enjoy much longer lives than our forebears, we accept that even if we avoid accident or
30 illness, our bodies will wear out and we will eventually die of 'old age'. However, humans don't have a 'death gene' which triggers the ageing process; the process is the result of malfunctioning cell reproduction. From the immortalists' point of view, instead of being an inevitable part of human biological destiny, death is something
35 which can be avoided if we can only find cures for the illnesses which threaten our lives. Given that we are talking about diseases such as cancer, this is a very big 'if' – but medicine's success in eradicating polio in the twentieth century shows how quickly today's incurable illness can become tomorrow's medical success story.

40 Already, advances in technology are raising previously unimaginable possibilities in medical science. For example, scientists at the Wake Forest University Medical School in America are working to grow twenty different tissues and organs, including blood vessels and hearts, in the laboratory using human cells. This procedure could,
45 one day, help combat diseases such as cancer, by simply replacing the diseased organs with 'spares' supplied by the recipients' own cells, with therefore no risk of rejection. In this way, humans might become much like cars – with every part replaceable and immortality guaranteed.

50 Perhaps the real question is not whether eternal life will one day be possible, but whether the quest itself is misdirected. In his short story, *The Immortal*, the Argentinean writer Jorge Luis Borges writes of a man who goes in search of a river which cleanses people of death. The immortal people whom he finds there are inert and
55 apparently miserable. Since they will live for an infinite number of years, they reason that everything that can happen to them will do at some point. As a result they can hardly bring themselves to move. 'I remember one who I never saw stand up,' says Borges' narrator. 'A bird had nested on his breast.'

60 This raises the question: what incentive would there be to do anything if we knew that we had an endless number of days ahead of us in which to accomplish all our goals? Indeed, would our lives have any meaning at all? As humans, we only seem able to understand our feelings when they are balanced against opposing
65 emotions. When we feel happy, it is in contrast to being sad; when we feel at peace, it is a respite from being anxious. How then could we feel glad to be alive, to savour our existence day to day, if there

3 Read the rest of the text and choose the best summary. What is wrong with the other two summaries?

A
Many scientists now believe that death is not biologically inevitable and could be avoided if there were cures for all life-threatening diseases. However, living for ever would create its own problems. People might become apathetic and the planet would be overcrowded.

B
Scientists are developing new ways to combat serious diseases, like cancer, and may soon be able to replace parts of the body, just like a mechanic replaces parts of a car. However, living for ever would have several disadvantages as well as advantages.

C
If scientists found a way of allowing humans to live for ever, the result would not necessarily be positive. As Borges illustrated in a short story, immortality would lead to a complete lack of motivation. It would also cause the planet to become over-populated.

4 According to the text, are the sentences true (T) or false (F), or is the answer not stated (NS)? Justify your answers.
1 Scientists believe that immortality may soon be a possibility.
2 Past attempts to find the secret of immortality failed because nobody fully understood the ageing process.
3 Everyone accepts that finding cures for illnesses will never be enough to prevent people from dying.
4 Advances in science make it almost inevitable that we will soon find a cure for cancer.

was no possibility that it might one day be snatched from us? All our emotions would become immaterial.

And what about the limitations of our memories which often fail us, even in the short lives currently allotted to us? It is frustrating enough to acknowledge that we have forgotten things which happened ten, twenty or thirty years ago. Imagine then the frustration of hundreds of years' worth of memories slipping away from us as we drift through the centuries – constantly losing sight of where we have been and what we have done.

There would be other problems too. Unless we began to colonise space, the Earth would soon be burdened with too many people and some sort of limit on the number of children we can have might be necessary. Perhaps we might only be allowed to reproduce if we undertook to die ourselves at some future point.

Given all this, it seems that longer life might come at a price much heavier than many of us are willing to pay. For most of us alive today, immortality may never be an issue – but for those who are at the start of their lives, or yet to be born, it is a decision they may well have to confront, and much sooner than any of us might have imagined.

5 Scientists can take what they learned from tackling polio and use it to find cures for other diseases.
6 Scientists at Wake Forest University Medical School are developing man-made organs to replace human organs.
7 The Borges story implies that achieving immortality would deprive us of the joy of being alive.
8 Deciding whether or not to choose immortality may be difficult, but it will probably never arise for anyone alive today.

5 Match the adjectives in red in the text with these definitions. Underline the negative prefix or suffix in each adjective.
1 _____ impossible to imagine
2 _____ not working properly
3 _____ not relevant
4 _____ with no interesting features
5 _____ having no conclusion
6 _____ not aimed at the correct goal

6 Complete the sentences. Make the words in brackets negative by adding the correct prefix or suffix from exercise 5. Use a dictionary to help you if necessary.
1 Cells can become _____ as a result of replicating themselves time and time again. (formed)
2 Knowing that you will never die could make your daily life _____ . (meaning)
3 One day, serious diseases could be rendered _____ (existent) by science.
4 Perhaps people who opt for cryonics are _____ to accept the reality of death. (willing)
5 Reviving people who have been frozen may prove to be scientifically _____ (feasible).
6 If you were revived centuries into the future, you might be _____ to life in that era. (adjusted)
7 Anyone who lived to be 200 would be _____ of remembering their own childhood. (capable)
8 Perhaps the very ambition of achieving immortality is _____ . (conceived)
9 Maybe the secret of immortality will remain _____ (penetrable) for ever.

7 **SPEAKING** Discuss the questions with the class.
1 What emotions might somebody who had been frozen for 200 years and then revived experience, in your opinion?
2 What might be the best and worst aspects of being immortal?
3 Would you personally choose to be immortal, if you could? Give reasons.

1 Read the text and explain in your own words how the Darwin Awards get their name.

The Darwin Awards

The various individuals **upon whom the Darwin Awards are bestowed** each year are, by definition, unaware of the honour, and even if they were, it certainly is not an award **of which any right-minded person could be proud.** This is because the people **to whom it is awarded** have inadvertently caused their own death through an act of reckless stupidity. (The famous scientist **that the awards are named after** put forward the theory of natural selection, **according to which inferior members of a species are less likely to survive long enough to pass on their genes.**) Each year, the Darwin Awards website publishes a number of such stories **which are then voted for by the public in order to select a winner.** Although the purpose of the award is, strictly speaking, to celebrate these bizarre deaths and the people **whose stupidity brought them about,** the website also includes 'near misses', **which people can receive an 'honourable mention' for.**

2 Read the information below. Then, where possible, rewrite the clauses in bold in exercise 1 with the preposition in a different position. If it is not possible, explain why.

LEARN THIS!

Prepositions in relative clauses

1 When a relative clause includes a preposition, we can often choose whether to put it at the beginning or at the end. The latter is more common and more informal.
*That's the man **from whom we bought our car.***
*That's the man **(who/that) we bought our car from.***

2 However, when the preposition is part of a phrasal verb, it always stays with the verb.
*He adopted three children, **whom he looked after well.***

3 Multi-word prepositional phrases can go at the beginning or end, but we don't separate the words.
*We saw a café, **in front of which sat several diners.***
*We passed a café, **which several diners sat in front of.***

4 We can't put a preposition at the beginning when the relative pronoun is the subject of the following verb.
*I bought a house **which hadn't been lived in for years.***

5 The relative pronoun may form part of a noun phrase such as *some of which, many of whom, the first of which* or an adverbial phrase like *at which point, for which reason, in which case.*
*I have three brothers, **the youngest of whom is five.***
*He recorded more than fifty songs, **many of which became hits.***
*The host fell asleep, **at which point we left.***

>>> GRAMMAR BUILDER 10.2: RELATIVE CLAUSES: PAGE 130 <<<

3 Write the story of Larry Walters by joining each group of two or three sentences into one complex sentence. When there are two possible positions for a preposition, choose the more formal.

1 Among the 'near misses' is the story of Larry Walters. Most fans of the Darwin Awards are familiar with his exploits.
2 In 1982, he attempted a daring flight using only an ordinary garden chair. He'd attached 45 helium balloons to it.
3 The plan was to float up to a height of about ten metres. He'd be able to enjoy a fine view of the surrounding terrain from that height. The plan had been worked out carefully.
4 Unfortunately, he rocketed into the air, climbing more than 5,000 metres. He remained at that altitude for more than fourteen hours.
5 Air traffic control received bewildered messages from passenger planes. Their pilots had seen Larry.
6 It was a terrifying flight. Larry had no control over it.
7 Luckily, Larry had brought his pistol. He burst some of the balloons with it.
8 He gradually descended to the ground. At this point, he was arrested by the police.

4 Work in pairs. Decide which of the complex sentences you wrote in exercise 3 could be rewritten in a less formal style by putting the preposition in a different position.

5 Add the information a–e to the correct place in the text 1–5 using one or more relative clauses.

One evening, Fabio was chatting to some friends. ¹☐ Fabio was a 28-year-old Italian truck driver. ²☐ He took a gadget ³☐ out of his pocket to show his friends. It looked like an ordinary pen, but was in fact a pistol ⁴☐. Keen to demonstrate the gadget to his friends, Fabio held it to his head and pulled the trigger ⁵☐.

a he'd recently become the proud owner of it.
b a single .22 calibre bullet could be fired from it.
c he was having a quiet drink with them.
d at this point, the gun fired and Fabio died.
e his hobby was spy gadgets. He had some of them with him.

6 **SPEAKING** Work in pairs. Student A: Briefly retell the story of Larry Walters in your own words. Student B: Briefly retell the story of Fabio in your own words. Try to use complex sentences. Which person deserved a Darwin Award more, in your opinion? Why?

1 SPEAKING Work in pairs. Read the task below. Discuss and decide on three things you might talk about. For each thing, think of two reasons why the world would be better off without it.

> Give a presentation about one thing which, in your opinion, the world would be far better off without.

 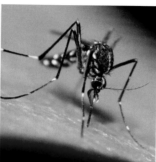

2 🎧 3.15 Listen to extracts from five students' presentations. For each speaker say what thing has been chosen and give one reason that is mentioned.

3 🎧 3.15 Listen again. Complete the phrases the students use when they forget a word. Then write the word that they have forgotten.

1 'The word has just _____ my mind.'   _____
2 'The correct word _____ me for the moment.' _____
3 'I can't quite remember what it's _____ .'   _____
4 'The word is on the tip of my _____ .'   _____
5 'I can't put my _____ on it at the moment.' _____

> **SPEAKING TIP**
>
> Try not to panic if you forget a word while you are speaking. Just use one of the phrases from exercise 4 to admit it, and then find a different way to describe it.

4 Read the *Speaking tip*. Then put the phrases below under the correct heading A–D.

It's quite similar to a...
It would come in handy for... *-ing*...
A (police officer) would probably have one of these.
It's a word that means...

A Specifying use
It's one of those things for *-ing* ...
It's something you might use for ...
It can be used to ...

B Describing appearance
It's one of those things that has (a handle)
It looks a bit like a ...
It's like a... only (smaller)

C Mentioning associations
You'd find it in/on/near ...
It's something you'd expect to see if you were ...
You might need one of these if you were ...

D Giving a definition
It's a type of ... that ...
It's another word for ...

5 SPEAKING Play a word game to practise coping when you forget a word. Use phrases from exercise 4.

- Everybody in the class writes three nouns on three pieces of paper.
- All the pieces of paper are put into one bag.
- One pair takes the bag and has one minute to score as many points as possible. Student A takes a piece of paper from the bag and describes the word to Student B without saying (or spelling) the word. Student B has to guess the word. The pair receives one point for each word correctly guessed. You are allowed to 'pass' if you cannot guess the word, but only twice.
- The pair with the most points wins. If there's a tie, the pair with the fewest passes wins.

6 Choose one idea from exercise 1 and expand your list of reasons why the world would be a better place without that thing.

> **SPEAKING TIP**
>
> Try not to repeat the same phrase too often in a presentation. Before you start, try to think of a few different ways of referring to the main idea. In addition, think about what adjectives you will need and note down a few synonyms.

7 Read the *Speaking tip*. Then study the box below. Can you add any phrases to it?

I'd	put a stop to put an end to put a halt to like to see the back of do away with	_____ because ...

8 SPEAKING Give your presentation to the class. Remember to carry on speaking if you forget a word, using phrases from exercises 3 and 4. You can also use the phrases below to help with fluency.

Correcting yourself
What I meant to say was ...
What I should have said was ...
Come to think of it, ...
Or rather, ...

Paraphrasing
Or to put it another way ...
In other words, ...
What I'm trying to say is ...
The point I'm trying to make is ...

1 Look at the photo. What are eBooks and how do they work? Read the first sentence of the essay in exercise 3 to check your ideas.

2 **SPEAKING** Work in pairs. Read the proposition below. Decide if you agree or disagree with it, and brainstorm ideas for and against the proposition.

> *eBooks will eventually make traditional books obsolete.*

3 Complete the essay with the phrases below, adding capital letters where necessary. (Some of the phrases can go in more than one gap, but there is only one set of correct answers.)

however	I accept that
I firmly believe that	in conclusion
it would be hard to deny that	moreover
of the opinion	the key question is

Over the past few years we have seen the introduction of eBooks: digital versions of paper books which can be downloaded from the Internet onto small hand-held devices called eBook readers. [1]_____ eBooks will inevitably have an enormous impact on the sales of traditional books, but [2]_____ , will they become so popular that they will eventually replace books?

Many of us already download more music than we buy from shops in CD form, and the same will soon be true of films. [3]_____ in the next decade or so it will be the turn of books. So what are the advantages of eBooks? A single eBook reader can hold hundreds of digital novels, which in their traditional form would occupy metres of shelving. [4]_____ , they are more environmentally friendly as they save paper and there are no transport costs.

[5]_____ eBook readers have two major drawbacks: they are currently very expensive and they rely on batteries. [6]_____ , they are sure to come down in price as they grow in popularity, as computers and mobile phones have done, and I'm convinced that battery-life will improve enough in the coming years for this no longer to be a serious concern.

[7]_____ , then, although eBooks are a relatively new phenomenon, I'm [8]_____ that it is only a matter of time before eBooks make traditional books uneconomical and therefore obsolete.

4 Work in pairs. Think of as many other phrases as you can that would fit in the gaps in the essay.

5 Did the writer mention any of the arguments which you discussed in exercise 2? Which of the writer's arguments do you find most persuasive? Give reasons.

6 In which paragraph does the writer:
1 state his/her own view for the first time?
2 reiterate his/her view?
3 give background information about eBooks?
4 focus on the proposition by turning it into a question?
5 give arguments supporting his/her view?
6 give counter-arguments?

7 **SPEAKING** Work in groups. Discuss the questions.
1 Do you think any of the things in the photos will become obsolete in the future? Give reasons.
2 Can you think of anything else which might become obsolete in the future? Justify your opinions.

1 **SPEAKING** Work in pairs. Discuss the proposition. Do you agree or disagree with it? Brainstorm ideas for and against.

Computers will soon make pens, paper and handwriting obsolete.

> **WRITING TIP**
>
> When you are expressing your own opinion in the essay, it is acceptable to use first person pronouns.
> *I am convinced that … I am of the opinion that …*
> However, to avoid over-use of personal pronouns, opinions, judgements and arguments can be introduced using impersonal language, for example passive structures (see page 98), or preparatory *it*.
> *It is interesting how much …*
> *It would appear that …*
> *It is undoubtedly true/highly likely that …*
> *It is usual/important/impossible, etc. for … to …*
> *It is right/wrong to suggest that …*

2 Read the *Writing tip*. Then rewrite the sentences using preparatory *it* and the words in brackets.

1 We have to remember that people have been using pen and paper for centuries. (bear in mind)
2 I'm pretty sure that paper won't become obsolete. (almost certainly true)
3 Some people say that it's a waste of time teaching children to write neatly. (be argued)
4 I simply cannot believe that paper will become obsolete. (inconceivable)
5 What surprises me is how few people can write neatly. (surprising)
6 I think children really should be taught to touch-type at school. (essential for children)
7 People who say that paper and pen will become obsolete are wrong. (wrong to suggest)

3 🎧 3.16 Listen to two people giving their opinions on the proposition in exercise 1. Which opinions do you agree with? Which do you disagree with? Give reasons.

4 Rephrase these extracts from the listening so that they would be stylistically appropriate for an essay. Use the words below to help you. Sometimes a passive construction is appropriate.

admittedly   considerably   continue to   currently
elderly   in a minority   increasingly   moreover the fact is

1 I mean, we now send loads more emails than traditional letters.
2 OK, so some old people will stick with paper and pen, but there won't be many of them.
3 Also, more and more often we're doing our schoolwork on computers.

although   granted   highly improbable   inconceivable
my own view   not too distant future

4 Sure, I admit that pretty soon they'll develop a computer that you can carry in a pocket.
5 People sometimes even say that handwriting will become obsolete, but I really don't reckon it's at all likely.
6 You simply cannot imagine they won't teach handwriting in schools in the future.

5 Plan an opinion essay about the proposition in exercise 1. Make notes under the headings using ideas from exercises 1 and 3.

Paragraph 1   Introduction
Paragraph 2   Points in support of your opinion
Paragraph 3   Points in support of the opposite opinion
Paragraph 4   Conclusion

6 Write the introduction and paragraphs 2 and 3 of your essay following your plan. Write no more than 210 words. Remember to use some impersonal language.

> **WRITING TIP**
>
> In an essay of 200–250 words, your conclusion shouldn't be more that 40–50 words long. A good strategy is to acknowledge the strength of the opposing argument and then to restate your own opinion. Do not introduce new arguments in the conclusion.

7 Read the *Writing tip*. Then write the conclusion to your essay. Use the phrases below to help you.

Acknowledging the opposing view and restating your opinion
While it's true to say that… , I really do think…
Even though some people maintain that… , I nevertheless believe that…
There's some truth in the view that,… Nevertheless, it doesn't alter my view that…

8 Work in pairs. Swap essays and check your partner's work using the list below.

> **CHECK YOUR WORK**
>
> **Has your partner:**
> ☐ followed the essay plan correctly?
> ☐ written the correct number of words?
> ☐ used expressions from the *Writing tip* and exercise 7?
> ☐ checked the spelling and grammar?

Vocabulary

1 Complete the sentences with the correct form of the verbs below. The answers may be active or passive.

breathe confide drop glean hear keep

1 The manager _____ a bombshell in the board meeting when he handed in his resignation.
2 Tell me what you know – I promise I _____ a word.
3 Anna _____ all the information she could about the job from the HR manager, who happens to be her cousin.
4 The identity of the jury members _____ under wraps in case they are blackmailed.
5 I told my best friend about my date with Dylan and now everyone knows. I _____ never _____ in her again!
6 _____ you _____ the latest? Martha's split up with Paul and she's going out with Andy!

Mark: ____ /6

2 Complete the sentences with the correct form of the words below.

accuse catastrophe censor nation person speak

1 Democratic countries believe in _____.
2 In many countries, there is state _____ of the press.
3 It's essential to be able to express your _____ opinion when discussing politics.
4 Opponents to totalitarian regimes are often imprisoned because of false _____.
5 _____ security is under threat from terrorist groups.
6 The results will be _____ if the problem is ignored.

Mark: ____ /6

3 Match 1–8 with a–h to make common collocations.

1	finalise	a	confidential
2	strictest	b	a contract
3	complete	c	a meeting
4	highly	d	arrangements
5	wind up	e	a Master's degree
6	cease	f	a word
7	terminate	g	industrial action
8	breathe	h	confidence

Mark: ____ /8

Grammar

4 Complete the sentences with the correct passive form of the verbs below.

decide evacuate lie rebuild record repair

1 Several towns _____ last night due to flood warnings.
2 The staff have been assured that the pay increase _____ during the next board meeting.
3 Pete couldn't watch the match because his TV _____.
4 You can't enter the studio right now because tonight's news programme _____ .
5 It took time to realise he _____ to by his wife.

Mark: ____ /5

5 Rewrite the sentences using the correct causative form of the verbs in brackets.

1 Someone mows my aunt's lawn once a fortnight. (have)
2 They're coming to change our windows next week. (have)
3 They'll refurbish the office when they can afford it. (get)
4 No one had serviced my father's car in years. (have)
5 Someone stole my boyfriend's wallet yesterday. (get)

Mark: ____ /5

6 Rewrite the sentences using the words below.

however whatever whenever ~~wherever~~ whichever whoever

No matter where you end up, please write to me.
Wherever you end up, please write to me.

1 The person who gave you that has impeccable taste.
2 John will never become an airline pilot, no matter how hard he tries.
3 Every time I'm in the UK I buy a load of tea bags.
4 She'll look stunning, no matter which dress she wears.
5 It doesn't matter what you do, but don't panic.

Mark: ____ /5

7 Join the two sentences using formal relative clauses.

A fight started in the club. At that point we went home.
A fight started in the club, at which point we went home.

1 She started to dust the desk. On top of it lay piles of papers.
2 He has won eleven medals so far. Most of them are gold.
3 The president will appoint a number of new ministers in the new session. Many of them are women.
4 That woman's an actress. My friend was mistaken for her.
5 I addressed my complaint to an employee. He was blatantly rude.

Mark: ____ /5

Total: ____ /40

Reading

1 Look quickly through the two excerpts from two emails, ignoring the gaps. Decide:

  a who each email is from.

  b what the relevance of the photo is.

2 Match sentences A–G with gaps 1–6 in the emails. There is one sentence that you do not need.

  A That would be a shame, because I've made some good friends here, including a really nice guy from Latvia called Edgars.

  B That's how I managed to earn enough money for the flat deposit.

  C This was a bit of a disaster, as I'd already found a flat and needed to pay my rent.

  D Ironically, she works for InterPost, the company who let me down over that job offer.

  E It's in a great location too, only a couple minutes from a tube station.

  F As it happens, my flatmate's sister, Rita, works in IT and would be an ideal business partner.

  G Who knows when another one might come along?

Everything is going well here. I'm sharing a flat with two other women, one from Lithuania and the other from Poland. The flat isn't huge, but it's big enough and in relatively good condition, with modern furniture and appliances. ¹____ (Everybody travels by tube here, it's the only way to avoid the traffic.) Work is going fine. In fact, I've recently been offered a promotion, which would mean more money as well as more responsibility. The downside is that I'd have to relocate to Edinburgh because that's where the company's head office is. ²____ We've really hit it off, and between you and me, I think he quite fancies me. And of course, my brother is here too. But I suppose I should do what's best for my career and accept the opportunity. ³____ Anyway, I haven't made a final decision yet.

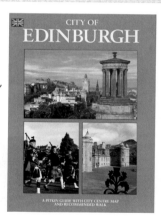

I've been in London for six months now. Can you believe that? The time has really flown by! I'm so sorry I haven't been in touch earlier, but I never seem to have time.

I haven't had a particularly easy time since getting here, for one reason or another. Having been offered a job at interview, I was then told that I didn't have the job after all. ⁴____ I decided to set up in business as a consultant, and it's really taken off. In fact, I'm so busy that I'm looking for somebody to work with me – either an employee or a partner. ⁵____ Not only is she really well qualified, but we also get on well together. However, she's currently in full-time employment, so I'd have to lure her away from her job. ⁶____ She hasn't been there long, so I doubt she'd want to leave.

Listening

3 🎧 3.17 Listen. Which three of the following four dialogues do you hear, and in what order?

  a Edgars and Tomas

  b Tomas and Rita

  c Rita, Edgars and Tomas

  d Edgars and Rita

4 🎧 3.17 Listen again, focusing on the speakers' intonation. Say how each speaker sounds when they say the words below. Then say what this implies about what they are thinking or feeling.

  1 Rita: 'Oh, I see. Professional.'

  2 Edgars: 'You don't have to say anything now.'

  3 Rita: 'I've just accepted a promotion.'

  4 Edgars: 'So you're moving to Edinburgh.'

  5 Tomas: 'No, she hasn't said anything to me.'

  6 Tomas: 'Nobody tells me anything.'

  7 Rita: 'His face went red and he couldn't speak.'

Speaking

5 Work in pairs. Role-play one of the following dialogues:

  • Edgars persuading Rita not to go to Edinburgh.

  • Rita telling her boss that she's leaving the company.

Writing

6 Read the statement below. Decide whether you agree or disagree with it. Make notes for and against. Use the words and phrases in the box to help you.

It is impossible to maintain a close friendship with somebody who lives a long way away.

body language   chat rooms   email   face to face hang out   physical contact   social networking sites

7 Write an essay of 200–250 words using your notes from exercise 6.

▶▶▶ **CHECK YOUR PROGRESS: PAGE 4** ◀◀◀

1 **Get ready to READ** Read the text in the Reading exam task, ignoring the gaps. In what order will the Sun turn into these types of star?

a a black dwarf **b** a red giant **c** a white dwarf

2 Do the Reading exam task.

READING exam task

Read the text carefully and decide which sentence (A–F) best fits each gap (1–5). There is one sentence that you do not need.

The end of the world

The Sun is now approximately half-way through its life span. It is in a 'dynamic equilibrium' – there is gravity on one hand and the fusion process that 'fuels' the Sun on the other hand. [1] Astronomers still don't know all the exact details but they know that the Sun will start to swell up and turn into a red giant with a diameter about 100 times greater than its current size. [2] The Earth will be scorched at this point, leaving the planet unsuitable for life. Pluto, in fact, would be the only place suitable for any life in the solar system. At the very end of its life cycle, the Sun is likely to blow off its outermost layers. It will then shrink to the size of the Earth, surrounded by a glowing bubble of gas called 'planetary nebulae'. [3] Astronomers have observed many Sun-like stars in their final stages, before becoming white dwarfs. The images of planetary nebulae are spectacular and each looks like no other. The expelled gas has intriguing symmetrical patterns as well as more chaotic structures.

A white dwarf derived from a star as massive as the Sun will be roughly the same size as the Earth. [4] The gravity on the surface will be over 100,000 times what we experience on Earth! Once the white dwarf has reached its minimum size, it will have a temperature of over 100,000 Kelvin and shine through residual heat. [5] Because the Universe is only 13.7 billion years old, there are no black dwarfs yet.

One thing is for sure: if the human race hasn't migrated to another solar system within the next five billion years, it is sure to become extinct.

A The star will gradually cool and eventually, after hundreds of billions of years of radiating, it will no longer be visible, becoming a black dwarf.

B The gases will eventually disperse in the course of several thousand years leaving behind a white dwarf.

C It will be so dense that a teaspoon of white dwarf material will weigh several tonnes.

D It will continue to burn in this stable condition for a further five billion years, when it will start to change.

E This means that the radiation, which initially will be very high, will lessen with time.

F It will be so big that it will engulf Mercury, while Venus will probably orbit just outside the Sun's surface.

3 Read the information about synonyms of *old* and complete the sentences with the adjectives in the correct form. Justify your choice of adjective.

SYNONYMS

old

elderly • aged • long-lived • mature

These words all describe sb who has lived for a long time or that usually lives for a long time.

old having lived for a long time; no longer young: *She's getting old—she's 75 next year.*

elderly (*rather formal*) used as a polite word for 'old': *She is very busy caring for two elderly relatives.*

aged (*formal*) very old: *Having aged relatives to stay in your house can be quite stressful.*

long-lived having a long life; lasting for a long time: *Everyone in my family is exceptionally long-lived.*

mature used as a polite or humorous way of saying that sb is no longer young: *clothes for the mature woman*

1 The _____ person in the world is 117.
2 A 400-year-old clam may be the _____ animal known.
3 There are over eleven million _____ people in the United Kingdom, according to the most recent census.
4 This particular dating agency is for men and women of _____ years.
5 Women have traditionally borne the brunt of supporting _____ relatives.

4 Do the Speaking exam task.

SPEAKING exam task

Compare and contrast the two photographs. Answer the questions.

1 In your opinion, at what age do people become 'old'?
2 What effect will increasing life expectancy have on society?
3 What, if anything, can we learn from talking to elderly people? Give examples.

Grammar Builder and Reference

1.1 Talking about habitual actions

Present simple

We use the present simple with an adverb of frequency to talk about repeated actions, habits and routines.
She **often goes** to work by bicycle.

Present/Past continuous

We use the present/past continuous with the adverbs *always*, *constantly*, *continually* and *forever* to talk about annoying repeated behaviour.
She's **always complaining** about her job.
They **were forever shouting** at each other.

Will / would

Will and *would* can be used to talk about habitual actions and behaviour. When they are stressed in spoken English, it suggests criticism. *Would* refers to the past.
She'll **often forget** to buy milk.
He **would play** records so loud we couldn't have a conversation.

Used to

We use *used to* + infinitive to describe past states **or** habits that someone did in the past but does not do now.
We **used to live** in New York.

Would

Would can also be used to talk about past habits, but it can't be used to talk about past states. We use *used to* to do that.
We **would go** to stay with our grandparents every summer.

1 Choose the correct words to complete the sentences. One, two or three answers may be correct.

1 Before my brother had children he _____ a motorbike.
   a used to have   b would have   c had

2 My sister often gets annoyed with her husband – he
   _____ .
   a would wind the children up
   b 's always winding the children up
   c will wind the children up

3 When I was little my mother _____ nursery rhymes to me at bedtime.
   a used to sing   b would sing   c sang

4 I moved out of Isaac and Maisie's house – they _____
   when I was around.
   a were constantly arguing
   b would argue
   c will argue

5 Before she got married she _____ in Germany for two years.
   a used to live   b lived   c would live

6 If it's not raining, I _____ to work.
   a usually walk   b used to walk   c 'll walk

2 Rewrite the sentences using the word in brackets.

1 We used to spend hours playing hide-and-seek when we were kids. ('d)
   We'd spend hours playing hide-and-seek when we were kids.

2 My mother will cook something special whenever we go round. (usually)

3 Gina will take my CDs without asking. (constantly)

4 We had no pets when we were little. (use)

5 Ben would always leave his dirty dishes all over the place when he lived with us. (leaving)

6 Every summer we made sandcastles on the beach. (used)

1.2 Phrasal verbs

Phrasal verbs combine verbs with adverbs or prepositions (or sometimes both) to create a new meaning. Phrasal verbs can be divided into four main types:

Two-part verbs with no object.
My car **broke down** on the motorway last night.

Two-part verbs whose object can come between or after the two parts. However, when the object is a pronoun, it must come between the two parts.
He **turned down** the job offer he received.
He received a job offer but he **turned** it **down**.

Two-part verbs whose object cannot come between the parts.
We have to **allow for** different opinions from staff members.

Three-part verbs whose object cannot come between the parts.
How do you **put up with** his comments?

1 Complete the sentences with the correct form of the phrasal verbs below. Where possible use an object pronoun.

cheer sb up   come across sth   get away with sth
go for sb   pass out   put up with sth   set off   tear sth up

1 My old school reports were in a box – I came across them in the attic yesterday.

2 Carol's children are very badly behaved – I don't know how she _____ .

3 We're going to have an early night as we _____ at 6 a.m. tomorrow.

4 Matt's girlfriend has left him, so his friends are trying to _____ .

5 Nobody could prove that Bill had stolen the car and so he _____ .

6 It's too hot and I'm feeling dizzy. I think I _____ .

7 The letter made Karl furious, so he _____ and put it in the bin.

8 Emma's dog bit her last night – it _____ as she was opening the door.

Grammar Builder and Reference

2 Complete the sentences with the phrasal verbs below. Use an object pronoun where necessary.

do away with sth   drop off   fall out with sb   get away
go through sth   let sb down   run into sb   turn sb down

1 'Did you watch the film all the way through?'
  'No, I dropped off in the middle.'
2 'Did you see Becky yesterday?'
  'Yes, I _____ in the supermarket.'
3 'Does your boyfriend think he'll get the job? '
  'No, he thinks they _____ .'
4 'Do you know where you went wrong in the exam?'
  'Yes, my tutor _____ with me.'
5 'Does your school still have a uniform?'
  'No, they _____ .'
6 'Did they catch the thief?'
  'No, he _____ .'
7 'Do you still see your old neighbours?'
  'No, I _____ .'
8 'Does Harry always turn up for football practice?'
  'No, he often _____ .'

1.3 Phrasal verbs: passive and infinitive forms

Some phrasal verbs that have an object can be used in the passive. As in all passive structures, the subject comes before the verb. This means the two or thee parts of the phrasal verb always stay together. This also applies to infinitive structures:
Please **switch** your computer off when you leave the office.
Please make sure your computer is **switched off** when you leave the office.
It's very difficult to **get through to** him. He never listens.

1 Rewrite the second sentence with a suitable passive form of the phrasal verb in brackets.

1 A gang attacked Tom on his way home. (beat up)
  Tom was beaten up on his way home.
2 They've cancelled the match. (call off)
  The match _____ .
3 Her grandparents took care of her. (bring up)
  She _____ by her grandparents.
4 A local builder is doing the work. (carry out)
  The work _____ by a local builder.
5 500 workers will lose their jobs. (lay off)
  500 workers _____ .
6 The police stopped the riot. (break up)
  The riot _____ by the police.
7 An accident is delaying the traffic. (hold up)
  The traffic _____ by an accident.
8 His boss has refused his transfer request. (turn down)
  His request _____ .

2 Complete the sentences with the infinitive form of the phrasal verbs below and an object pronoun.

do sth up   drop sb off   get round to doing sth
get through to sb   give sth up   go with sth   put sb up

1 Jim was going past the station so I asked him to drop me off outside.
2 If they want to rent out the cottage, they'll have _____ first.
3 I haven't washed the car – I hope _____ soon.
4 We've thoroughly enjoyed our stay. It was so kind of you _____ .
5 Jane's phone is always engaged – it's impossible _____ .
6 Once you start smoking, it's very hard _____ .
7 Keira bought a dress but couldn't find shoes _____ .

2.1 *as* and *like*

Like is a preposition and it is used with a noun or a pronoun to describe similarities.
My brother's just **like** my dad.

Unlike is also a preposition and it is used with a noun or a pronoun to describe differences.
Unlike Jack, I don't enjoy watching reality shows.

As is a conjunction and it is used with a subject and a verb to describe similarities.
He's a good player, **as** his father was when he was younger.

However, in informal speech *like* is also often used as a conjunction.
She doesn't dress **like** you do. She hasn't got your style.

In written English, when *as* is followed by an auxiliary or modal verb the word order of questions is often used.
He went, **as** did his brothers, to a boarding school.

As is used to talk about the job a person has. In this case it operates in the same way as a preposition.
As your doctor, I recommend you give up smoking.

If we replace *as* with *like* in this sentence it changes the meaning. *As* means 'I am your doctor' and *like* means 'I have the same opinion as your doctor'.
Like your doctor, I recommend you give up smoking.

In very informal speech *like* can be used to introduce reported speech.
My dad was **like**, 'What time do you call this?'

Notice how the function of *like* can change depending on whether it comes before or after a negative clause.
Like my sister, I'm not keen on comedies.
(She doesn't like them and neither do I.)
I'm not keen on comedies, **like** my sister.
(My sister likes them but I don't.)

Grammar Builder and Reference

1 Choose the correct words to complete the sentences. (Sometimes both are correct.)

1 I prefer Italian food, ___ pizza and pasta.
   a as   **b** like

2 The weather was superb, ___ was the hotel.
   a as   **b** like

3 ___ you, I don't enjoy staying in all day. You never move from the sofa!
   a Like   **b** Unlike

4 My boyfriend's ___ yours in some respects.
   a as   **b** like

5 I don't work out every day, ___ you do.
   a as   **b** like

6 '___ your doctor, I recommend you to try and lose weight,' said Dr White.
   a As   **b** Like

7 My sister's ___ , 'Where's my jacket?'
   a as   **b** like

8 '___ your doctor, I think you should lose some weight,' his mum said.
   a As   **b** Like

2 Complete the sentences with *as*, *like* or *unlike*. Sometimes two answers may be possible.

1 Owen enjoys playing team sports, _____ basketball and volleyball.

2 '_____ the rest of the family, I'm fed up with your moods,' her mum said.

3 _____ my brother, I'm not very good at maths. He always gets top marks!

4 Your dad doesn't go away on business _____ mine does.

5 You've got a car _____ mine, haven't you?

6 We got lost on the way, _____ did most of the guests.

7 '_____ your father I think you should seriously consider your future,' said Connor's dad.

8 My boyfriend's _____ , 'Where have you been?'

2.2 Narrative tenses

We use past tenses to narrate past events.
We use the past simple to refer to short actions and events that are soon finished, longer actions and events and to repeated actions.
He **walked** down the street and bought a newspaper.
We **lived** in Manchester for 20 years.
I **went** to the gym every week last year.

We use the past continuous to set the scene of a situation in the past. It is often used to describe a background event in conjunction with the past simple, which describes an event or action that interrupted it.
The sun **was shining** and the birds were singing.
They **were cleaning** the car when it started to rain.

We use the past perfect to talk about an event that happened before another event in the past.
I started the exercise and realised I **had done** it before.

We use the past perfect continuous to talk about longer events that were happening before another event in the past.
I'd been waiting for an hour before she arrived.

We use *used to* + infinitive to describe past situations or habits that are different now and *would* + infinitive is used to describe past habits that are different now.
She **used to go out** with Tom.
We **would go** to the cinema every Saturday morning.

We use the future in the past to talk about things that were in the future when we were talking about them. We express these ideas by using structures similar to the ones we normally use to talk about the future but changing the verb forms.
I thought you **were going** away for the weekend.
He said he **would see** me next week.

1 Correct the mistake with narrative tenses in each sentence.

1 Although the storm had passed, the roads were still treacherous because it <u>had snowed</u> all night.
   had been snowing

2 He climbed the stairs stealthily and was entering the bedroom.

3 She crossed a field when she spotted a bull grazing by the gate.

4 They couldn't take the flight because they had been forgetting their passports.

5 As a child, I was sitting in the kitchen for hours watching my mother cook.

6 They used to be married in the spring, but war broke out and he was called up.

7 My parents would live in a cottage in the country before they moved to the city centre.

8 Our arms were aching as we had shifted boxes all day. We weren't looking forward to continuing the next day.

2 Complete the mini dialogues with the correct form of the verbs in brackets.

1 'Why didn't she answer the phone?'
   'Because she was lying in the bath.' (lie)

2 'Why are you late?'
   'Because I _____ my train.' (miss)

3 'Have you got any pets?'
   'Not now, but I _____ a dog.' (have)

4 'Why were they so lethargic?'
   'Because they _____ TV all day.' (watch)

5 'Do you remember your grandparents well?'
   'Yes, we _____ every summer with them as kids.' (spend)

6 'Why was Annabel crying?'
   'Because her boyfriend _____.' (walk out)

7 'Why didn't you book a hotel?'
   'Because we had decided we _____ camping.' (go)

8 'When did you have your bag snatched?'
   'While I _____ at the traffic lights.' (wait)

2.3 Simple and continuous forms

We use simple forms to talk about habits, repeated actions and states.

We **play** tennis every week.
I **was** in the army.
We**'ve** always **lived** here.

We use continuous forms to talk about something happening at a particular moment.

He **was** still **sleeping** at 10a.m.
This time tomorrow I**'ll be lying** on a beach.
He**'s working** at the moment.

We use simple forms to talk about permanent situations.

He **worked** for the company all his life.

We use continuous forms to talk about temporary situations.

I**'d been staying** with Jack until the house was finished.

We use simple forms to talk about finished situations.

We **cleaned** the office and then we **went** home.

We use continuous forms to talk about unfinished situations.

I**'ve been reading** this book for two months.

There are two types of verbs, dynamic and state. Dynamic verbs are verbs that describe actions. They can be used in simple and continuous forms.

She **eats** lunch at home every day.
I **was eating** lunch at home when I **heard** the news on the radio.

We don't usually use state verbs in continuous tenses.

They **want** to visit the cathedral.

Some common state verbs are: *believe, belong, enjoy, forget, hate, like, love, need, prefer, remember, understand, want.*

1 Choose the correct words.

1 They **'d only known / 'd only been knowing** each other for three weeks when they got married.
2 The teacher refused to repeat the explanation because some students **hadn't listened / hadn't been listening**.
3 I adored my new shoes – they were just what I **'d looked for / 'd been looking for**.
4 We voted for the opposition party because we **thought / were thinking** they might change our foreign policy.
5 Ruby **didn't enjoy / wasn't enjoying** the party, so she decided to leave early.
6 The fish **smelt / was smelling off**, so we threw it away.
7 The ring **had belonged / had been belonging** to my grandmother before it was handed down to my mother.

2 Complete the two sentences with a simple and a continuous form of the verb given.

1 RUN
   a He was out of breath because he 'd been running.
   b He was out of breath because he 'd run all the way.

2 EAT
   a Ruth got food poisoning because she _____ something strange.
   b Daisy had greasy fingers because she _____ fish and chips.

3 JOG
   a I _____ in the park when I twisted my ankle.
   b I didn't have much time so I _____ once round the park.

4 STUDY
   a George passed his exams because he _____ every night.
   b Charlie had a headache because he _____ .

2.4 Speculating

We use the following structures to speculate about people and things:

look (and *seem, sound, feel,* etc.) *like* with a noun.
She **looks like** a student.
It **feels like** silk.

look (*seem, sound, feel,* etc.) with an adjective.
They **look upset**.
She **seems angry**.

wonder + if followed by a subject and verb.
I **wonder if** they have had problems.

modal verbs to talk about possibility, probability and certainty in the present and the past.
He **must** be at home now.
They **might** have gone out last night.

1 Rewrite the example sentence using the words in brackets.

1 I wonder if he's a sailor.
   a He looks like a sailor. (look)
   b He might have been a sailor. (might)

2 She might be ill.
   a _____ . (wonder)
   b _____ . (look)

3 It looks like they're going to a football match.
   a _____ . (wonder)
   b _____ . (must)

4 I wonder if he's passed his exams.
   a _____ . (not look)
   b _____ . (can't)

2 Complete the sentences with one word.

1 The lights are on. She must be home.
2 You _____ awful! What's wrong?
3 I _____ what time it is.
4 Her boyfriend didn't stop. He _____ have seen her.
5 Rudi looks _____ he didn't sleep last night.
6 Sara's not at school today. I suppose she _____ be ill.
7 What's that noise? It _____ like a fire alarm.
8 My mother didn't call me on my birthday. She _____ have forgotten.

3.1 Present perfect simple and continuous

We use the present perfect:
- **continuous** for something which has been happening repeatedly in the very recent past.
- **simple** when something has happened on several occasions over a period of time and may happen again.
- **continuous** with *for* or *since* to say how long an action has been in progress.
- **simple** with *for* or *since* only if the verb is one which is not commonly used in continuous tenses.
- **simple** for a recent action that is now complete.
- **continuous** for a recent action that is ongoing.

1 Complete the two sentences in each pair with the present perfect simple and the present perfect continuous form of the verbs given. Use contractions where possible.

1 SWIM
   a William _____ 50 lengths today.
   b We _____ in a mountain stream and now we're frozen.

2 SEE
   a I _____ all of Woody Allen's films.
   b Lily _____ Adam for over two years now.

3 STAY
   a Daisy _____ in rented accommodation since she arrived in London.
   b We _____ at this guesthouse a few times before.

4 DISAPPEAR
   a My car isn't where I parked it. It _____ !
   b Bags _____ from the changing rooms for several weeks now.

5 STOP
   a Now you _____ arguing perhaps you can tell me what happened.
   b The police _____ pedestrians to ask them about the burglary.

2 Complete the formal letter with the present perfect simple or continuous form of the verbs in brackets.

Dear Albert,

I am writing to complain about your proposed changes to our agreement regarding business flights. Employees from TNN [1]_____ (fly) with BusyAir for over twenty years now, and our relationship until now [2]_____ (be) more than cordial. Each year we [3]_____ (negotiate) a reasonable increase in fares and every month our accounts department [4]_____ (deal) promptly with your invoice.

I fail to understand why on this occasion you [5]_____ (choose) to communicate your proposal in this impersonal manner.

Regarding the price increase itself, I can only hope you [6]_____ (make) a mistake. This year we [7]_____ (pay) on average nearly 80 per cent of the full business rate and you are now proposing that we pay the full fare.

Since receiving your fax, my colleagues and I [8]_____ (discuss) our relationship with BusyAir and we wish to express our indignation at the lack of respect we have suffered at your hands.

Yours sincerely,

Benjamin Murray

3.2 Verb patterns (1)

Some verbs are followed by an infinitive.
We **wanted to leave** early but we couldn't.

Some verbs are followed by + object + infinitive.
I won't **allow the children to stay up**.

Some verbs are followed by + object + base form.
Will they **let us stay** and see the end?

Some verbs are followed by + (object) + -*ing* form.
We **enjoy coming** to see you.

Some verbs are followed by + object + past participle.
She **had her nails polished** at the hairdressers.

Verbs which are only followed by an infinitive: *afford, agree, appear, decide, expect, fail, happen, hope, manage, mean, pretend, promise, refuse, seem, want*.

Verbs which are only followed by an -*ing* form: *admit, appreciate, avoid, can't stand, consider, contemplate, delay, deny, dislike, enjoy, escape, face, feel like, finish, forgive, mention, miss, practise, put off, resent, risk, suggest, understand*.

Some verbs are followed by both an infinitive or an -*ing* with little or no change in their meaning: *begin, like, love, hate, prefer, start*.

Grammar Builder and Reference

Some verbs are followed by both an infinitive or an -ing with a change in their meaning: *forget, go on, try, regret, remember, stop.*

We can also use infinitives and -ing forms directly after some nouns.
I need a **key to open** the door.
It's not **worth worrying** about.

1 **Complete the sentences with the correct form of the verbs in brackets.**

1 Most people tend to take their summer holiday in August. (take)
2 Angie volunteered _____ the money for Gina's leaving present. (collect)
3 Because of the crisis they had difficulty _____ their house. (sell)
4 The inheritance enabled him _____ a yacht. (purchase)
5 Ryan's parents wouldn't let him _____ a tattoo. (get)
6 It's not worth _____ the doctor – he'll only give me some pills. (consult)
7 Peter stopped in a car park _____ a phone call. (make)
8 Last year we spent a month _____ around Europe. (travel)
9 I'm so glad I remembered _____ my mum's birthday card yesterday. (post)

3.3 Verb patterns (2)

When a verb is followed by another verb, the infinitive or -ing form can include the passive, perfect and continuous forms.

1 **Complete the sentence with the correct alternative.**

1 After her ordeal, she described _____ in the jungle.
   a to be held   b being held
2 If he starts another fight at school, he risks _____ .
   a to be expelled   b being expelled
3 She was unlucky that she happened _____ in the wrong place.
   a to be standing   b being standing
4 They admitted _____ the car.
   a to have stolen   b having stolen
5 The actress agreed _____ on TV.
   a to be interviewed   b being interviewed
6 We appear _____ an agreement.
   a to have reached   b having reached
7 The politician denied _____ .
   a to have been mistaken   b having been mistaken
8 The painting seems _____ by a professional.
   a to have been stolen   b having been stolen

2 **Complete the sentences with *to be*, *being*, *to have* or *having*.**

1 My sister avoids being seen with her glasses on.
2 I don't recollect _____ been bullied at school.
3 She resents _____ treated like an idiot when she takes her car to the garage.
4 The accident appears _____ been caused by leaves on the track.
5 I refuse _____ spoken to like that.

4.1 Comparative and superlative forms

Some comparatives can be used with *the* to say that two changes happen at the same time or are linked.
The bigger the pizza, **the happier** I am.
The richer you are, **the more successful** you are.

We can use two comparatives to express the idea of continuing change.
What he says is **less and less interesting**.
He's getting **taller and taller!**

We use the following words to modify comparatives: *very much, a lot, lots, any, rather, a little, a bit.*
Is he **any happier** than when I last saw him?
That restaurant was **very much nicer** than the other one we went to.

1 **Complete the sentences with a comparative or superlative form of the adjectives in brackets. Be careful of negatives!**

1 The _____ (long) you wait for something, the more you appreciate it.
2 Good health is one of _____ (important) things in life.
3 The _____ (fast) he speaks, the _____ (intelligible) he becomes.
4 Most mothers are at their _____ (low) when their children leave home.
5 The more time he spends at home, the _____ (good).
6 Life is _____ (hard) in Europe as it is in Africa.

2 **Complete the sentences with the words below.**

awful bit deal far mile quite slightly very

1 Mallorca isn't _____ as popular as Ibiza with young people.
2 I'd like to introduce you to my _____ best friend, Katie.
3 My mother spent a good _____ more time with us as kids than my father did.
4 My younger brother is a little _____ taller than me.
5 Daniel Craig is _____ better as James Bond than Sean Connery.
6 In my opinion, Cristiano Ronaldo is _____ and away the most talented footballer in the world.
7 JK Rowling is an _____ lot richer than Philip Pullman.
8 Nico is the most intelligent student in our class by a _____ .

Grammar Builder and Reference

4.2 Reduced relative clauses

We can sometimes form reduced relative clauses from identifying relative clauses. In a reduced relative clause we drop the relative pronoun and auxiliary verb that helps form the verb tense.

A lot of the people **(who were) sitting at the table** were my relatives.
The buildings **(which were) constructed in the seventies** are ugly.

Reduced relative clauses cannot be used if the relative pronoun is not the object of the verb in the relative clause.
A lot of the people **who I talked to at the table** were my relatives.

1 Join the two sentences using a reduced relative clause.

1 Some information was given in the leaflet. It was wrong.
Some information given in the leaflet was wrong.
2 A player was injured in the match. He was rushed to hospital.
3 Some boys are hanging around outside the shopping centre. They live on my estate.
4 A man was arrested last night. He is now in police custody.
5 Some hostages are being held by the hijackers. They are all members of the crew.
6 Several employees were dismissed for bad conduct. They have all been reinstated.
7 A lifeguard is jumping into the sea. He's going to rescue someone.
8 Some measures have been enforced by the government. They seem to be working.
9 A woman is standing on the podium. She's my mother.
10 Some houses were destroyed in the earthquake. They're going to be rebuilt.

4.3 Conditionals

Second conditional

We use the second conditional to talk about an imaginary situation or event and its result in the present or future.
We form the second conditional with the past simple in the conditional *if* clause and *would* + bare infinitive in the result clause. It's also possible to put the *if* clause at the end of the sentence. Furthermore, *were* can be used instead of *was* in the conditional clause with *I*, *he* and *she*.

conditional clause	result clause
if + past simple	*would* + bare infinitive

If you lived in Paris, **you'd learn** French quickly.

Third conditional

We use the third conditional to talk about the imaginary result of things that didn't happen in the past. It is often used it to express criticism or regret.
We form the third conditional with *if* + past perfect, *would have* + past participle. It's also possible to put the *if* clause at the end of the sentence.

conditional clause	result clause
if + past perfect	*would have* + past participle

If you had left earlier, **you wouldn't have missed** the plane.

Mixed conditional

We use mixed conditionals to say how an imaginary situation in the present depended on an imaginary event in the past taking place.

We form mixed conditionals with *if* + past perfect and *would* + bare infinitive in the result clause. It's also possible to put the *if* clause at the end of the sentence.

conditional clause	result clause
if + past perfect	*would* + bare infinitive

If she had gone shopping, **she wouldn't have** an empty fridge now.

Inversion

In a more formal style the auxiliary verbs *should*, *were* and *had* can replace *if* at the beginning of a conditional sentence.
If I had seen him, **I would have told** him.
Had I seen him, **I would have told** him.

We can use *unless* instead of *if... not* when we want to say we'll do the first thing if the second condition does not happen.
We'll have a barbecue **unless** it rains.

We can sometimes use *as long as* instead of *if* in first conditional sentences.
We can watch the film **as long as** it's not too late.

1 Decide if the sentences are correct or not. Correct the sentences that are incorrect.

1 You'd have passed your test if you hadn't been so nervous.
2 If I'd spoken better English, I got the job.
3 She wouldn't have called unless she had a problem.
4 Suppose I hadn't been to the bank, how did we pay for that meal?
5 Had they arrived any later, the show would start.
6 You wouldn't be so tired if you went to bed earlier last night.
7 Should you require any help, our call centre is open 24 hours a day.
8 If they'd been driving more slowly, they wouldn't crash.

2 Choose the first, second, third or a mixed conditional to complete the sentences.

1 You spent all your money in the sales. You're broke now.
If you hadn't spent all your money in the sales, you wouldn't be broke now.
2 I didn't know you liked Coldplay. I didn't buy you a ticket for the concert.
If _____ .

Grammar Builder and Reference **121**

3 You didn't lose your glasses. You'll be able to read the menu.
Had _____ .

4 John didn't pack the sandwiches. He's starving now.
If _____ .

5 If they don't ban tourists from the ancient city, it will be ruined in no time.
Unless _____ .

6 Mary doesn't work at home. She doesn't spend much time with her children.
Mary _____ .

5.1 *for* + noun/pronoun + infinitive

We use *for* + noun/pronoun + infinitive after certain adjectives. These sentences are often introduced by *it*.

With adjectives used to express importance or the lack of it:
It's **vital for us to win** the match.
It's **unnecessary for the students to memorise** everything.

With adjectives used to express frequency:
It's **normal for** lorry drivers **to** get tired.
It's **rare for** my students **to** do all their homework.

With adjectives used to express reactions to future events:
I'm **eager for** the play **to** start.
We're **keen for** the children **to** return.

This structure can be more formally expressed by using a *that* clause:
It's **vital that** we win the match.
It's **normal that** lorry drivers get tired.
I'm **eager that** the play should start.
This structure is also used with some nouns:
It's **time for** us **to** start work.

1 Complete the sentences using the words in brackets.

1 It's a shame for you to miss (you / miss) the party.
2 Her father's plan was _____ (she / take over) the medical practice.
3 They're reluctant _____ (he / leave) the company.
4 _____ (they / win) would be a miracle.
5 She's anxious _____ (we / go) and stay in her new house.
6 It's impossible _____ (I / start) work next week.

2 Rewrite the *that-* clauses using *for* + noun/pronoun + infinitive.

1 It's important that Grace arrive before the other speakers.
It's important for Grace to arrive before the other speakers.
2 Mum's plan was that the whole family go camping together.
3 It's essential that he shouldn't turn up late.
4 He's eager that his girlfriend accompany him to Jo's wedding.
5 It seems unnecessary that we stay until the boss leaves.
6 Our host's idea was that we shouldn't set off until after lunch.

5.2 Ellipsis

We can leave words out when the meaning is clear without them and also to avoid repetition.

We can sometimes just use *to*, a reduced infinitive, instead of repeating the whole expression again.
He wants me to go to the cinema with him and I **would like to** (go to the cinema with him).

We sometimes leave out the whole infinitive.
You don't have to tell me if you **don't want** (to tell me).

We sometimes leave out the main verb after an auxiliary or modal verb.
We didn't finish the work but we **should have** (finished the work).
I can't fix it this morning, but I **can** (fix it) this afternoon. Is that OK?

In these cases, the second auxiliary verb is stressed in spoken English.

1 Cross out the words that can be omitted from the sentences because of ellipsis.

1 Millie agreed to peel the potatoes although she didn't want to peel them.
2 Maria is going to try to get the books I want but I'm sure she won't be able to get the books.
3 I didn't ask after Pam's mother when I should have asked after her.
4 Alfie's always upsetting his girlfriend although he doesn't mean to upset her.
5 My brother didn't go out last night although he could have gone out.
6 Andy doesn't know if he'll be able to beat Rafa, but he certainly hopes to beat him.
7 Max goes horse-riding now, but he didn't use to go horse-riding.
8 When Liam asked Grace to go out for a drink, she said she'd love to go out for a drink.

6.1 Talking about the future

We use *will* + infinitive when we decide to do things as we are speaking (instant decisions, offers, promises).
I'm going now. I'll **phone** you this evening.
You don't look well. I'll **take** you home.
We'll **bring** you that book tomorrow.

We also use *will* to make predictions about the future.
He'll **never get** all that work finished by Friday.

We use *going to* + infinitive for plans and intentions that we have already decided on before speaking.
We've already decided where we want to go. We're **going to visit** Brazil.

We also use *going to* to make predictions about the future. In this case, the prediction is based on some present evidence.
It's five to nine and he's only just left. He's **going to be** late for school again!

Grammar Builder and Reference

We use the **present continuous** to talk about arrangements we have already made, usually at a specific time in the future and with somebody else.

I'm meeting the boss in her office at nine o'clock tomorrow morning.

We use the **present simple** to talk the timetables of future activities and events.

Your plane leaves at 5 p.m. tomorrow.

We use the **future continuous** (*will* + *be* + *-ing*) to talk about actions that will be in progress at a certain time in the future. It suggests that the future event has already been decided on.

I'll be working in our Sydney office next month.
Will he be staying with you at Christmas?

We use the **future perfect** (*will* + *have* + past participle) to talk about actions or events that will have finished in the future.

We'll have finished the course in June.
I hope you'll have left the office by seven o'clock.

1 Choose the correct alternatives.

1 Sophie's gone very pale, I think _____ out.
   a she's going to   b she'll pass

2 Come and stay with us, the fresh air _____ you good.
   a is going to do   b will do

3 Dave's been saving up. _____ a new car.
   a He's going to buy   b He'll buy

4 There's a documentary on TV tonight. _____ at 7.30.
   a It's starting   b It starts

5 Alex can't see his girlfriend tonight. _____ with her friends.
   a She'll go clubbing   b She's going clubbing

6 This time next year _____ around the world.
   a we'll be travelling   b we're travelling

7 By the time you get home _____ the cases.
   a I'll pack   b I'll have packed

8 Don't cry. By this time next week _____ someone new.
   a you'll be meeting   b you'll have met

2 Complete the mini dialogues with a suitable future form of the verbs in brackets.

1 'Can you call me before midnight?'
   'OK. I'm sure I 'll have arrived by then.' (arrive)

2 'Shall we go out for a coffee after class?'
   'Sorry, I can't. I _____ tennis.' (play)

3 'Why are you slowing down?'
   'Because I can see the traffic lights _____ .' (change)

4 'Shall I pick you up at eight tonight?'
   'No, We _____ dinner then. Come round at 8.30 instead.' (have)

5 'What time do you have to get up?'
   'At six. The bus _____ at 7.15.' (leave)

6 'When will you be able to hand in your project?'
   'I'm sure I _____ it by Friday.' (finish)

6.2 Particles and their meanings

Phrasal verbs are formed from two (sometimes three) parts: a verb followed by a preposition or adverb. The prepositions or adverbs are sometimes referred to as particles. These particles often add a particular meaning to a phrasal verb and they usually have more than one meaning.

back = repeating or looking into the past
Could you **play back** the telephone message, please?
The tennis club **dates back** to the 19th century.

down = record in writing or reducing
Could you **write** these dates **down**?
House prices have finally **gone down**.

off = departing or ending
He quickly said goodbye and then **ran off** to catch the bus.
The two countries have **cut off** diplomatic relations with each other.

on = continuing or attacking
She spent the whole time **going on** about her new partner.
Those bullies are always **picking on** Dave.

out = disappearing or solving, searching
The forest fire finally **died out** after two days.
Can you **work out** the answer to this maths question?

over = visiting or considering, examining
We **popped over** to my mum's but she was out.
Let's **go over** the report before the meeting.

up = approach or improve
He always **creeps up** on me. He just appears, without making a noise.
I want to **brush up** on my computer skills this year.

1 Choose the correct meaning for the underlined particle.

1 Have you sorted <u>out</u> what you're doing at the weekend?
   a disappearing   b solving, searching

2 We're going to ask some friends <u>over</u> for dinner on Saturday.
   a visiting   b considering, examining

3 Hannah cheered <u>up</u> as soon as she saw her boyfriend's message on her mobile.
   a approach   b improve

4 Janice is going to stay <u>on</u> at school to do the university entrance exam.
   a continuing   b attack

5 Every now and then we look <u>back</u> at our wedding photos.
   a repeating   b looking into the past

6 Matt's mum asked him to turn <u>down</u> the TV.
   a record in writing   b reducing

7 The old man is always telling the kids to clear <u>off</u>.
   a departing   b ending

2 Choose a particle that can be used in both sentences. Decide which meaning from exercise 1 is used in each sentence.

1 back – (a) looking into the past, (b) repeating.
   a This song takes me _____ to our first family holiday in Greece.
   b Paola played _____ the CD to make sure it had recorded properly.

2 _____
   a When my aunt had finished criticising my sister, she started _____ me.
   b They kept _____ working until they finished the report.

3 _____
   a Let's invite some friends _____ to see our holiday photos.
   b I'm going to think _____ the job offer before I accept it.

4 _____
   a Tom noted _____ her number and arranged to call that afternoon.
   b They played the incident _____ to prevent the crowd from panicking.

5 _____
   a The weather soon brightened _____ and we were able to go out for a walk.
   b The castle loomed _____ at us through the fog.

6 _____
   a We set _____ for the beach as soon as the sun came out.
   b Anne's waiting for Stephen to log _____ so she can use the phone.

7 _____
   a We need to find _____ what time our train leaves tomorrow.
   b The government is phasing _____ analogue TV.

6.3 Reporting structures

We use direct speech to repeat the exact words that someone said. We use reported speech to report what someone has said, but without using the exact words.

Anne said, 'It was an incredible concert. We had a fantastic time.'
Anne **said they had really enjoyed the concert**.

When we change direct speech to reported speech we usually change the tense of the sentence, the pronouns and possessive adjectives from first and second person to third person and the time expressions.

'I had an interview yesterday', said John.
John **said he had had an interview the day before**.

Reporting verbs

We can use a number of other reporting verbs to introduce reported statements apart from *say* and *tell*. These verbs are used with a variety of structures. A few verbs are used with more than one structure:

verb + infinitive: *agree, ask, claim, offer, promise, refuse, threaten*
He **promised to help** us.

verb + object + (not) infinitive: *advise, beg, dare, order, remind, urge*
He **advised us to apply** for a visa.

verb + gerund: *deny, mention, recommend, suggest*
He **recommended visiting** the museum.

verb + preposition + gerund: *accuse, admit, boast, confess, congratulate, insist*
He **confessed to copying** my work.

verb + object + preposition + gerund: *accuse, blame, warn*
They **accused me of stealing** their car.

verb + *that* + (*should*) clause: *demand, propose, recommend, request, suggest*
She **suggests that** we should get up early.

verb + (object) + question word + infinitive with *to*: *ask, tell*
He **asked where** to go.

1 Complete the sentences with the correct form of the verb in brackets. Use an object pronoun where necessary.

1 Tyler's friends dared **him to do** a bungee jump. (do)
2 I've only lent Holly the money because she's agreed _____ by the end of the week. (pay back)
3 As soon as Beth mentioned _____ to a theme park, her brother and sister wanted to join her. (go)
4 The teacher kept the whole class behind until someone confessed _____ her mobile. (steal)
5 Nathan's parents urged _____ home. (not leave)
6 The head teacher gave the student her prize and congratulated _____ the competition. (win)
7 The protesters are demanding that the government _____ taxes. (reduce)
8 The muggers threatened _____ Amy's boyfriend if she didn't reveal her PIN number. (beat up)

2 Choose the correct alternative.

1 They warned me **against crossing** / **not to cross** the park at night.
2 Tom's girlfriend reminded **to call her at midday** / **him when to call her**.
3 He accused me **to use** / **of having used** all the milk.
4 Millie advised us where **to stay** / **we stay** in Mykonos.
5 The teacher suggested **Dan to stop** / **that Dan stop** and think about it.
6 Mum insisted **on giving** / **to give** us more cake.

6.4 Adverbs and adjectives

Adjectives

The order of adjectives before a noun usually depends on their meaning. Adjectives which describe attitudes and opinions usually come before all other adjectives.
It's an **incredible** old French painting.

Adjectives referring to size, length and height often come before age, colour, origin, material and purpose.
He's got an **enormous** black Japanese motorbike.

Numbers usually go before adjectives and the words *first*, *next* and *last* go before numbers.
These are my **first** two old British stamps.

Adverbs

We can usually use adverbs in three positions: at the beginning, in the middle or at the end of a sentence. However, most adverbs are only used in one or two of these positions.

We use adverbs that show our thoughts or feelings about something at the beginning of a sentence.
Personally, I'm not really interested in his ideas.
Unfortunately, we won't be able to come to the wedding.

We use adverbs of frequency in the middle of a sentence. They go after the verb *to be*, between an auxiliary verb and a main verb, and before all other verbs.
He was **often** late.
They've **always** lived here.
We **usually** play at the weekends.

We also use adverbs of degree like *almost*, *nearly* and *quite* in the middle of a sentence.
We are **nearly** there.
She **almost** won the race.

When we want to say something was unexpected we use *even* before a verb.
Mike **even** cooked lunch. And it was good!
She didn't **even** return the money I had lent her.

We usually use adverbs of manner with the verbs they describe. If the verb has an object, the adverb follows it.
She has always sung opera **beautifully**.
The children ate **quickly** and went out to play.

1 Complete the sentences putting the adjectives in brackets in the correct order. You may also need to add an article.

1 They purchased a charming little thatched cottage in the auction. (thatched, charming, little)
2 She looked very stylish in _____ evening gown. (silk, black, long)
3 John drives _____ sports car. (fast, Italian, elegant)
4 They're going to pull down that _____ building on the corner. (concrete, grey, hideous)
5 Grace is hoping to meet _____ stranger while she's away. (tall, dark, gorgeous)
6 Susan's down-and-out father wore _____ suit to her wedding. (check, old-fashioned, scruffy)

2 Decide if the sentences are correct or not. Sometimes there is more than one possibility. Correct the incorrect sentences.

1 We'd luckily booked a table for dinner the day before. Luckily, we'd booked a table.
2 Zoe spent her childhood in Moscow and she can still speak fluently Russian.
3 Unfortunately, the young people in my area rarely put their litter in a bin.
4 I lost my job almost yesterday.
5 Basically, we never are going to finish on time.
6 She's been trying to eat healthily for the last week or so.
7 They occasionally in the summer go camping.
8 My cousin even didn't say thank you when we put her up last weekend.

7.1 -ing forms after preparatory *it*, nouns and adjectives

It can be used as a preparatory subject or object for an *-ing* form, especially in informal style.

We often use *it* with adjectives.
It was interesting hearing what he had to say.
It will be great seeing you all again.

We often use *it* with the noun *worth*.
Is it really worth buying those jeans?
It was worth asking for help.

The object of the *-ing* form can sometimes become the subject of the sentence.
It's worth seeing **Regent's Park**.
Regent's park is worth seeing.

It is also often used negatively with the noun *use*.
It won't be any use waiting here for him.

Some nouns and adjectives can be followed by *-ing* forms. A preposition usually joins the *-ing* form with the noun or adjective.
I hate **the idea of getting** bad exam results.

Grammar Builder and Reference

1 Complete the sentences with the words below and the *-ing* form of the verb in brackets.

~~good~~ ~~nice~~ ~~pointless~~ ~~tiring~~ ~~use~~ ~~worth~~

1 It's no use reporting the crime. Your wallet will never be found. (report)
2 It was _____ your mother out for lunch. She didn't eat anything. (take)
3 It's no _____ on at school if you aren't going to study. (stay)
4 It's been _____ to you. Thank you for your time. (talk)
5 It was _____ with the same old problems, day in and day out. (deal)
6 It isn't _____ our house right now. (sell)

2 Complete the sentences using the word in brackets and an *-ing* form.

1 Nobody wants to have an operation. (thought)
   People don't like the thought of having an operation.
2 Of course I'll pass all my exams. (confident)
   I'm _____ .
3 Everybody thinks that Nadal will win. (chance)
   Nadal has _____ .
4 Her main concern is that her children may get lost. (worried)
   She's _____ .
5 I've never spent the night in an igloo before. (strange)
   It'll be _____ .
6 Kids rarely like thinking that their parents might split up. (thought)
   Most children hate _____ .

7.2 Emphasis

We add emphasis to written English by using special structures.

Cleft sentences

We can use *It is/was… that…* to emphasise different parts of a sentence from the verb.
Jack lost the camera.
It was Jack who lost the camera.
It was the camera that Jack lost.

We can use *What… is/was…* to emphasise the subject or object of a sentence.
Kate sold her flat.   **What** Kate sold **was** her flat.

Inversion

Some negative adverbs can be used at the beginning of a sentence to add emphasis. In these cases the auxiliary verb is put before the subject. If there is no auxiliary verb *do*, *does* or *did* is used.
I've never seen such an animal.   **Never have I seen** such an animal.
We rarely arrived on time.   **Rarely did we arrive** on time.

We use *not only… but also…* to emphasise that two negative events have happened.
He lost his job and his wife left him.
Not only did his wife leave him, **but he also** lost his job.

Adverbial expressions of place

Adverbial expressions of place can be put at the beginning of a sentence for emphasis, especially when they are followed by intransitive verbs such as *come*, *sit*, *stand* or *walk*.
He walked up the hill.
Up the hill he walked.
We can also use phrases such as the *problem/trouble/truth/fact/question is*.
The problem is he doesn't do any work.
We sometimes use the auxiliary verb *do* to add emphasis to the main verb.
We really **do** enjoy his recitals at the concert hall.

1 Complete the second sentence adding emphasis.

1 The four officers jumped into a waiting police car.
   Into a waiting police car jumped the four officers.
2 The party had hardly got going when the lights went out.
   Hardly _____ .
3 We got completely carried away. That's the truth.
   The truth is _____ .
4 The captain reported the fault as soon as we took off.
   No sooner _____ .
5 They need to improve public transport to solve the congestion problem.
   What _____ .
6 I miss my older sister the most.
   It's _____ .
7 Two armed soldiers stood outside the palace.
   Outside _____ .
8 We didn't pay for the flight. We paid for the hotel. (do)
   We didn't _____ .

2 Rewrite the underlined phrases in the text to add emphasis. Use the words in brackets for 3, 4, 6 and 7.

[1] A solitary figure stands in front of the ruins of his house. [2] Neither a bomb nor a fire caused the destruction, but a formidable tornado, which roared through the French town of Hautmont last Sunday night. [3] The storm ripped houses apart and killed three people. [4] Nobody knows what turned a thunderstorm into a devastating tornado.
Paul Knightley, at the Tornado and Storm Research Organisation, believes that [5] a supercell struck the north of France. Supercells are exceptionally powerful thunderstorms. They rotate like a slowly spinning carousel but deep in their centre a faster-spinning column of air drops down to the ground as a tornado. [6] These storms occur frequently in the USA, but [7] they haven't been seen in northern Europe before.

1 In front of the ruins of his house stands a solitary figure.
2 What _____
3 _____ (not only)
4 _____ (question)
5 It _____
6 _____ (do)
7 _____ (not until)

8.1 would

We can use *would* to:

- express examples of what was typical behaviour in the past.
  People **would wear** their best clothes on Sundays.

- express examples of willingness in the past or in a hypothetical present.
  He **wouldn't help** me with my homework last night.
  I **wouldn't want** to visit Egypt at this time of year.

- make a deduction about the present or past.
  I heard someone at the door. That **would be** the postman.
  We **would have been** at university when we saw that film.

We express preferences using *would* + *like*, *love*, *prefer* and *rather*.
I'd **like** a black coffee, please.

We use *would* with the verbs *say* and *think* to make our opinions more tentative.
I'd **say** that you should try and improve your performance.
I'd **think** you'll have a difficult time.

1 Complete the sentences using *would* and the verbs in brackets. Then match the sentences to the uses on page 82 of this Student's Book.

1 The children didn't like vegetables when they were little. (eat)
  They wouldn't eat vegetables when they were little.

2 As a child I always made my own birthday cards. (create)
  When _____ .

3 Can't we get a takeaway instead? (rather)
  I _____ .

4 It never occurs to my brother to call me. (think)
  My brother _____ .

5 In my opinion about twenty people turned up. (say)
  I _____ .

6 I guess you were tired after your journey. (been)
  You _____ .

7 Going to the Emeli Sandé concert's a great idea! (love)
  I _____ .

8 Of course her boyfriend stood up for her! (defend)
  Her _____ ?

8.2 Modals

Modal verbs are used to talk about obligation, permission, willingness, ability and future possibility. They are also used to talk about the possibility or probability of something happening.

Ability

We use *can* and *am/are/is able to* to talk about ability in the present.
I'm **able to** drive very big lorries.
Can your daughter swim?

We use *could* and *was/were able to* to talk about ability in the past. We use both structures to talk about repeated activities in the past.
He **could** dance very well.
We **weren't able to** speak French then.

We only use *was/were able to* (i.e. not *could*) to talk about something that only happened once in the past.
The party finished late but I **was able to** take a taxi.

Permission

We use *can* to say something is permitted in the present and *could* to say something was permitted in the past. *Can't* and *couldn't* are the negative forms.
We **can leave** work at 5 p.m. every Friday.
I **can't** use the Internet at home after 10 p.m.
My dad **could** only eat chocolate on Sundays.
I **couldn't** wear long trousers to school when I was a boy.

Obligation

We use *must* and *have to* to talk about obligation in the present. We usually use *have to* when we are talking about rules, *must* when it's a personal obligation.
You **have to** wear a swimming cap at the public swimming pool.
I **must** study more English before I go to live in Chicago.

We use *mustn't* when something is prohibited.
Students **mustn't** eat and drink in the library.

We use *needn't* and *don't have to* to say there is no obligation to do anything. You may choose to do or not to do something.
We **needn't** do these exercises but I think it would be a good idea to.
He **doesn't have to** help his old neighbour but he likes to.

Possibility

We use *may*, *might* and *could* to discuss the possibility of something happening. *May* suggests that the chances of something happening are slightly greater than *could* and *might*.
I think it **may** rain this evening.
She said she **might** come, but she didn't sound very enthusiastic.

Logical deductions about the present

We use *may/might/could* + infinitive to say something is possible.
Tom **might** win the race. He's in good form.

We use *must* + infinitive to say something is certain.
Mike is soaking. It **must** be raining.

We use *can't* + infinitive to say something is impossible.
It **can't** be true. Sam was with me last night.

Logical deductions about the past

We use *may/might/could* + *have* + past participle to say something was possible in the past.
It's strange that he hasn't phoned. He **might have** lost his mobile.

We use *must* + *have* + past participle to make a strong supposition about something in the past.
John was off work last week. He **must have** been ill.

We use *can't* + *have* + past participle to say it was impossible that something happened in the past.
They didn't know anything about the film so they **can't have** seen it.

1 Cross out the modal verb that cannot complete the sentence. Try to justify your choice.

1 He ____ walk for a year after his accident. He went around in a wheelchair.
  a couldn't   **b** wasn't able to   **c** shouldn't
  c – **couldn't** and **wasn't able to** express no ability, **shouldn't** is normally used for advice

2 She ____ have left her mobile in the coffee shop. Her mum called while she was there.
  a might   **b** can   **c** could

3 I ____ get my hair cut – it looks awful.
  a must   **b** can't   **c** have to

4 You ____ park on a double yellow line or you'll get a fine.
  a don't have to   **b** can't   **c** mustn't

5 ____ I stay at your house tonight? I've missed the last bus home.
  a Can   **b** May   **c** Must

6 They ____ wait in the queue. They had already bought their tickets.
  a mustn't   **b** didn't need to   **c** didn't have to

7 We ____ buy a leaving present for Mary. She's been such a good boss.
  a ought to   **b** should   **c** would

8 It's 2.30 p.m. George ____ have arrived in Beijing by now.
  a can   **b** must   **c** will

2 Complete the sentences with a suitable modal verb and the verb in brackets. More than one answer may be possible.

1 I don't mind our school uniform because we _____ a tie. (wear)
2 To reduce carbon emissions people _____ public transport more. (use)
3 My mother _____ until she was 40. She passed her test on her birthday. (drive)
4 It _____ John that called. He said he would. (be)
5 You _____ your mobile phone while you're driving. It's illegal. (use)

6 _____ I _____ a pen? I want to write down your email address. (borrow)
7 I'm not sure why they're so late, but they _____ . (get lost)
8 Jessica isn't going out tonight because she _____ for tomorrow's exam. (study)

9.1 Colloquial omissions

In informal spoken English we can sometimes leave out words at the beginning of a sentence if the meaning is very clear. These words are not stressed in spoken English when they are included in a sentence.

Articles
Why did you catch the bus? **(The)** Trains aren't running today.

Possessive pronouns
Are you OK? No. **(My)** Head hurts. I think I've got a migraine.

Subject pronouns
What did you say? **(I)** Can't hear you! The music's too loud.

Auxiliary verbs and personal pronouns at the beginning of questions
(Have you) Been to the cinema recently?
No. What's on?

Negative forms can be replaced by *not*
How's John?
(He isn't) Not happy, I'm afraid.

9.2 The passive

We make passive forms with the verb *be* + past participle.

	The school
Present simple	is decorated every summer.
Present continuous	is being decorated at the moment.
Present perfect	has been decorated recently.
Past simple	was decorated last month.
Past continuous	was being decorated until the bad weather started.
Past perfect	had been decorated only once before
will	will be decorated soon.
going to	is going to be decorated next month.
modal verb	may be decorated in the next few months.

The passive is used to talk about processes.
The cars **are taken** from the factory and then they **are transported** all over Europe.

The passive is used when we don't want to say or we can't say who performed the action.
This book **was written** in the 17th century but the author **is unknown**.

The passive is used when it's obvious who performed the action.
The fire **has** finally **been put out**.

The passive is also used to put the main focus at the beginning of the sentence. If we want to say who carried out the action we introduce the person's name with the preposition *by*.
These emails **have been sent** by someone in this office, and I want to know who!

1 Complete the article with the correct passive form of the verb in brackets.

A study into the future of the world's monkeys
[1] has been carried out (carry out) recently by animal experts, the results of which [2]_____ (release) at an international conference last month.

During the survey it [3]_____ (find) that 303 of the 634 primates studied may soon become extinct in the wild; 69 species [4]_____ (classify) as critically endangered since the results became known.

The main reason for the rapid decline in numbers [5]_____ (identify) in the report as deforestation. However, in some areas more damage [6]_____ (do) by local people who hunt the animals for food. Monkeys [7]_____ (eat) in several regions of Africa and Asia.

Conservationists want world leaders to take urgent measures to protect these animals in the hope that they [8]_____ (save) from extinction in the near future.

9.3 Passive structures with *consider*, *believe*, etc.

We sometimes use passives with an introductory subject to talk about things in a general sense. Some the verbs most frequently used in this way are *believe*, *consider* and *feel*.
This man **is considered** extremely dangerous.
It **is felt** that the government must do something about inflation.

1 Rewrite the sentences in the passive using the words in brackets.

1 National security is of paramount importance. (believe firmly)
It is firmly believed that national security is of paramount importance.

2 Human actions are responsible for global warming. (accept widely)
It _____ .

3 Monsoons are a tropical phenomenon. (regard usually)
Monsoons _____ .

4 Wind power is the best solution to the global energy crisis. (say often)
It _____ .

5 Oil is running out. (consider generally)
Oil _____ .

6 Public transport is too unreliable. (see usually)
Public transport _____ .

7 Commercial flights cause a great deal of pollution. (acknowledge widely)
Commercial flights _____ .

8 Flooding has worsened in recent years. (report frequently)
It _____ .

10.1 *whatever*, *whoever*, *wherever*, *however*, etc.

We use *whatever*, *whoever*, *wherever*, *however*, etc. to say it doesn't matter what, who, where, how, etc. because the outcome will be the same. As these expressions are conjunctions, they can come at the beginning or in the middle of a sentence.
Whatever you say, I won't change my mind.
We had a great time in Italy, **wherever** we went.

We can also use *however* with an adjective or adverb to mean it doesn't matter to what extent. In these sentences we can sometimes leave out the verb *to be*.
However interesting (it is), I don't want to see the play.

1 Complete the sentences using the words below.

however   whatever   whenever   wherever   whichever   whoever

1 I'm not telling you my phone number, _____ you are.
2 Don't go out with Mandy's brother, _____ you do.
3 We can meet up _____ day is best for you.
4 People are seldom satisfied with their salary _____ much they earn.
5 We can meet _____ you've got time, I've got a flexible schedule.
6 My little brother follows me _____ I go.

10.2 Relative clauses

Relative pronouns

	defining relative clauses	non-defining relative clauses
people	who/that	who
things	which/that	which
places	where	where
dates	when	when
possessive	whose	whose

Defining relative clauses

Defining relative clauses give essential information about the person, thing or place in the main clause. Without this information the sentence would be incomplete.

That's the flat **that we want to buy**.
I met the person **who is going to take** over the department.
I've bought you the book **which I told** you about.

We can omit the relative pronoun when it is the object of the defining relative clause but not when it is the subject.

That's the flat (**that**) we want to buy.
I met the person **who** is going to take over the department.
I've bought you the book (**which**) I told you about.

Non-defining relative clauses

Non-defining relative clauses give non-essential information about the person, thing or place in the main clause. This extra information must always go between commas.

The Queen, **who was wearing a blue summer dress**, opened the new hospital in Manchester.
My car, **which I bought last year**, is always breaking down.

We cannot omit non-defining relative pronouns from the sentence. Neither can we use the relative pronoun *that* in place of *which* or *who*.

Prepositions in relative clauses

If a relative clause includes a preposition we can often choose to put it at the beginning or the end of the clause. If it is used at the beginning of the clause it sounds more formal.

This is the church (which) we got married in.
This is the church in which we got married.

We usually use the formal relative pronoun *whom* instead of *who* when a preposition comes before it.

The people who I spoke to were really helpful.
The people to whom I spoke were really helpful.

If the preposition is part of a phrasal verb it stays with the verb.
I met the man who set up the company with my father.

1 Join the sentences with a suitable relative clause. Omit the pronoun where possible.

1 A man answered the phone. He refused to listen to my complaint.
The man who / that answered the phone refused to listen to my complaint.
2 Some medicine got rid of my cough. It tasted of liquorice.
3 The Golden Gate Bridge is an impressive sight. We crossed it yesterday.
4 He's a pilot. His plane crashed yesterday.
5 The lift is being repaired. It broke down yesterday.
6 I asked a woman for information. She was very helpful.
7 Britney Spears is hoping to make a comeback. She sang *Baby one more time*.
8 The hotel was full. We had booked it.

2 Rewrite these relative clauses in a more formal style. It is not possible to rewrite two of the sentences.

1 The land which the river runs through belonged to my family in the past.
The land through which the river flows belonged to my family in the past.
2 My grandfather, who I have the utmost respect for, died fighting for his country.
_____.
3 Applications which are filled in incorrectly will be rejected.
_____.
4 My mother's glasses, which she cannot see without, look quite stylish.
_____.
5 William's best friend, who he has always confided in, has just moved abroad.
_____.
6 They gave away some old toys which hadn't been played with for years.
_____.
7 The wall which Ryan was standing on top of looked like it would topple over.
_____.
8 The boy who Sarah fell in love with turned out to be a thief.
_____.

1 SPEAKING **Work in pairs. What do you know about Shakespeare? Can you name any of his plays?**

2 **Read the Fact file. Compare your ideas from exercise 1. Is there anything that surprises you?**

▶ **FACT FILE**

- ▶ Born 23 April 1564. Died 23 April 1616.
- ▶ Married at eighteen and had three children.
- ▶ Wrote 37 plays: history plays (e.g. *Julius Caesar, Henry V*), tragedies (e.g. *Hamlet, King Lear, Othello,*) and comedies (e.g. *As You Like It, Twelfth Night*).
- ▶ Regarded as the greatest writer in the English language.
- ▶ Many of his plays were first performed at the Globe Theatre, London. The theatre was destroyed by fire in 1613 – and reconstructed in 1997!
- ▶ Few records of Shakespeare's private life survive.

3 **Read the information about *Romeo and Juliet*.**

The play is set in Verona in Italy. Romeo, from the Montague family, and Juliet, who is a Capulet, have fallen in love, but their families are sworn enemies and would never consent to their marriage. They can't see each other openly, so Romeo comes at night to Juliet's balcony …

4 🎧 TRCD **Listen to a modern version of part of a famous scene from Romeo and Juliet. Choose the correct words to complete the summary.**

Juliet is ¹**aware / unaware** that Romeo is there. She wishes that Romeo could change his ²**name / family**. She wishes that names were ³**more / less** important and reasons that if a rose were given another name it ⁴**would still be a rose / would be quite different**. Romeo is ⁵**unwilling / willing** to reveal his identity to Juliet, but in any case she recognises his ⁶**voice / face**.

5 🎧 TRCD **Now read the original text and match the underlined words and phrases with the modern English equivalents below. Then listen and read again.**

from now on   hidden   I don't know   if he weren't   if I had
it is only   private thoughts   remove   speech   why
why are you   will   young woman   you   your   yourself

6 SPEAKING **Match the phrases to make famous Shakespeare quotes. Then translate and explain them.**

1 To be, or not to be:
2 All the world's a stage
3 Neither a borrower
4 Love is blind
5 The course of true love
6 Good Night, Good night!

a nor a lender be.
b never did run smooth.
c that is the question.
d Parting is such sweet sorrow.
e and lovers cannot see.
f and all the men and women are merely players.

7 SPEAKING **Act out the extract from Romeo and Juliet.**

Juliet   O Romeo, Romeo! ¹Wherefore art thou Romeo?
Deny ²thy father and refuse thy name.
Or, if thou ³wilt not, be but sworn my love,
And I'll no longer be a Capulet.

5 Romeo   [*aside*] Shall I hear more, or shall I speak at this?

Juliet   ⁴'Tis but thy name that is my enemy.
Thou art ⁵thyself, though not a Montague.
What's Montague? It is nor hand, nor foot,
10   Nor arm, nor face, nor any other part
Belonging to a man. O, be some other name!
What's in a name? That which we call a rose
By any other word would smell as sweet.
So Romeo would, ⁶were he not Romeo called,
15   Retain that dear perfection which he owes
Without that title. Romeo, ⁷doff thy name,
And for that name, which is no part of ⁸thee
Take all myself.

Romeo   I take thee at thy word.
20   Call me but love, and I'll be new baptized.
⁹Henceforth I never will be Romeo.

Juliet   What man art thou that, thus ¹⁰be screen'd in night,
So stumblest on my ¹¹counsel?

25 Romeo   By a name
¹²I know not how to tell thee who I am.
My name, dear saint, is hateful to myself
Because it is an enemy to thee.
¹³Had I it written, I would tear the word.

30 Juliet   My ears have not yet drunk a hundred words
Of that tongue's ¹⁴uttering, yet I know the sound.
Art thou not Romeo, and a Montague?

Romeo   Neither, fair ¹⁵maid, if either thee dislike.

1 SPEAKING In pairs, answer the quiz questions about the British royal family.

1 How many children does Queen Elizabeth have? Can you name any of them?
2 What is the relationship between Prince William and the Queen?
3 Assuming William has children, who will become monarch after his death?
  a his younger brother
  b his eldest son or daughter
  c his eldest son (even if he has a daughter first)
4 Does the Queen have any political power in the UK? Choose the best answer.
  a Yes, in theory, but he/she never uses it.
  b Yes, and she uses it occasionally.
  c No, her political powers were abolished years ago.
5 The next head of the Commonwealth of Nations
  a will be the Queen's eldest son.
  b has yet to be decided.
  c will be from a country other than the UK.

2 🎧 TRCD Listen and check your answers to the quiz.

3 🎧 TRCD Listen to the information. What does the map below show? Is it (a) the British Empire, (b) the Commonwealth, or (c) the Commonwealth Realms?

4 🎧 TRCD Listen again and choose the correct answers.
1 The Commonwealth of Nations is an organisation made up of 54 independent states, nearly all of which were:
  a in NATO b part of the British Empire c in Africa
2 Sixteen members, including the UK, are Commonwealth Realms, which means that they all share the same:
  a constitution   b president   c monarch

3 Which of these countries is not a Commonwealth realm?
  a Australia b Canada c India d the UK
4 More than 54 countries enter the Commonwealth Games because:
  a ex-members of the Commonwealth can enter.
  b non-members can enter by invitation only.
  c countries which are part of a larger state can enter separate teams.

5 Read the text about the kind of English spoken in the Commonwealth country of Ghana. Match the words below with their synonyms underlined in the text.

copy   freedom   inheritance   language   reaction
rules   status

Question: 'Have you eat?' Reply: 'No I go eat after small small.' This is just one of the turns of phrase Ghanaians use, in the words of one local commentator, 'to give the Queen's English a good beating'. But as Ghanaians begin to speak their inherited colonial ¹tongue with growing creative ²licence, a row is breaking out about what really is the proper way to speak English. On one side of the fence are the old-school Ghanaians who were taught throughout their education to ³mimic received pronunciation – or BBC English, as it is popularly known – with varying degrees of success. On the other side, a ⁴backlash is growing against the old mentality of equating a British accent with ⁵prestige.

'The idea that intelligence is linked to English pronunciation is a ⁶legacy from colonial thinking,' said Delalorm Semabia, 25, a Ghanaian blogger. 'People used to think that if you speak like the British then you are as intelligent as the British. But now we are waking up to the fact that we have great people here who have never stepped outside the borders.'

'In the 90s many local artists wanted to sound like Usher or Jay-Z, but now they are taking local names and branding themselves locally,' said Semabia. 'For us, English is our language – we want to break away from the old ⁷strictures, to personalise it, mix it with our local languages, and have fun with it. The whole point of language is that it's supposed to be flexible and it's meant to be fun.'

6 🎧 TRCD Listen to five sentences about the text in exercise 5. Are they true (T) or false (F)?

1	2	3	4	5

7 SPEAKING Discuss these questions with your partner.
1 How important is, or was, the royal family in your country? How much do you know about them?
2 Is there such a thing as a 'modern royal family' or is the whole idea old-fashioned?

1 SPEAKING Look at the photo. How much do you know about this character? Compare your ideas in pairs.

2 TRCD Listen to the information about the novel *Frankenstein*. Complete the notes in the fact file. Write one or two words in each gap.

▶ **FRANKENSTEIN FACT FILE**

▸ The novel was written and published near the beginning of the ¹_____ century.
▸ The author, Mary Shelly, later married a famous ²_____ .
▸ Mary and some friends decided to write stories on holiday because of ³_____ .
▸ The idea for the story came to Mary in ⁴_____ .
▸ In the novel, Frankenstein is the name of ⁵_____ .
▸ The novel's themes reflect concerns of the day, such as the fear that ⁶_____ were becoming too powerful.

3 Read the extract opposite. Match the underlined words (1–10) with the definitions below (a–j).

a confusion
b healthy-looking features
c cloth for wrapping the dead
d work
e tiredness
f dead body
g arms and legs
h drops of water
i passion, eagerness
j miserable person

4 SPEAKING In pairs, discuss how the extract is made more effective by:

a the weather and time of night.
b the detailed description of the creature's face.
c Victor's dream.
d the creature's inability to speak clearly.

5 SPEAKING Work in pairs. How many different characters from horror films or stories can you think of? What makes them scary? Do they have any other qualities which make them appealing or sympathetic?

It was on a dreary night of November that I beheld the accomplishment of my ¹toils. With an anxiety that almost amounted to agony, I collected the instruments of life around me, that I might infuse a spark of being into the lifeless thing that lay at my feet. It was already one in the morning; the rain pattered dismally against the panes, and my candle was nearly burnt out, when, by the glimmer of the half-extinguished light, I saw the dull yellow eye of the creature open; it breathed hard, and a convulsive motion agitated its ²limbs.

How can I describe my emotions at this catastrophe, or how delineate the ³wretch whom with such infinite pains and care I had endeavoured to form? His limbs were in proportion, and I had selected his features as beautiful. Beautiful! – Great God! His yellow skin scarcely covered the work of muscles and arteries beneath; his hair was of a lustrous black, and flowing; his teeth of a pearly whiteness; but these ⁴luxuriances only formed a more horrid contrast with his watery eyes, that seemed almost of the same colour as the dun white sockets in which they were set, his shrivelled complexion and straight black lips.

The different accidents of life are not so changeable as the feelings of human nature. I had worked hard for nearly two years, for the sole purpose of infusing life into an inanimate body. For this I had deprived myself of rest and health. I had desired it with an ⁵ardour that far exceeded moderation; but now that I had finished, the beauty of the dream vanished, and breathless horror and disgust filled my heart. Unable to endure the aspect of the being I had created, I rushed out of the room, and continued a long time traversing my bedchamber, unable to compose my mind to sleep. At length ⁶lassitude succeeded to the ⁷tumult I had before endured; and I threw myself on the bed in my clothes, endeavouring to seek a few moments of forgetfulness. But it was in vain: I slept, indeed, but I was disturbed by the wildest dreams. I thought I saw Elizabeth, in the bloom of health, walking in the streets of Ingolstadt. Delighted and surprised, I embraced her; but as I imprinted the first kiss on her lips, they became livid with the hue of death; her features appeared to change, and I thought that I held the ⁸corpse of my dead mother in my arms; a ⁹shroud enveloped her form, and I saw the grave-worms crawling in the folds of the flannel. I started from my sleep with horror; a cold ¹⁰dew covered my forehead, my teeth chattered, and every limb became convulsed: when, by the dim and yellow light of the moon, as it forced its way through the window shutters, I beheld the wretch – the miserable monster whom I had created. He held up the curtain of the bed; and his eyes, if eyes they may be called, were fixed on me. His jaws opened, and he muttered some inarticulate sounds, while a grin wrinkled his cheeks. He might have spoken, but I did not hear; one hand was stretched out, seemingly to detain me, but I escaped, and rushed down stairs.

1 SPEAKING **Describe the photo and answer the questions below.**

1 In your opinion, what might be:
  a the attitude of the boys on the right towards the boys on the left?
  b the reason why the boys on the left are not looking at the boys on the right?
2 What does the photo tell you about British society at the time?

2 Complete the text with suitable words.

The British are particularly aware of – and fascinated ¹_____ – their class system. While many other societies around the world have a comparable structure, in Britain it seems to permeate every aspect of life, from food to fashion and ²_____ sports to speech.

A hundred years ago, the British class system was well-defined and there ³_____ little movement between the classes. In broad terms, society was divided into three social groups. The upper class consisted ⁴_____ people with inherited land or wealth who ⁵_____ no need to work. The middle class were professional people, generally well-educated, with jobs which paid a monthly salary: teachers, architects and doctors, for example. The working class were people who did unskilled work or skilled manual work for ⁶_____ they were paid a daily or weekly wage.

Although the basic structure of the class system remains the ⁷_____, some important aspects of it have changed. Firstly, the proportions. For most of the nineteenth century, the upper and middle classes together constituted only about 15% of the population. But the middle classes grew rapidly ⁸_____ the economy grew, with more and more people becoming merchants, businessmen, financiers and civil servants. Secondly, inequalities in wealth have become ⁹_____ pronounced. Before the 20th century, ordinary workers earned so little that even a moderately wealthy member of the middle classes ¹⁰_____ afford to employ servants. This changed as workers began to demand a reasonable wage. Thirdly, ideas of status have changed and people tend to be proud of their origins rather than aspiring to move up the class ladder.

3 🎧 TRCD **Listen to the radio programme about the British class system and speech. Which of these topics are mentioned?**

grammar   pronunciation   spelling   vocabulary

4 🎧 TRCD **Listen again. Using information from the programme, try to follow the instructions below.**

1 Choose the option (a–c) which rhymes with the word on the left when it is spoken in an upper class accent.
  getting   a shutting   b patting   c sitting
  just   a fist   b chest   c past
  catch   a pitch   b fetch   c clutch
2 In an upper class accent, say: 'Let's get ready for the match!'
3 In a working class London accent, say: 'I think I'll have some butter.'
4 Translate this sentence into standard English: 'My mate went into the boozer to use the bog.'
5 Translate this sentence into London working class language: 'You were lucky I'm not a police officer.'

5 SPEAKING **Read the fact file about a popular British TV show. Then discuss the questions below in pairs.**

▶ **FACT FILE**

▸ *Downton Abbey*, one of the most popular shows on British TV, is shown in more than 100 countries worldwide.
▸ First screened in 2010, it became an instant hit.
▸ *Downton Abbey* is the fictional home of an aristocratic family, the Crawley family, in the north of England.
▸ The events take place in the early part of the twentieth century.
▸ There are two sets of characters: the upper-class family who own the Abbey and the servants who work there.
▸ Highclere Castle is used for the setting. Its owner, the Earl of Carnarvon, is a personal friend of the show's writer.

1 In what way does the popularity of *Downton Abbey* reflect an interest in the class system?
2 In your opinion, is it morally wrong to have servants? Why?/Why not?
3 Do you think society would be better without a class system of any kind? Why?/Why not?

I can read and understand an early nineteenth century novel.

1 SPEAKING Think about the plots of two romantic comedies and answer the questions. Use two from the list or your own ideas.

*Definitely Maybe   Forgetting Sarah Marshall
Hit and Run   The Five Year Engagement   Marley and Me*

1 Is it usually clear from the start which characters will end up together? How can you tell?
2 How well do these characters get on earlier in the film? What happens between them?

2 Read the information about Jane Austen and *Pride and Prejudice*. Complete the text with suitable words.

Although Jane Austen (1775–1816) is one of the most famous writers in the English ¹_____ , she was not regarded as a major figure in English literature until a century ²_____ her death. Her six novels are generally regarded as romantic fiction, but they also show the reality of contemporary society and customs, particularly from a female perspective. In Austen's day, women were financially ³_____ on men, living at home until they got married. For families with several ⁴_____ , it was a daunting task finding a 'good match' (that is, a suitable husband) for them all. In *Pride and Prejudice*, Austen's best-known novel, Mr and Mrs Bennet have five daughters, and ⁵_____ the girls all have certain qualities, they have no private wealth to ⁶_____ them more attractive to would-be husbands. So when Mr Bingley, a handsome, rich and charming bachelor, moves to the area, it naturally causes great excitement in the Bennet family. His friend, Mr Darcy, is also handsome (and even ⁷_____) but his behaviour is far from charming. Elizabeth Bennet, the second eldest daughter, immediately dislikes him. This dislike grows throughout the novel – exacerbated by various deceptions and misunderstandings – until, eventually, the inevitable happens: they fall desperately in ⁸_____ .

3 Read the extract from *Pride and Prejudice*. Underline parts which either show or imply that:

1 Mrs Bennet is protective towards her daughters.
2 Jane Austen believes gossip leads to exaggeration.
3 Bingley and Darcy are close friends.
4 Darcy has a high opinion of himself.
5 Darcy is feeling particularly unsociable on this occasion.

4 🎧 TRCD Listen to an extract from *Pride and Prejudice*. Does Mr Bennet break his word to his wife? Why?/Why not ?

5 🎧 TRCD Listen again. Find evidence to show that these statements are true.

1 Mrs Bennet is very keen for her daughter to marry.
2 Mr Bennet is used to his wife being over-dramatic.
3 Mr Bennet has a low opinion of Mr Collins.
4 Mr Bennet has a close relationship with Elizabeth.

Mr Bingley had soon made himself acquainted with all the principal people in the room; he was lively and unreserved, danced every dance, was angry that the ball closed so early, and talked of giving one himself at Netherfield. Such amiable qualities must speak for themselves. What a contrast between him and his friend! Mr Darcy danced only once with Mrs Hurst and once with Miss Bingley, declined being introduced to any other lady, and spent the rest of the evening in walking about the room, speaking occasionally to one of his own party. His character was decided. He was the proudest, most disagreeable man in the world, and everybody hoped that he would never come there again. Amongst the most violent against him was Mrs Bennet, whose dislike of his general behaviour was sharpened into particular resentment by his having slighted one of her daughters.

Elizabeth Bennet had been obliged, by the scarcity of gentlemen, to sit down for two dances; and during part of that time, Mr Darcy had been standing near enough for her to overhear a conversation between him and Mr Bingley, who came from the dance for a few minutes to press his friend to join it.

'Come, Darcy,' said he, 'I must have you dance. I hate to see you standing about by yourself in this stupid manner. You had much better dance.'

'I certainly shall not. You know how I detest it, unless I am particularly acquainted with my partner. At such an assembly as this, it would be insupportable. Your sisters are engaged, and there is not another woman in the room whom it would not be a punishment to me to stand up with.'

'I would not be so fastidious as you are,' cried Bingley, 'for a kingdom! Upon my honour I never met with so many pleasant girls in my life, as I have this evening; and there are several of them, you see, uncommonly pretty.'

'You are dancing with the only handsome girl in the room,' said Mr Darcy, looking at the eldest Miss Bennet.

'Oh! she is the most beautiful creature I ever beheld! But there is one of her sisters sitting down just behind you, who is very pretty, and I dare say very agreeable. Do let me ask my partner to introduce you.'

'Which do you mean?' and turning round, he looked for a moment at Elizabeth, till catching her eye, he withdrew his own and coldly said, 'She is tolerable; but not handsome enough to tempt me; and I am in no humour at present to give consequence to young ladies who are slighted by other men. You had better return to your partner and enjoy her smiles, for you are wasting your time with me.'

Mr Bingley followed his advice. Mr Darcy walked off; and Elizabeth remained with no very cordial feelings towards him.

6 SPEAKING Discuss this question: How has the relationship between men and women changed now that women can work and support themselves financially?

1 SPEAKING Work in pairs. Look at the photos above. How has the BBC changed over the years? Do you know any BBC programmes?

2 Read the text. Which of these media is not mentioned?

books   the Internet   magazines   radio   television

3 Match these headings (A-F) to paragraphs 1–5 of the text. There is one extra heading.

A   A false start
B   A multi-platform provider
C   Commercial beginnings
D   Radio's heyday
E   The launch of BBC News

4 TRCD Listen to the information about the BBC World Service. Answer the questions.

1   How confident was the director general of the BBC that the new Empire Service would be successful?
2   What event did the same director general describe as 'the most spectacular success in BBC history'?
3   What did the Empire Service change its name to in 1939?
4   Why did General Charles de Gaulle broadcast such strange messages from London?
5   How did the BBC respond when the Communists attempted to block their broadcasts?
6   How did Vaclav Havel get around efforts to prevent him speaking on the BBC's Czech Service?
7   What happened to Bulgarian journalist Georgi Markov on his way to work in London?
8   In what way did the BBC World Service inadvertently help the KGB?

5 SPEAKING Discuss this statement in pairs: *Television and radio belong to the past and will soon be replaced by the Internet and social media.* **Do you agree or disagree? Give reasons.**

The story of the BBC

1 ___

The BBC (British Broadcasting Corporation), the most famous public service broadcaster in the world, began life as the British Broadcasting Company, owned and managed by a consortium of six radio manufacturers. By establishing a network of radio transmitters around the country and broadcasting a popular mix of news, weather, children's entertainment and music, they hoped to achieve their main goal: selling more radios! It worked, and by 1926, more than two million households in the UK owned at least one radio set. Newspapers refused to print details of the programmes on offer for fear their readers would desert them, so they were listed in a new BBC magazine called The Radio Times.

2 ___

In 1927, the company evolved into a national institution rather than a business venture, and its General Manager at that time, John Reith, had a clear vision of the BBC's role: it was to educate, inform and entertain. Their output increased massively during the 1930 as did their number of listeners, and in 1936 they began experimenting with a new and exciting form of technology: television. Sport immediately became an important part of the TV schedules and in 1937 they broadcast tennis from Wimbledon. But when Europe went to war in 1939, the BBC's television service closed down.

3 ___

During World War II, BBC radio played a crucial role, not only by broadcasting public service announcements and reporting news, but also by providing morale-boosting entertainment for the troops abroad and their families back home. During that period, the BBC also broadcast news programmes in all European languages and these were an important part of the propaganda war against Nazi Germany. After the war finished in 1945, radio continued to flourish and became a central part of British culture.

4 ___

Today, the BBC is the largest broadcasting company in the world employing about 23,000 people. Although its main activity is still making and broadcasting radio and TV programmes, it also maintains a huge website which includes a news service, an on-demand video service (BBC iPlayer) and a wide range of educational resources.

1 **SPEAKING** Work in pairs. Can you name any Romantic writers, artists or composers? Can you describe any of their work or say why you like or dislike it?

2 Read the text about Romanticism. Answer the questions.

1 What did the Enlightenment (a) react against? (b) value?
2 What did the Romantic poets dislike about modern life?
3 How did Romantic artists differ from those who preceded them?

Romanticism

Romanticism was a movement in the arts which started in the late eighteenth century and lasted for about 50 years. It revolutionised the way people thought about the world. In the eighteenth century the Enlightenment (or 'Age of Reason') had emphasised the importance of knowledge and reason, and had championed freedom of thought over despotism, medieval religion and superstition. It placed a special value on science, invention and discovery, and paved the way for the Industrial Revolution at the end of the eighteenth century.

Although in sympathy with many of the aims and achievements of the Enlightenment, poets like William Wordsworth reacted against industrialised urban life. These Romantics, as they came to be known, stressed the importance of 'nature' in contrast to the 'monstrous machines' in the new cities. They placed a high value on emotions; for Wordsworth, poetry was 'the spontaneous overflow of powerful feelings'. Whereas in the period before Romanticism artists had often followed 'rules' and tried to create beautiful works of art, the Romantics despised conventions and valued above all originality and imagination. The artist was a lonely figure, a talented 'genius', with a special mission in the world. He or she often shunned the company of others to be alone with nature. Through the power of imagination and memory, he or she was able to create works of art which spoke directly to the reader and invited them to identify with the artist and share his or her feelings.

3 **TRCD** Read and listen to Wordsworth's poem *Daffodils*. Choose the best summary:

1 The poet saw some daffodils but soon forgot them.
2 The poet saw some daffodils and takes great pleasure in the memory.
3 The poet didn't see real daffodils but created a beautiful image of them in his imagination.

4 **TRCD** Read and listen again. Identify parts of the poem which show:

1 the poet alone with nature.
2 the poet spending time at home alone with his thoughts.
3 the importance of memory and imagination in quiet moments.

5 What does the poet compare the daffodils with in:
(a) lines 7–10   (b) 11–13?

6 What is the poet's mood or moods in:
(a) lines 15–16   (b) lines 19–20   c) lines 23–24?

7 What is the rhyme scheme of the poem?

1 A B C A B C   3 A B A B C C
2 A A B B C C   4 A B A B A B

8 **SPEAKING** Do you like the poem? Give reasons.

Daffodils

I wandered lonely as a cloud
That floats on high o'er <u>vales</u>¹ and hills,
When all at once I saw a crowd,
A host, of golden daffodils;
5 Beside the lake, beneath the trees,
Fluttering and dancing in the breeze.

Continuous as the stars that shine
And twinkle on the milky way,
They stretched in never-ending line
10 Along the <u>margin</u>² of a bay:
Ten thousand saw I at a glance,
Tossing their heads in sprightly dance.

The waves beside them danced; but they
Out-did the sparkling waves in glee:
15 A poet could not but be gay,
In such a jocund company:
I gazed—and gazed—but little thought
What wealth the show to me had brought:

For oft, when on my couch I lie
20 In <u>vacant</u>³ or in pensive mood,
They flash upon that <u>inward eye</u>⁴
Which is the <u>bliss</u>⁵ of solitude;
And then my heart with pleasure fills,
And dances with the daffodils.

Glossary ¹over valleys ²edge ³without thoughts
⁴mind or imagination ⁵joy

1 SPEAKING Work in pairs. What do you know about these famous streets?

1 Downing Street 2 Oxford Street 3 Carnaby Street

2 TRCD Listen to the radio advertisement for a sightseeing tour and check your ideas.

3 Find these words and phrases in the texts below. Explain them.

1 draw a big crowd
2 blockbuster shows
3 flagship stores
4 independent boutiques
5 bring into the mainstream
6 fashion house
7 residence
8 accession

4 What nouns do these adjectives qualify in the text? Think of other nouns that they could be used with. Use a dictionary to help you.

1 ceremonial   4 iconic   7 refined
2 edgy   5 prestigious 8 upmarket
3 fashionable   6 principal   9 world-renowned

5 SPEAKING Work in pairs. Discuss these questions.

1 Which of the places mentioned in the text would you like to visit? Which not? Why?

2 Have you ever seen a play or a musical? If so, tell your partner about it. If not, would you like to see one? Why?/Why not?

3 Describe
   a the most important shopping streets in your town/capital city/country.
   b the main residence of your country's president or monarch.

Theatreland

'Theatreland' is London's principal theatre district. Situated in the heart of the West End, it contains approximately 40 theatres. The first, The Theatre Royal, was established in 1663 in Drury Lane and is still open, although the building itself has been demolished and rebuilt several times. The works staged at West End theatres are predominantly classics, comedies and musicals, often starring world-renowned film actors like Nicole Kidman and Orlando Bloom, who draw big crowds. The success of blockbuster shows like *Cats*, *Phantom of the Opera* and *Les Misérables* has helped the West End overtake New York's Broadway as the world capital of musical theatre.

Shopping

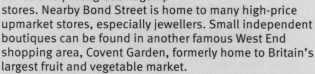

Stretching two and a half kilometres through the West End, Oxford Street is Europe's longest and busiest shopping street, with about 300 shops, including major department stores and prestigious flagship stores. Nearby Bond Street is home to many high-price upmarket stores, especially jewellers. Small independent boutiques can be found in another famous West End shopping area, Covent Garden, formerly home to Britain's largest fruit and vegetable market.

Fashion

London is one of the four big fashion capitals of the world, the others being Paris, Milan and New York. London is a relative newcomer, only rising to prominence in the 1960s when Carnaby Street in the West End and the King's Road in

Chelsea became centres of youth culture. Fashion designers Mary Quant, who invented the mini-skirt and hotpants, and Vivienne Westwood, who brought punk fashion into the mainstream, both opened boutiques there. In recent years, edgy young London designers such as John Galliano, Alexander McQueen and Stella McCartney, daughter of Beatle Paul McCartney, have landed top jobs at the most famous fashion houses, such as Givenchy and Christian Dior, and become some of the industry's most revered and fashionable figures. While Milan and Paris are famous for haute-couture and refined elegance, London-based designs have gained a reputation for quirkiness and extravagance.

Government

The British Prime Minister resides at Britain's most famous address: 10 Downing Street. Nearby, the Palace of Westminster, on the north bank of the Thames, contains the two Houses of Parliament (the Commons and the Lords), Big Ben – probably London's most iconic landmark – and Westminster Hall, which has been used for trials, coronations and ceremonial banquets for over 900 years. Not far away stands another world-renowned building: Buckingham Palace, the principal residence of British monarchs since the accession of Queen Victoria in 1837.

1 SPEAKING **Work in pairs. Match the sentence halves to make epigrams by Oscar Wilde. Which ones do you like? Say why.**

1 Always forgive your enemies;
2 I am not young enough
3 I can resist everything
4 Some cause happiness wherever they go;
5 One should always be in love.
6 Experience is simply

a but temptation.
b That is the reason one should never marry.
c nothing annoys them so much.
d the name we give our mistakes.
e others whenever they go.
f to know everything.

2 **Complete the information about *The Importance of Being Earnest* and Oscar Wilde with the nouns below.**

crime   customs   health   play   plot   release   success   trial

The Importance of Being Earnest is Oscar Wilde's best known and most popular ¹_____ . First performed in 1895, it was subtitled 'A trivial comedy for serious people' and in many ways it is, for despite the light-hearted ²_____ and witty dialogue, it mocks late-Victorian ³_____ and morality, especially marriage and love. In the play the two main characters have secret identities so that they can behave differently in different places. *The Importance* was an immediate ⁴_____ , but it proved to be Wilde's final play. Shortly after it opened in London, Wilde was put on ⁵_____ , accused of being homosexual, which was then a ⁶_____ in Britain. He was found guilty and sentenced to two years' hard labour. His ⁷_____ suffered greatly in prison and he died destitute in Paris in 1900, three years after his ⁸_____ . He was just 46 years old.

3 **Check the meaning of the words below, which all appear in the extract from *The Importance of Being Earnest* that you will listen to in exercise 4.**

candidly   demonstrative   destined   get christened
ideal (n)   indifferent   plain   propose to sb (vb)
speculation   thrill (vb)

4 🎧 TRCD **Now listen to the extract. Does Gwendolen accept Jack's proposal? What does she find most attractive about him? Why is this a problem for Jack?**

5 🎧 TRCD **Listen again. Find evidence of:**

1 Gwendolin's   **a** confidence. **b** cynicism.
2 Jack's   **a** nervousness. **b** romantic nature.

6 🎧 TRCD **Read and listen to the next part of the play. Identify comic moments and say why they are funny. (Look at both the characters' lines and the stage directions.)**

Lady Bracknell Mr Worthing! Rise, sir, from this semi-recumbent posture. It is most indecorous.

Gwendolen Mamma! [*He tries to rise; she restrains him.*] I must beg you to retire. This is no place for you. Besides, Mr Worthing has not quite finished yet.

Lady Bracknell Finished what, may I ask?

Gwendolen I am engaged to Mr Worthing, mamma. [*They rise together.*]

Lady Bracknell Pardon me, you are not engaged to any one. When you do become engaged to some one, I, or your father, should his health permit him, will inform you of the fact. An engagement should come on a young girl as a surprise, pleasant or unpleasant, as the case may be. It is hardly a matter that she could be allowed to arrange for herself. And now I have a few questions to put to you, Mr Worthing. While I am making these inquiries, you, Gwendolen, will wait for me below in the carriage.

Gwendolen [*Reproachfully*] Mamma!

Lady Bracknell In the carriage, Gwendolen! [*Gwendolen goes to the door. She and Jack blow kisses to each other behind Lady Bracknell's back. Lady Bracknell looks vaguely about as if she could not understand what the noise was. Finally turns round.*] Gwendolen, the carriage!

Lady Bracknell [*Sitting down*] You can take a seat, Mr Worthing. [*Looks in her pocket for note-book and pencil.*]

Jack Thank you, Lady Bracknell, I prefer standing.

Lady Bracknell [*Pencil and note-book in hand.*] I feel bound to tell you that you are not down on my list of eligible young men, although I have the same list as the dear Duchess of Bolton has. We work together, in fact. However, I am quite ready to enter your name, should your answers be what a really affectionate mother requires. Do you smoke?

Jack Well, yes, I must admit I smoke.

Lady Bracknell I am glad to hear it. A man should always have an occupation of some kind. There are far too many idle men in London as it is. How old are you?

Jack Twenty-nine.

Lady Bracknell A very good age to be married at. I have always been of opinion that a man who desires to get married should know either everything or nothing. Which do you know?

Jack [*After some hesitation.*] I know nothing, Lady Bracknell.

Lady Bracknell I am pleased to hear it. I do not approve of anything that tampers with natural ignorance. [...] The whole theory of modern education is radically unsound. Fortunately in England, at any rate, education produces no effect whatsoever. If it did, it would prove a serious danger to the upper classes, and probably lead to acts of violence in Grosvenor Square.

7 **What does the extract tell us about the nature and purpose of marriage in late-Victorian England?**

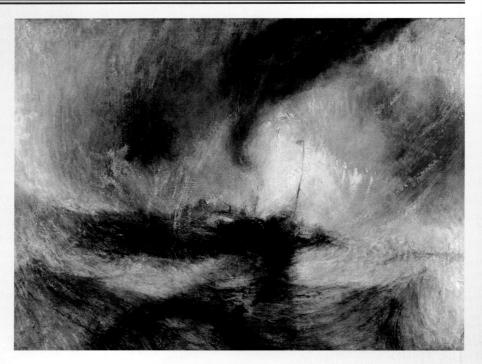

Joseph Mallord William Turner was born in London in 1775. He came from a modest background; his father was a barber and wig maker and his mother was from a family of butchers. He showed a very early talent for drawing and painting, and began to sell his pictures from his father's shop. By the age of 14, young Joseph was already an accomplished artist and enrolled at the Royal Academy of Arts school, the most prestigious painting school in Britain.

In the 1790s Turner spent the summers travelling widely in Britain, sketching in the open air, and spent the winters painting in his studio. His paintings soon began to appear in exhibitions in London alongside works by much older, well-established painters. In 1802 he made the first of many trips to mainland Europe, visiting France and Switzerland. He was very influenced by French painters and imitated their style. But he soon began to experiment and to develop a very individual style of his own.

Turner was particularly attracted to dramatic, romantic subjects like shipwrecks, fires and natural disasters. He was fascinated by the destructiveness of nature and in particular the violent power of the sea. In this painting, 'Snow storm – steamboat off a harbour's mouth', exhibited in 1842, the boat is caught in the middle of a terrible storm and is trying to reach the safety of the harbour. Turner is not trying here to paint realistically. He has imagined the scene rather than painted it from nature, and attempts to make it as dramatic and as striking as possible. He is giving us an impression of the tiny boat in the swirling rain and mountainous seas. He is trying to show us how helpless we are when faced with the destructive powers of nature.

Turner was recognised by his contemporaries as an artistic genius. His romantic, dramatic paintings were very popular and sold well, making him a very wealthy man. On his death, he left all his paintings to the British government and most of them are kept at the Tate Gallery in London. Turner had a big influence on the French impressionist painters in the second half of the nineteenth century. What they admired in Turner was the 'impressionistic' atmosphere in his paintings and the way that he painted light.

1 SPEAKING Look at the painting. Discuss these questions. Give reasons for your opinions.

1 What does the painting depict?
2 When do you think it was painted?
3 Describe the atmosphere of the painting.

2 Read about the painting and the artist. In your own words tell your partner about the following aspects of the artist.

1 family background
2 early career
3 travel
4 subject matter of his paintings and style
5 success during his lifetime
6 influence on later artists

3 SPEAKING Work in pairs. Discuss these questions.

1 Do you like the painting in exercise 1? Why?
2 Do you generally prefer figurative art (art that attempts to represent with some accuracy its subject matter) or abstract art (art that in some ways departs from the reality of the subject)? Why?
3 Tell your partner about a work of art or an artist that you admire. Give reasons for your views.

I can read and understand poems about war.

1 SPEAKING When was the First World War? Which countries were involved?

2 🎧 TRCD Read and listen to the poems. Which poem:
1 glorifies dying for your country?
2 highlights the horror of dying in war?

3 🎧 TRCD Read and listen again. Use the adjectives below to describe the tone and content of each poem. Give reasons for your opinions.

angry bitter compassionate depressing gruesome
hard-hitting nostalgic patriotic peaceful powerful
realistic sentimental shocking soothing uplifting

4 Read the Fact file. In what way do the two poems reflect each poet's experience of war?

> ▶ **FACT FILE**
>
> ▶ Rupert Brooke and Wilfred Owen both died in the First World War. Brooke was 27 and died of an infected mosquito bite on a naval ship in the Mediterranean. Owen was 26 and was killed in action in France on 4 November 1918, exactly a week before the war ended.
> ▶ *The Soldier* was written in 1914 at the start of the war. Brooke had not experienced any fighting.
> ▶ *Dulce Et Decorum Est* was written in 1917 after Owen had experienced a number of years of trench warfare. The poem was written to Jessie Pope, who wrote poems encouraging young people to join the army.

5 Match each of the four stanzas of *Dulce Et Decorum Est* with a summary sentence below. There is one sentence that you don't need.

a the image of the soldier dying recurs in the poet's dreams
b a direct address to the reader challenging him/her not to glorify war
c a warning not to join the army
d sudden action as the soldiers come under chemical weapon attack
e a description of tired soldiers returning from battle

6 Consider and contrast the imagery used in the poems.
1 In *The Soldier*, find:
 a references to the English landscape.
 b tranquil images in lines 12–14.
2 In *Dulce Et Decorum Est*, find:
 a two similes in lines 1–2 describing the soldiers.
 b four adjectives in lines 6–8 describing the soldiers.
 c shocking images describing the dying soldier in lines 16–24.

7 SPEAKING Do you like the poems? Which one do you prefer? Give reasons.

THE SOLDIER by Rupert Brooke

If I should die, think only this of me:
That there's some corner of a foreign field
That is for ever England. There shall be
In that rich earth a richer dust[1] concealed;
5 A dust whom England bore, shaped, made aware,
Gave, once, her flowers to love, her ways to roam[2],
A body of England's, breathing English air,
Washed by the rivers, blest[3] by suns of home.
And think, this heart, all evil shed away[4],
10 A pulse in the eternal mind, no less
Gives somewhere back the thoughts by England given;
Her sights and sounds; dreams happy as her day;
And laughter, learnt of friends; and gentleness,
In hearts at peace, under an English heaven.

> **Glossary** [1]'a richer dust' i.e. the soldier's body
> [2]paths and roads to wander [3]blessed [4]removed

DULCE ET DECORUM EST by Wilfred Owen

Bent double, like old beggars under sacks,
Knock-kneed, coughing like hags, we cursed through sludge,
Till on the haunting flares we turned our backs
And towards our distant rest began to trudge.
5 Men marched asleep. Many had lost their boots
But limped on, blood-shod[1]. All went lame; all blind;
Drunk with fatigue; deaf even to the hoots
Of gas-shells dropping softly behind.
Gas! GAS! Quick, boys! – An ecstasy of fumbling,
10 Fitting the clumsy helmets just in time;
But someone still was yelling out and stumbling,
And flound'ring like a man in fire or lime …
Dim, through the misty panes and thick green light,
As under a green sea, I saw him drowning.
15 In all my dreams, before my helpless sight,
He plunges at me, guttering, choking, drowning.
If in some smothering dreams you too could pace
Behind the wagon that we flung him in,
And watch the white eyes writhing in his face,
20 His hanging face, like a devil's sick of sin;
If you could hear, at every jolt, the blood
Come gargling from the froth-corrupted lungs,
Obscene as cancer, bitter as the cud
To children ardent for some desperate glory,
25 The old Lie: *Dulce et decorum est
Pro patria mori*[2].

> **Glossary** [1] 'shod' wearing on one's feet
> [2] Latin: 'It is sweet and fitting to die for one's country'.

1 Work in pairs. Answer the quiz questions.

1 When did the Aboriginal people first arrive in Australia?
a about 50,000 years ago   b about 25,000 years ago
c about 5,000 years ago
2 In which century did Britain first colonise Australia?
a 17th century   b 18th century   c 19th century
3 What did the British establish in Botany Bay?
a a cricket club   b a holiday resort   c a penal colony
4 The British colonists took Aboriginal land principally to
a grow crops.   b raise livestock.   c build new towns.
5 What made Australia much richer in the mid-19th
century?
a livestock farming   b the arrival of immigrants
c the discovery of gold
6 Australia gained independence from Britain in
a 1851   b 1901   c 1951

2 🎧 TRCD   Listen and check your answers to the quiz.

3 🎧 TRCD   Listen again. Answer the questions.

1 What information is given about the early indigenous
people?
2 What unfortunate effect did the arrival of the European
colonists immediately have on the Aboriginal people?
3 What caused conflict between the colonists and the
indigenous people?
4 What effect did the Gold Rush have on the population?

4 Complete the text with the adjectives below.

common   first   free   ideal   overcrowded   penal
poor   reluctant   useful

5 🎧 TRCD   SPEAKING   Work in pairs. Listen to part of a song
called Botany Bay, written in the 19th century. Discuss the
questions.

1 Who is 'we' in the song?
2 What do they find depressing?
3 Who else is on the ship besides them?
4 What warning is contained in the third verse?

BOTANY BAY

It's not leaving old England we care about,
Nor sailing for shores far away,
It's the bloomin' monotony wears us out
And the prospect of Botany Bay.

　Oh, too-roo-lie, oo-roo-lie, oo-roo-lay,
　Too-roo-lie, oo-roo-lie ay.
　Too-roo-lie, oo-roo-lie, oo-roo-lay,
　Too-roo-lie, oo-roo-lie-ay.

Oh, the Captain and all the ship's officers
The Bo's'n and all of the crew,
The first- and second-class passengers,
Knows what us poor convicts go through.
　Chorus

Now, all you young dukes and you duchesses,
Take warning from what I've to say:
Be sure that you own all you touchesses
Or they'll land you in Botany Bay.
　Chorus

TRANSPORTATION

By the late eighteenth century, Britain's prisons had
become very ¹_____ , and transportation to the
American colonies had become a ²_____ punishment
for many crimes. In the 1770s Britain lost her American
colonies and was forced to look elsewhere. Australia, which
had recently been claimed for Britain by Captain James Cook,
was the ³_____ location for a new ⁴_____ colony. Conditions
on the transport ships were ⁵_____ and many prisoners
died before reaching their destination. For the few decades
after the arrival of the ⁶_____ settlers, convicts made up the
majority of Australia's population. Approximately 161,700
convicts, of whom 25,000 were women, were sent to Australia
between 1788 and 1868. As time went by, however, they were
increasingly seen as a ⁷_____ source of labour rather than
simply as prisoners undergoing punishment. Opposition to
transportation grew among the free settlers, who resented the
convicts taking their jobs. It was the discovery of gold that
finally led to the abolition of transportation. Free settlers were
understandably ⁸_____ to share the new-found wealth with
convicted criminals, and argued that transportation was no
longer a punishment but a ⁹_____ ticket to riches. The last
convict ship arrived in Australia in 1868.

1 SPEAKING **Work in pairs. What do you know about:**
1 the Russian Revolution? 2 Stalin?
3 life in the Soviet Union before the fall of Communism?

2 TRCD **Listen to information about *Animal Farm* and George Orwell. Answer the questions.**
1 In which countries did Orwell live before returning to England in the 1930s?
2 In which war did he fight, and on which side?
3 Why did he have to flee from Spain?
4 Why was he critical of left-wing people in Britain?
5 Did Orwell believe that the Russian Revolution was totally wrong? Why?/Why not?
6 What other famous books did he write?

3 **Read the extract from *Animal Farm*. Answer the questions.**
1 How does the animals' fear and wonderment manifest itself as they look round the farmhouse?
2 What do the animals resolve to do with the house?
3 What have the pigs done that demonstrates how much cleverer they are than the other animals?
4 What does Snowball first use the paint for?
5 The commandments are designed to unite the animals, and to emphasise the distinction between them and what else?

(The animals have just taken control of the farm and expelled Farmer Jones.)

They filed back to the farm buildings and halted in silence outside the door of the farmhouse. That was theirs too, but they were frightened to go inside. After a moment, however, Snowball and Napoleon butted the door open with their shoulders and the animals entered in single file, walking with the utmost care for fear of disturbing anything. They tiptoed from room to room, afraid to speak above a whisper and gazing with a kind of awe at the unbelievable luxury, at the beds with their feather mattresses, the looking-glasses, the horsehair sofa, the Brussels carpet, the lithograph of Queen Victoria over the drawing-room mantelpiece [...] A unanimous resolution was passed on the spot that the farmhouse should be preserved as a museum. All were agreed that no animal must ever live there.

The animals had their breakfast and then Snowball and Napoleon called them together again.

'Comrades,' said Snowball, 'it is half-past six and we have a long day before us. Today we begin the hay harvest. But there is another matter that must be attended to first.'

The pigs now revealed that during the past three months they had taught themselves to read and write from an old spelling book which had belonged to Mr Jones's children and which had been thrown on the rubbish heap.

4 SPEAKING **Discuss this question in pairs: What do you think might happen later in the story with regard to the Seven Commandments?**

5 TRCD **Listen to an extract from near the end of the story. Did you make any correct predictions in exercise 4?**

6 TRCD **Listen again and answer the questions.**
1 Which of the first six commandments have the pigs broken? In what way?
2 What other resolution described in the text in exercise 3 have the pigs also broken?
3 What role do (a) the sheep (b) the dogs have on the farm?
4 How has the seventh commandment been altered?
5 In what way is this new single commandment nonsensical and contradictory?

7 SPEAKING **Do you think allegories are an effective way of conveying a political message? Give reasons.**

Napoleon sent for pots of black and white paint and led the way down to the five-barred gate that gave on the main road. Then Snowball (for it was Snowball who was best at writing) took a brush between the two knuckles of his trotter, painted out MANOR FARM from the top bar of the gate and in its place painted ANIMAL FARM. This was to be the name of the farm from now onwards. After this they went back to the farm buildings, where Snowball and Napoleon sent for a ladder which they caused to be set against the end wall of the big barn. They explained that by their studies of the past three months the pigs had succeeded in reducing the principles of Animalism to seven commandments. These seven commandments would now be inscribed on the wall; they would form an unalterable law by which all animals on Animal Farm must live for ever after. With some difficulty (for it is not easy for a pig to balance himself on a ladder) Snowball climbed up and set to work, with Squealer a few rungs below him holding the paint-pot. The commandments were written on the tarred wall in great white letters that could be read thirty yards away. They ran thus:

THE SEVEN COMMANDMENTS
1 Whatever goes upon two legs is an enemy.
2 Whatever goes upon four legs, or has wings, is a friend.
3 No animal shall wear clothes.
4 No animal shall sleep in a bed.
5 No animal shall drink alcohol.
6 No animal shall kill any other animal.
7 All animals are equal.

1 SPEAKING **Describe the photo below and answer the questions.**

1 Where do you think these people were going and why?
2 What problems do you think they might have faced on the journey?

2 **Read the text and find the answers to the questions in exercise 1. What is the connection between the photo below the text and the photo in exercise 1?**

3 **Are these sentences true (T), false (F), or is the answer not stated (NS)?**

1 The word 'pioneers' refers to the first European settlers in North America.
2 The most likely cause of death for members of a wagon train was illness.
3 Some rumours about life in the west were not true.
4 Malaria was a big killer in the swamps of the mid-west.
5 Few of the pioneers who made the journey west regretted their decision.
6 People who make 'road trip movies' are a modern incarnation of the pioneer spirit.

4 🎧 TRCD **Listen to the true story of an ill-fated wagon train called the Donner Party. Who was mostly to blame for their problems?**

5 🎧 TRCD **Listen again. Answer the questions.**

1 Why were the group called the Donner Party?
2 Why did the party choose to follow Lansford Hastings's new route from Fort Bridger to California?
3 How many people and wagons were in the group?
4 Why did the party stop and wait several days before entering the Wasatch Mountains?
5 Why did the delays during their journey become more important when they reached the Sierra Nevada?
6 What are members of the party rumoured to have done to escape starvation while trapped in the mountains?

6 SPEAKING **Discuss examples of the 'pioneer spirit' in the modern world. Do you think it is something specifically American or do all nations have it?**

PIONEERS

The earliest European settlers in North America established colonies on the east coast, where they had landed. But as the population increased, many felt the urge to move westwards in search of new lands and a new life. The vast expanses of the continent were largely unpopulated, except for scattered tribes of indigenous Indians. Those who headed west were called pioneers, and they travelled in lines of wagons for up to six months in order to reach California or Oregon on the west coast.

The pioneers faced many dangers on their journey. Some Indians were hostile, although not as blood-thirsty as Hollywood films tend to suggest. Injury and illness were far more likely causes of death. Crossing rivers was perilous, as were storms and wild animals, and since distances between watering holes could be great, they were always at risk of running out.

Given the hazardous nature of the journey, why did so many Americans choose to make it? Partly, they were tempted by exaggerated descriptions of how wonderful life could be in the west; many had heard tales of crops growing taller than a man. But they were also escaping very real hardships in the Mid West, where the swamps of Missouri and Mississippi were infested with disease-carrying insects.

Once they had arrived at their destination, pioneers used any money they had brought with them to buy land. They cleared trees and prepared the land for farming, and built simple houses. The pioneers needed to be largely self-sufficient, making their own clothes, tools and furniture. Life was certainly hard but communities were close-knit and supportive, and most families were glad they had made the journey.

In modern America, people still talk of the 'pioneer spirit', meaning a willingness to face hardships and danger in order to achieve a better life for yourself and your family. Many of the immigrants who come to the USA each year are a testament to this spirit. And although these days Hollywood makes few films about wagon trains, the modern 'road trip movie' taps into the same urge to escape your surroundings and follow your dreams across a vast and exciting continent.

I can read and understand part of a classic American novel.

1 SPEAKING Work in pairs. Can you think of any films or TV shows in which the two main characters are close friends but very different? Why is it an appealing kind of story?

2 Complete the text with the words below.

as   enduring   particularly   peacefully   previously
temporary   while   wholly

At the beginning of the 1930s, the United States entered a long period of economic depression, ¹_____ did most other countries in the developed world. Economic output declined sharply, ²_____ unemployment soared. There was widespread poverty, ³_____ in areas which depended on heavy industry, construction and farming. The people who had ⁴_____ been employed as farm labourers, builders and factory workers now found themselves without jobs, without money, without homes – and often without hope. Against this background, the Nobel Prize-winning novelist John Steinbeck created some of his most powerful and ⁵_____ fiction. *Of Mice and Men* is a novella which tells the tragic story of two migrant workers struggling to make a living by wandering from farm to farm in search of ⁶_____ employment. The two men could hardly be more different: George Milton is a survivor, small and quick-witted, while Lennie Small is mentally disabled, ⁷_____ dependent on his friend and yet immensely strong physically. The two friends share a dream of one day living ⁸_____ on a small farm of their own, where Lennie, who loves pets, can look after the rabbits. But Lennie's habit of getting into trouble means that the dream is destined never to come true.

3 Read the extract from *Of Mice and Men*. What does it tell you about Lennie's physical and mental qualities? Justify your answer with words and phrases from the text.

4 Find the following words in the text. How do you write the words correctly? Why are they written this way here?

1 ya	3 yella	5 'im	7 tol'	9 han'
2 gonna	4 'um	6 leggo	8 ever'	

5 🎧 TRCD Listen to an extract from near the end of the novel. Lennie has run away after accidentally killing a young woman, but George has caught up with him. Why do you think George:

1 tells Lennie to take his hat off?
2 talks about the rabbits one more time?
3 pauses several times while he's talking to Lennie?
4 wants Lennie to looks straight ahead, across the river?
5 insists he isn't, and has never been, angry with Lennie?

6 SPEAKING In pairs, discuss why George shoots Lennie. Do you think he is right to do it? What does it tell you about their relationship?

Curley stepped over to Lennie like a terrier. 'What the hell you laughin' at?'

Lennie looked blankly at him. 'Huh?'

Then Curley's rage exploded. 'Come on, ya big bastard. Get up on your feet. No big son-of-a-bitch is gonna laugh at me. I'll show ya who's yella.'

Lennie looked helplessly at George, and then he got up and tried to retreat.

Curley was balanced and poised. He slashed at Lennie with his left, and then smashed down his nose with a right. Lennie gave a cry of terror. Blood welled from his nose. 'George,' he cried. 'Make 'um let me alone, George.' He backed until he was against the wall, and Curley followed, slugging him in the face. Lennie's hands remained at his sides; he was too frightened to defend himself.

George was on his feet yelling, 'Get him, Lennie. Don't let him do it.'

Lennie covered his face with his huge paws and bleated with terror. He cried, 'Make 'um stop, George.' Then Curley attacked his stomach and cut off his wind.

Slim jumped up. 'The dirty little rat,' he cried, 'I'll get 'um myself.'

George put out his hand and grabbed Slim. 'Wait a minute,' he shouted. He cupped his hands around his mouth and yelled, 'Get 'im, Lennie!'

Lennie took his hands away from his face and looked about for George, and Curley slashed at his eyes. The big face was covered with blood. George yelled again, 'I said get him.'

Curley's fist was swinging when Lennie reached for it. The next minute Curley was flopping like a fish on a line, and his closed fist was lost in Lennie's big hand. George ran down the room. 'Leggo of him, Lennie. Let go.'

But Lennie watched in terror the flopping little man whom he held. Blood ran down Lennie's face, one of his eyes was cut and closed. George slapped him in the face again and again, and still Lennie held on to the closed fist. Curley was white and shrunken by now, and his struggling had become weak. He stood crying, his fist lost in Lennie's paw.

George shouted over and over. 'Leggo his hand, Lennie. Leggo. Slim, come help me while the guy got any hand left.'

Suddenly Lennie let go his hold. He crouched cowering against the wall.

'You tol' me to, George,' he said miserably.

Curley sat down on the floor, looking in wonder at his crushed hand. Slim and Carlson bent over him. Then Slim straightened up and regarded Lennie with horror. 'We got to get him in to a doctor, he said. Looks to me like ever' bone in his han' is bust.'

1 Read part of a song about the Vietnam War. What is the songwriter's attitude to the war? Find evidence in the lyrics to support your answer.

Saigon Bride by Joan Baez

Farewell my wistful Saigon bride
I'm going out to stem the tide
A tide that never saw the seas
It flows through jungles, round the trees
5 Some say it's yellow, some say red
It will not matter when we're dead

How many dead men will it take
To build a dike that will not break?
How many children must we kill
10 Before we make the waves stand still?

2 Discuss the questions. Give reasons for your opinions.
1 Who is the singer, do you think?
2 Who is the Saigon bride?
3 What is the significance of the words *yellow* and *red* (line 5)?

3 Read the text about the Vietnam War and answer the questions below in your own words.
1 Why did Britain and the USA help create South Vietnam?
2 Who were the Viet Cong?
3 Why was it difficult for the US government to resolve the conflict?
4 In what sense did the Americans lose the war, bearing in mind their original aims?

4 🎧 TRCD Listen to an extract from *Catch-22*, in which the main character Yossarian explains his fear of combat to another soldier, Clevinger. Which character gets angry and why?

5 🎧 TRCD Listen again and write Yossarian's two missing lines. Do you think his argument makes sense? Why?/Why not?

'No one's trying to kill you,' Clevinger cried.
'_____ ?' Yossarian asked.
'They're shooting at everyone,' Clevinger answered. 'They're trying to kill everyone.'
'_____ ?'

6 SPEAKING In pairs, look at the titles of some films about the Vietnam War. Then discuss the questions below.

Apocalypse Now   *Good Morning Vietnam*
AWOL   *Missing in Action*
Born on the Fourth of July *Platoon*
The Deer Hunter   *The Walking Dead*
Full Metal Jacket   *We Were Soldiers*

1 Do you enjoy watching war films? What do you like or dislike about them?
2 Why is the theme of war so popular with film-makers and audiences?
3 Can a war film ever convey an anti-war message? How?

WHEN WORLD WAR TWO ended in 1945, the small South-East Asian country of Vietnam, which had been under French control for many years, hoped to gain independence at last. But the French had other ideas. Britain and the USA were also unhappy with the idea of an independent Vietnam because they feared it could embrace Communism, seen as the big enemy by the West at that time. So when the French were defeated by the Vietnamese in 1954, the Americans stepped in. Vietnam was split in two, and an anti-Communist state was formed in the south, supported financially and militarily by the USA.

North Vietnam's ambition was to reunite the two halves of the country, and they were aided by various groups within South Vietnam too, who were known as the Viet Cong. South Vietnam needed more and more American assistance, until the USA found itself fighting a full-scale war in South-East Asia. Casualties were high on both sides, but there was no clear way to resolve the conflict. An anti-war movement formed in the USA, mainly among singers, musicians, artists and students, but with a few high-profile celebrities from Hollywood and the media adding their voices to the protests. As more and more American troops were killed, the government struggled to find a peaceful solution which wouldn't look like a defeat.

In 1972, the Americans intensified their bombing campaign against North Vietnam while at the same time seeking a peace settlement. In 1973, the Paris Peace Treaty was agreed and US troops left Vietnam. However, two years later North Vietnam took control of the south and the country was reunited as a Communist state which survives to this day. According to Joseph Heller, author of the famous anti-war novel Catch-22, the Americans brought peace to Vietnam 'in the same way Napolean brought peace to Europe: by losing.'

I can read and understand poems by a twentieth century poet.

1 **SPEAKING** Discuss this statement in pairs: *Song lyrics are a form of poetry*. **Do you agree or disagree? Give reasons.**

2 🎧 **TRCD** Listen to a short biography of Sylvia Plath. Complete the key facts below. Write one word in each gap.

1 Sylvia Plath was born and grew up in the _____ .
2 She studied _____ at Smith College.
3 Plath underwent treatment for _____ .
4 She met Ted Hughes while at _____ .
5 As a poet, Hughes often chose _____ as a theme.
6 Plath and Hughes _____ in 1962.
7 Plath's death in 1963 was the result of _____ .
8 The final months of her life were a very _____ period.

3 🎧 **TRCD** Read and listen to the poems opposite. Which theme do they have in common, in your opinion?

a relatives   c day and night
b trees and plants   d death

4 In pairs, read the poems and check the meaning of any unknown words. Then answer the questions.

Which poem contains:
1 more rhymes?
2 a more regular rhythm?
3 more references to the natural world?
4 a clearer sequence of events?
5 more references to specific sounds?
6 more allusions to death?

5 Read the generalisations below about modern poetry. Find evidence for them by comparing the two Sylvia Plath poems with the poems on pages 137 and 141.

Compared to more traditional poetry, modern poems often:
• have more irregular line lengths.
• have a less regular rhythm.
• have fewer rhymes or none.
• contain more ambiguities and unclear meanings.
• focus more on the poet's own experiences and feelings.

6 **SPEAKING** Which of the two poems on this page do you prefer? Can you explain why?

Family Reunion (CIRCA 1953)

Outside in the street I hear
A car door slam; voices coming near;
Incoherent scraps of talk
And high heels clicking up the walk;
The doorbell rends the noonday heat
With copper claws;
A second's pause.
The dull drums of my pulses beat
Against a silence wearing thin.
The door now opens from within.
Oh, hear the clash of people meeting —
The laughter and the screams of greeting:

Fat always, and out of breath,
A greasy smack on every cheek
From Aunt Elizabeth;
There, that's the pink, pleased squeak
Of Cousin Jane, our spinster with
The faded eyes
And hands like nervous butterflies;
While rough as splintered wood
Across them all
Rasps the jarring baritone of Uncle Paul;
The youngest nephew gives a fretful whine
And drools at the reception line.

Like a diver on a lofty spar of land
Atop the flight of stairs I stand.
A whirlpool leers at me,
I cast off my identity
And make the fatal plunge.

I am vertical (1961)

But I would rather be horizontal.
I am not a tree with my root in the soil
Sucking up minerals and motherly love
So that each March I may gleam into leaf,
Nor am I the beauty of a garden bed
Attracting my share of Ahs and spectacularly painted,
Unknowing I must soon unpetal.
Compared with me, a tree is immortal
And a flower-head not tall, but more startling,
And I want the one's longevity and the other's daring.

Tonight, in the infinitesimal light of the stars,
The trees and the flowers have been strewing their cool odors.
I walk among them, but none of them are noticing.
Sometimes I think that when I am sleeping
I must most perfectly resemble them —
Thoughts gone dim.
It is more natural to me, lying down.
Then the sky and I are in open conversation,
And I shall be useful when I lie down finally:
Then the trees may touch me for once, and the flowers have time for me.

1 🎧 TRCD Listen. Match the six music clips with the musical styles below. Which do you like or dislike?

blues   gospel   jazz   ragtime   rap   soul

2 SPEAKING Work in pairs. Match the singers and performers below with the musical styles in exercise 1 that they are associated with.

1 Louis Armstrong
2 Aretha Franklin
3 Snoop Dogg
4 Scott Joplin
5 B. B. King
6 Mahalia Jackson

3 How many more black American musicians and singers can you name? What do you know about them?

4 Read the texts. Which type(s) of music:

1 possibly has a bad influence on young people?
2 was sung by black slaves?
3 is sung in churches?
4 was at its most popular in the first two decades of the twentieth century?
5 developed in New Orleans?
6 often has as its subject matter problems experienced by black people in the USA?

5 SPEAKING Read the texts again. Tell your partner in your own words two interesting facts you discovered about the music.

Spirituals and gospel

Spirituals are religious folk songs that were created by black slaves in the USA in the eighteenth and nineteenth centuries. The slaves were converted to Christianity, and the songs were an expression of their religious faith and also communicated the hardship and suffering they endured. Black gospel music has its roots in spiritual music, originating in churches in northern cities in the 1920s. It has survived as the most important music in churches with predominantly black congregations.

Ragtime

Ragtime had its origins in the marching music played by African-American bands in the 1890s. It is characterised by a syncopated or 'ragged' rhythm, hence its name. It was at the height of its popularity between about 1900 and 1918, after which it fell out of favour. Scott Joplin, a virtuoso pianist, became famous as a composer of ragtime music. Many of his pieces, such as *The Entertainer* are still widely played today.

Blues

Blues originated in the African-American communities in the southern states of the USA in the late nineteenth century. The lyrics are usually sad, often describing troubles experienced in African-American society. Early blues songs were typically sung with a guitar or banjo and harmonica accompaniment. In the 1950s, blues had a huge influence on mainstream popular music and inspired white British musicians such as Eric Clapton in the 1960s.

Jazz

Jazz developed in the last decade of the nineteenth century in New Orleans from blues, ragtime, and brass band music usually heard at festivals and funerals. There was a strong 'party atmosphere' in the city and music was always in demand. Scores of jazz bands formed and played in the city's bars and dancehalls, often competing with one another to play the most demanding and entertaining music. Improvisation also became an important part of New Orleans jazz.

Soul

Soul originated in the 1950s and 1960s, in northern US cities like Chicago. It combines elements of gospel music and blues and, like the blues, reflects the experience of young African-Americans. In the 1960s, Detroit-based Motown Records produced a number of soul hits by artists such as Stevie Wonder, Gladys Knight, Marvin Gaye and the Temptations.

Hip hop

Hip hop evolved in the 1970s in New York at parties held by groups of young black people. It has its roots in the strong driving rhythms of soul and disco music, and is often accompanied by 'rapping', chanted rhyming speech. The lyrics are frequently political or deal with social issues like poverty and racism, but have often been criticised for being misogynistic and glorifying gun culture. It is often claimed that hip hop music provides a voice for disenfranchised youth in poor urban areas.

1 SPEAKING In pairs, write a definition of the term 'science fiction'. Then compare your ideas with the class and improve your definition.

2 TRCD Listen to a synopsis of Margaret Atwood's novel *The Handmaid's Tale*. How well does it fit your definition from exercise 1? Explain your answer.

3 TRCD Listen again. Are these statements about the plot of *The Handmaid's Tale* true (T) or false (F)?

1 The novel is set after the USA has been invaded by another state.
2 Offred can only achieve total privacy in her own room.
3 Offred's name reflects the fact that she is the Commander's possession.
4 When Offred becomes separated from her husband and daughter, she stays with another relative.
5 Offred becomes a member of a secret organisation called Mayday.
6 The novel does not say what Offred's ultimate fate is.

4 Read the extract opposite. What does Aunt Lydia mean when she says 'Now you are being given freedom from'?

5 Explain in your own words what the following phrases from the text tell us about the Republic of Gilead.

1 'Gilead', said Aunt Lydia, 'knows no bounds. Gilead is within you.'
2 There are no lawyers anymore …
3 … and the university is closed.
4 Luke and I used to walk together … Such freedom now seems almost weightless.
5 … the striped dress … that mark the women of the poorer men. Econowives, they're called.
6 … no man shouts obscenities at us, speaks to us, touches us.

6 SPEAKING Discuss why science fiction so often shows the future as a 'dystopia'. Say whether you agree or disagree with the statements below and add your own ideas.

1 It's easier to invent stories about dystopias.
2 It's more interesting to read or watch stories about dystopias.
3 Dystopias are more realistic because the world is becoming a worse place to live.

This is the heart of Gilead, where the war cannot intrude except on television. Where the edges are we aren't sure, they vary, according to the attacks and counterattacks; but this is the center, where nothing moves. 'The Republic of Gilead,' said Aunt Lydia, 'knows no bounds. Gilead is within you.'

Doctors lived here once, lawyers, university professors. There are no lawyers anymore, and the university is closed.

Luke and I used to walk together, sometimes, along these streets. We used to talk about buying a house like one of these, an old big house, fixing it up. We would have a garden, swings for the children. We would have children. Although we knew it wasn't too likely we could ever afford it, it was something to talk about, a game for Sundays. Such freedom now seems almost weightless.

We turn the corner onto a main street, where there's more traffic. Cars go by, black most of them, some gray and brown. There are other women with baskets, some in red, some in the dull green of the Marthas, some in the striped dresses, red and blue and green and cheap and skimpy, that mark the women of the poorer men. Econowives, they're called. These women are not divided into functions. They have to do everything; if they can. Sometimes there is a woman all in black, a widow. There used to be more of them, but they seem to be diminishing. You don't see the Commanders' Wives on the sidewalks. Only in cars.

The sidewalks here are cement. Like a child, I avoid stepping on the cracks. I'm remembering my feet on these sidewalks, in the time before, and what I used to wear on them. Sometimes it was shoes for running, with cushioned soles and breathing holes, and stars of fluorescent fabric that reflected light in the darkness. Though I never ran at night; and in the daytime, only beside well-frequented roads.

Women were not protected then.

I remember the rules, rules that were never spelled out but that every woman knew: Don't open your door to a stranger, even if he says he is the police. Make him slide his ID under the door. Don't stop on the road to help a motorist pretending to be in trouble. Keep the locks on and keep going. If anyone whistles, don't turn to look. Don't go into a laundromat, by yourself, at night.

I think about laundromats. What I wore to them: shorts, jeans, jogging pants. What I put into them: my own clothes, my own soap, my own money, money I had earned myself. I think about having such control.

Now we walk along the same street, in red pairs, and no man shouts obscenities at us, speaks to us, touches us. No one whistles.

'There is more than one kind of freedom,' said Aunt Lydia. 'Freedom to and freedom from. In the days of anarchy, it was freedom to. Now you are being given freedom from. Don't underrate it.'

1 SPEAKING Work in pairs. Look at the photos. Do you know:

a where it is?
b how old it is?
c why it was built?

2 Read the text about Stonehenge. Did you find the answers to any of the questions in exercise 1?

Stonehenge is a Neolithic monument

situated near Salisbury in southern England. At first, it was just a circular bank and ditch, about 110 m in diameter, within which stood another circle of upright wooden posts. Radiocarbon dating on deer antlers used to dig the ditch reveal that it was constructed between 3000 and 2920 BC.

By about 2500 BC huge stones started to arrive, the largest of which weigh over 40 tonnes. The amazing thing is that these stones were brought from two sites: one 30 km away, the other an astonishing 240 km away, in Wales. There is no doubt about their origin: the mineral composition of the stones can be matched precisely. But how were they transported such enormous distances? It is thought that they were brought by boat and then dragged across the land on rollers. They were arranged in a circle and capped with horizontal stones. Only seventeen of the original stones are still standing, with five horizontal stones in place.

The arrival of these stones marked a period of 800 years of construction and alteration stretching into the Bronze Age, when the first metal tools and weapons were made. By this time Stonehenge was the largest and probably the most important monument in Britain, but it was just one part of a remarkable ancient landscape. It is surrounded by hundreds of burial mounds and a number of smaller ceremonial sites. The most remarkable burial is the skeleton of a man of about 30, found surrounded by flint arrowheads.

Archaeologists know that he met a violent death because the missing tips of the arrowheads were found embedded in his bones. But he was carefully buried, and is believed to have been either a warrior who died in battle, or possibly a human sacrifice.

Stonehenge was finally abandoned in 1500 BC, but just as no one knows for sure why it was built, and what it was used for, no one knows why it fell into disuse. These unanswered questions have inspired people through the ages to make up their own stories to explain Stonehenge, from medieval myths of magic, to the Victorian theory that it was built by Celtic Druids. But it is archaeology and modern science that provide the best hope of unlocking the mysteries of Stonehenge.

3 Work in pairs. What in your opinion are the two most interesting pieces of information in the text? Tell your partner and explain your choices.

4 🎧 TRCD Listen to a radio report about Stonehenge. Answer the questions.

1 In what way does Stonehenge appear to function as a calendar?
2 What kind of people are gathered today at Stonehenge?
3 What do the owners of the site allow visitors to do on the solstices?
4 How does attendance at the winter solstice compare with that at the summer solstice?
5 What kinds of crop did the people who built Stonehenge grow, and what kinds of animal did they raise?
6 What does George think their feelings would have been on the shortest day of the year?
7 What reasons does George give for his celebrating the winter solstice?

5 SPEAKING Work in pairs. Discuss these questions.

1 Would you like to visit Stonehenge? Give reasons.
2 What do you think of people who still celebrate the solstices at Stonehenge?
3 Do you know of any other ancient monuments whose origin or purpose is still a mystery? Describe them.

Communicative Activities

Photo comparison Unit 2F

1 Work in pairs. Take it in turns to do the task. The student who is listening should think of two questions to ask when his/her partner has finished speaking.

Compare and contrast the photos. Answer the questions.

1 What do you think life is like for these people?
2 What experiences might they have had in their lives?
3 Do you agree that the elderly have a lot to offer society? Why?/Why not?
4 Do you think we treat the elderly with enough respect? Why?/Why not?

Photo comparison Unit 6F

1 Work in pairs. Take it in turns to do the task. The student who is listening should think of two questions to ask when his/her partner has finished speaking.

Compare and contrast the photos. Answer the questions.

1 What do you think these people have done to achieve their awards?
2 Which person do you admire more, and why?
3 What does it take to be successful?
4 What do consider success to be?

Stimulus-based discussion Unit 8F

1 Present the information in relation to the topic.

Sharp rise in childhood obesity brings call for action

15% decline in school meal uptake following introduction of low-fat menu

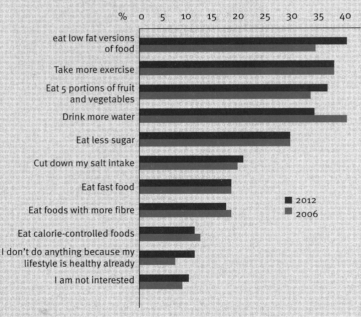

Teenagers' attitudes to healthy eating

2 Discuss the questions.

1 What kinds of fast food are available where you live? How often do you eat them?
2 What are the pros and cons of fast food?
3 Are young people's tastes in food becoming more healthy or more unhealthy, in your opinion?
4 How could we encourage young people to have healthier diets?

Photo comparison Unit 9F

1 Work in pairs. Take it in turns to do the task. The student who is listening should think of two questions to ask when his/her partner has finished speaking.

Compare and contrast the photos. Answer the questions.

1 What steps has each person taken in order to make himself hard to see?
2 Why do you think they have taken those steps?
3 How would you feel if you were in each person's situation?
4 Which of the photos do you find the most interesting and why?